Liberty and Power

Liberty and Power

A LIBERTARIAN APPROACH TO THE PAST

Edited by

Anthony Comegna

CATO INSTITUTE
WASHINGTON, D.C.

eBook ISBN: 978-1-944424-55-8
Print ISBN: 978-1-944424-54-1

Library of Congress Cataloging-in-Publication Data

Names: Comegna, Anthony, editor.
Title: Liberty and power : a libertarian approach to the past / [compiled by]
    Anthony Comegna.
Other titles: Liberty and power (Cato Institute)
Description: Washington, D.C. : Cato Institute, 2017. | Includes
    bibliographical references and index.
Identifiers: LCCN 2017022719 (print) | LCCN 2017039891 (ebook) | ISBN
    9781944424558 (ebook) | ISBN 9781944424541 (pbk. : alk. paper)
Subjects: LCSH: Libertarianism--History--Sources. | Libertarianism--United
    States--History--Sources.
Classification: LCC JC585 (ebook) | LCC JC585 .L4243 2017 (print) | DDC
    320.51/2--dc23
LC record available at https://lccn.loc.gov/2017022719

Printed in the United States of America.

CATO INSTITUTE
1000 Massachusetts Avenue, N.W.
Washington, D.C. 20001
www.cato.org

TABLE OF CONTENTS

Introduction:
Class, Civilization, and
Cycles—The Liberal
"Model" of History

The history of the world can largely be understood as generations of individuals struggling to acquire both liberty and power. Classical liberal historians have long attempted to divine the mechanics of change over time, explaining events largely with reference to cyclical social contests between individuals' interests in liberty and power. In what may be called the "thin" version of the liberal theory, arbitrary *political* power over one's fellow beings divided society into conflicting classes, whereas the "thick" version popular in the 19th century saw *all* attempts by individuals to exercise power as potentially problematic manipulations of nature.

Whereas the "thin" view hardly needs further explanation, it is perhaps appropriate to note that "thick" liberal thinkers identified politics as *merely* one facet of individual and social life, one small slice of human history. To the "thick," even using one's power to expand individual liberty may produce historical outcomes entirely unexpected and unwanted. Well-intended revolutions often lead to catastrophic war and even the rise and fall of civilizations. Should one indulge the desire to shape reality in pleasing ways, the impulse tends to corrupt one's virtue. As individuals tilt their value scales to favor the use of power over the enjoyment of liberty, they may shortly find themselves under the judgment of the ages.

Whether thick or thin, the liberals argued that political institutions created distinct classes in society: those with influence in the halls of state, and those subject to the state's rule.[1] Those who rule are driven by the fundamental social force of *power*; those who are ruled strive to exercise the fundamental force of *liberty*. When the two interests clash, a wide-scale battle ensues, and society's institutional, cultural, economic, and ideological composition shifts into new, syncretic forms. Throughout this book, we will survey the origins of classical liberal historiography, the liberal historian's view of the world, and the lessons we might glean from innumerable human generations, each desperately searching for greater liberty or greater power.

The classical liberal historian marches into the field of ideological and scholarly battle armed with methodological individualism (the individual is the fundamental social unit, the sole source of human agency) *and* a political-institutional concept of *class formation*. Every individual acts according to his or her own ideas and interests, and when power-wielding institutions actually exercise their power, the result is a discrimination of one sort or another. Because political decisions are made and enforced on the population without its consent, political actions always benefit one party at the expense of another. The use of political power automatically divides the population into those who benefit and those who are harmed; those who exercise and enhance their privilege and those who suffer exploitation at the hands of the powerful. The exploited usually wish simply to enjoy their liberties but find that to do so, they must resist the powerful. In overthrowing the aristocracy, the exploited absorb a great deal of power and privilege, which they then tend to use once again to pursue their own ideas and interests. The cycle begins anew.

The classical liberal, *cyclical* theory of historical change held sweeping appeal across the Western world for much of the modern era. From Kant, Hegel, and Marx to Guizot, Acton, and Mises, the idea that historical change is the direct result of man's dual nature as an individual and a social being was only seriously supplanted in the mid-20th century. Midcentury historians found far too much romanticism and cartoonishness in all of this, especially given their graduate training under Progressive Era academic luminaries. Simple binaries (like capitalist vs. proletariat or liberty vs. power) could not explain the vast complexities of human life and interactions they held.

It would be much more useful, historians began arguing, to simply collect massive amounts of data and tell the story of the past *as it actually happened*. Rather than impose our own theoretical story of history *on* the data, the data will *impress themselves on us,* and the narrative will be revealed through the numbers. Empirical historians found that history worked in exactly the opposite fashion claimed by the dialecticists: history was in fact the story of a grand, gradually expanding political-ideological consensus. Louis Hartz in particular noted the staggering importance of John Locke in defining modernity to the point that virtually all American intellectual traditions owe him their fundamental allegiances. As a socialist himself, Hartz was mortified by the idea that American society was destined to stagnation. The colonies' exceptional break from European feudalism may have provided Americans with a fast track to bourgeois society, but progress and change required discontent and conflict.

This volume revives the story of perpetual and generative conflict, undergirded by the constant rejuvenation of the species through new generations of individuals shaped by new historical contexts. Each successive generation strikes out to explore its liberty, expand its power, and reshape the world it inherited, fulfilling its own liberal imaginings or flattering itself with pretensions to greatness.

Since the late 1960s—and especially after the Soviet collapse—historians have attempted to reconcile the conflict and consensus interpretations of change over time. Although the Progressives denied that ideas and interests may in fact unite vast portions of society in a sweeping "consensus," midcentury historians stubbornly refused to admit that deep and serious conflicts did indeed separate Americans into distinct classes. As academic historians reconsidered the generative roles of consensus and conflict, many have returned to the battle-tested cyclical model. Even the lone individual has made a comeback, as many have recognized that individuals functioning *as such* are not equivalent to isolated atoms in a vacuum.

Although we will encounter a variety of liberal theorists and activists, historians Carroll Quigley (see the following paragraph), William Strauss, and Neil Howe (see the conclusion) in particular offer compelling, influential, and liberal-compatible models for historical change that include important narrative roles for both deep ideological consensus *and* sharply divisive social conflicts. In our attempt to restore to some prominence the liberal theory of history, then, we begin by engaging with one of the most influential academic teachers in the 20th century.

Historian Carroll Quigley was born in Boston, Massachusetts, in 1910. From very early in life, he showed a certain academic restlessness and ambition of the sort that sets apart the greatest academic scholars from those of us suffered to be more common in our abilities and talents. Although originally drawn toward the physical sciences, Quigley the undergraduate found history challenging and enlightening. He swiftly excelled in the field and moved rapidly through Harvard's elite doctoral program. Always captivated by big and synthetic as well as comparative history, Quigley was not suited to the staid atmosphere of the Ivies. As his friend and student Harry Hogan wrote, Harvard "offered little opportunity for the development of cosmic views and he was less than completely content there."[2] Once employed at Georgetown University, Quigley "became an almost legendary teacher," especially renowned for his course on the West and the Development of Civilization, which was required for all incoming students. Quigley's interpretation of history, therefore, "was a vital intellectual experience for young students, a mind-opening adventure. Foreign Service School graduates, meeting years later in careers around the world, would establish rapport with each other by describing their experience in his class."[3] His influential students were legion, plucked from elite families around the globe and reared to rule from birth. His influence as an educator and thinker in recent history can hardly be overstated.

Yet Carroll Quigley the historian would likely have been the first to admit that his theories and perspectives were anything but original. Indeed, he and his closest students saw themselves carrying forth the broad but well-defined mantle of Augustinian rationalism, a tradition millennia in the making. In his personal life, Quigley drifted far from his native Roman Catholicism, but he retained the church's cosmological perspective and connection with ancient times. Hogan writes: "He never swerved from his search for the meaning of life. He never placed any goal in higher priority." Quigley devoted himself to the peculiarly Western tradition of rationalism, and his historical works "addressed the problem of explaining change in the world around us, first examined by Heraclitus in ancient Greece."[4]

In a world characterized by constant change, Quigley sought some kind—any kind—of stable principles influencing the course of history. Quigley's answer to the historians' perpetual problem took the form of a "model" for the evolution of civilizations and large changes over the broad course of human history. As was so intellectually fashionable in his era, Quigley found great beauty in the explanatory power of modeling. In his view, transformational changes in and between civilizations occurred when "social 'instruments'" calcified into standing institutions, "that is, the transformation of social arrangements functioning to meet real social needs into social institutions serving their own purposes regardless of real social needs." Because Western civilization, like Carroll Quigley himself, possessed "an open-ended epistemology" in which all knowledge was subject to change, the West possessed a curious capacity to reform and rebirth itself.[5]

According to Quigley's model, socioeconomic and political systems like feudalism and kingship eventually ceased serving wide social goals, being diverted instead to the stagnant private interests of powerful classes. Westerners believed, however, that no institutions were sacred (even the church itself), and feudalism fell to "municipal mercantilism in the period 1270–1440." The 16th and 17th centuries were periods of entrenchment for new regimes, most notably modern imperial states and monopoly corporations. These, too, outwore whatever usefulness they may ever have had, and Westerners discarded early modern institutions as well. In the 18th and 19th centuries, democratic-republican governments proliferated. The political crisis seemed to be solved in favor of democracy by the mid-20th century, but the economic clash between corporate capitalism and the further devolution of economic power remained unresolved.

During Quigley's tenure at Georgetown University, humanity and Western civilization remained as threatened by potential stagnation as ever. Hogan writes, "With access to an explosive technology that can tear the planet apart, coupled with the failure of Western civilization to establish any viable system of world government, local political authority will tend to become violent and absolutist." Should irrationalism triumph over the rationalist's impulse, "states will seize upon ideologies that justify absolutism.

The 2,000-year separation in Western history of state and society would then end. Western people would rejoin those of the rest of the world in merging the two into a single entity, authoritarian and static." For fully two generations, Carroll Quigley taught classes of future world leaders, bureaucrats, activists, and business leaders that the triumph of irrationalism "would end the Western experiment and return us to the experience of the rest of the world—namely, that history is a sequence of stages in the rise and fall of absolutist ideologies."[6]

Quigley believed that the post–New Deal United States rested on the brink of disintegration and potentially rapid dissolution. With it would fall the course of Western civilization generally. Whereas Franklin Roosevelt captivated Americans with his optimism and vision, his death left Americans like Quigley and Hogan "in shock." They and many of their fellow hopeful Americans felt, "We had lost our shield." Without Roosevelt's unique leadership, new generations of Americans, "acting for Western civilization, must find within the history of that civilization the intellectual and spiritual reserves to renew itself within the tradition."[7] His somewhat desperate sense of danger for the future of Western life paired well with his self-image as an academic warrior for a better future. Always a man of rather moderate politics, Quigley's thinking grew steadily more radical as depression and world war wreaked their havoc, sparing virtually no one. His research led him deep into the rabbit holes of recent intellectual and geopolitical history, including the shadowy, secretive corporate and political forces behind so much of what was wrong with the world. In his history of civilization, the Georgetown professor perhaps hoped to raise up a new Franklin Roosevelt, an inspired youth who could prepare the American people to shoulder the burdens of history and triumph over decadence and decay.[8]

Carroll Quigley was hardly the first professional historian to formulate a general theory of historical change. In fact, it is a testament to his body of work that it manages to synthesize so well two millennia of Western liberalism into compelling new directions. Almost exactly a century before Quigley began his career, the American landscape artist Thomas Cole painted the very same liberal theory of history onto his canvases. Cole's radical liberal activist friends and contemporaries used their peculiar understanding of America's place in history to fuel a host of reformist causes and movements. Across the ocean, philosophers and historians like William Godwin and François Guizot expanded upon the long history of liberal reactions against calcified powerful interests. Their work explained change over time with reference to individuals, political bodies, and civilizations in contact and conflict with one another and themselves.

In so many ways, the entire corpus of classical liberal history and activism was perhaps best represented by Thomas Paine. As a revolutionary and a rationalist both, Paine inculcated a millennia-long tradition of Western thought, which he then perfectly translated into popular calls for popular action. Paine fused ideas and action like virtually no one else before or since, and like the figures explored in this volume, Paine believed himself both a student and a shaper of history. In his view, "the cause of America is in a great measure the cause of all mankind."

The patriots fought "universal" battles "through which the principles of all Lovers of Mankind are affected, and in the Event of which, their Affections are interested."

Paine's *Common Sense* made the plainest and most straightforward presentation of Lockean theory that most Americans had ever encountered, and his steady dismantling of statist principles ensured a revolutionary critical mass. In Paine, readers found a bold declaration that *it was government* that divided them into classes; *it was government* that brought them to war with one another and against foreigners with whom Americans otherwise had no quarrel; and *it was government* first and foremost that threatened future prosperity. By contrast, all the fruits of civilization one could practically list were the result of social forces that remained essentially ungoverned and undirected.

Although Paine lamented the Britons' long slide from ancient liberties into monarchical and aristocratic tyranny, he believed that a proper understanding of history could restore free society to his contemporaries and their children. A full and frank knowledge, for example, that the line of English kings in fact descended from "a French bastard landing with an armed banditti, and establishing himself king of England against the consent of the natives."[9] As such, neither nature nor history in fact, justified the British government as it existed in 1776—it was simply a lumbering mass of interconnected privileges, powers, immunities, charters, and usurped authorities. Americans, Paine declared, must do their historical part "to begin government at the right end" of society by reviving the ancient liberties, restoring individual sovereignty, and placing reason at the center of intellectual and political life.

He predicted that the Revolution would affect human history "even to the end of time," and to this end, he implored his fellows:

> O ye that love mankind! Ye that dare oppose, not only the tyranny, but the tyrant, stand forth! Every spot of the old world is overrun with oppression. Freedom hath been hunted round the globe. Asia, and Africa, have long expelled her.—Europe regards her like a stranger, and England hath given her warning to depart. O! receive the fugitive, and prepare in time an asylum for mankind.[10]

Although political writers and activists like Paine and his revolutionary compatriots pioneered much of the modern radical tradition, they also leaned heavily on religiously inclined writers like John Ponet. During Ponet's lifetime, the Reformation tore across Europe and affected virtually all aspects of daily life. As traditional powers lost their grips on European life, cultural and political space opened through which Renaissance humanism flourished. The humanists cut through the long history of feudalism to recall supposedly ancient liberties and republican forms of government from the premedieval past. As historian Steve Davies writes: "The interest in the ancient world and the contrasts drawn between it and the centuries that had followed, as well as the present, made people more aware of the differences between the present and the past. It also led to an awareness of historical change." "The impact of humanism," Davies continues, "was to reinforce the view of history as a branch of literature."

The humanists' great-grandchildren developed rationalism, continuing the rebirth by dispelling what they termed "medieval mysticism" with the light of science. As Davies argues, "The decline of the notions of the providential and miraculous was an enormously significant event in the intellectual history of Europe, with wide implications." One such implication was that historical events had distinct causes that could ultimately be traced to individual human actors. Nonetheless, Paine's idealized version of history was characteristic of the Enlightenment "speculative histories": "These were large-scale accounts of the history of the world or some large part of it, or of some significant feature of human life. They were driven in the first instance not by the empirical facts of the *erudits*, but by theories or abstract models, of the past and of human nature."[11]

Modern empirical history developed with the careers of Barthold Niebuhr (1776–1831) and, most important, Leopold von Ranke (1795–1886). Ranke transformed professional history from the servant of popular narratives (like Paine's lament over lost liberties and overgrown tyranny) into a purportedly dispassionate attempt "merely to show what actually occurred."[12] The 19th-century devotees of Ranke embraced "historicism," the philosophical belief that the present can be explained only with reference to the specific facts of the past.

Historicists rejected aprioristic understandings of universal human nature or teleological narratives about historical "destiny." Generations of historicist entrenchment, however, invited reaction. From the perhaps more idealistic corners of the West, historians like Great Britain's Lord Acton; France's Michelet, Thierry, and Guizot; and the American George Bancroft pioneered "historical romanticism." According to the romantics: "History as much as art and literature, was both a development of, and reaction against, the classicism, universalism and rationalism of the Enlightenment. The emphasis is on sentiment and feeling as opposed to rational calculation, the particular and local as against the universal, and (frequently) the medieval in contrast to both ancient and modern."[13] Romantic historians remained passionately committed to reengaging with the activist world to positively shape the course of history toward greater good.[14]

As we see in our selections from Guizot in 19th-century France to his contemporaries across the Atlantic—the trio of Democratic editors, Levi Slamm, Michael Walsh, and John L. O'Sullivan—the grand humanistic vision of history-as-human-mission remained powerful beyond the Revolutionary era. To the cast of thinkers examined here, history was the long story of humanity's internecine battle between social forces seeking liberty and social forces seeking power. To writers like Guizot, civilization "was effectively a way of thinking about the emerging European society of the time that distinguished it both from the European past and that of the rest of the planet. An essential element was the belief that civilization, defined as a way of living and behaving, had emerged in Europe and was continuing to develop there and to spread to other parts of the world."[15] The Americans, for their part, were similarly convinced of their democratic-republican destinies in world history.[16]

The 19th century constituted a long period of existential crisis throughout the steadily industrializing, democratizing, and centralizing world, and individuals responded with frantic searches to define themselves and their positions in history.[17]

Liberal historians like Lord Acton built famed careers on the idea that individuals were citizen-soldiers in the grand battle of *liberty* against *power*.

Following Acton, the Italian Benedetto Croce was perhaps the most important liberal historian. Croce was born in Abruzzi in 1866 to a wealthy family, which assured lifelong involvement in Italian politics and a fortune large enough to support a career of independent study and scholarship. Croce wrote in the fields of aesthetics, literature, and philosophy, quickly earning acclaim in each. His work in history and historiography was, however, perhaps his most important contribution. Croce's corpus contains roughly 80 volumes in addition to his critical review, *La critica*, which he published personally from 1902 to 1944.

For his entire intellectual and political life, Croce maintained a sort of celebrity in the European liberal movement and Italian public life broadly. He became a senator for life (1910) largely as official recognition for his immense cultural contributions. He used his position to advance liberal policies, including opposition to Italy's involvement in the First World War. He later served as secretary of education for the year before Mussolini's 1922 March on Rome. Once the new regime consolidated power, the government blacklisted Croce for having written and signed an anti-fascist manifesto (1925). Croce biographer Claes Ryn writes that "Black Shirt troopers broke into Croce's home and raided his library," but Croce remained critical of both fascism and the Mussolini regime "at considerable risk."[18] The level of Croce's intellectual accomplishments shielded him from direct attack, but Mussolini had him surveilled at all times, forbade newspapers from mentioning his name, and removed all of Croce's books from Italian academia.

Croce believed that all history, correctly conceived and written, was the story of liberty. He argued that nationalist interpretations of history failed to account for the constant change and upheaval of events that constitute the historical process. Nationalists imposed static, collective identities on their subjects, producing works closer to poetry than history. Rather, history is the constant, ever-evolving, and social process through which individuals seek greater and greater liberty.

Croce considered himself part of the Rankean historicist tradition, although like Lord Acton, he believed that the narrative historians should tell is based on the romantic ideologies that inspire our work. The past—presented in the form of empirical evidence spliced together to form a strong narrative—should serve to inform humanists and activists about the true nature of their world. Human beings are in fact ideas-driven creatures, whose abstract understandings of reality order their actions, and although strict Rankean historicists might wish that evidence could speak for itself, all human experience is filtered through the minds of individual subjects.

Those who read Croce read of a world in which history presented constant and myriad changes in life over time and across space; but a world in which despite the occasional tyrant or fascist coup, the struggle for liberty has been the constant and ever-present fact of human existence. Croce published his book *History as the Story of Liberty* in 1938. A mere seven years later, Italy lay devastated by another world war, and Mussolini's regime was in ashes.

In late April 1945, Italian anti-fascists discovered, captured, and executed Benito Mussolini. The Italian people spent days desecrating Il Duce's corpse as it hung from a meat hook at a gas station outside Milan. Italy's interlude with fascism, bizarre and destructive as it was, faded into history, but liberty—as ever—remains the impetus for true historical progress. The new government invited Croce to serve as the provisional head of state, a position he declined. The venerable historian remained president of the Liberal Party until his death in 1952.[19]

This volume is an attempt to distill the liberal interpretation of history into a concise explanation of change over time as offered by centuries of liberal thinkers and activists. Part One examines the liberal interpretation of history from the theoretical perspective. We examine a slate of liberal writings in the Western tradition from Reformation England through the 19th-century triumph of democratic-republicanism in the United States. In particular, we explore the subjects of politics and state formation, social class, and violence against equal, individual rights.

In Part Two, we turn to examining the liberal theory of history put into practice by those who thought of themselves as positively advancing that theory. We trace the documentary and ideological origins of early modern states and monopoly corporations, the common population's desperate attempts to live freely in such a world, the gradual democratization and republicanizing of political regimes, and the calcification of modern politico-economic devices into institutions that demand greater and greater sacrifices of liberty for the well-being of the powerful few.

Finally, we will return to the cyclical nature of history in Part Three, where we will grapple with the dilemma so many classical liberal thinkers have faced: To what extent are those who understand the course of history able to influence its trajectory, and is it morally advisable to do so? Should we use the liberties and powers we do possess that we might remake our world into a better place, or are we best advised to uphold a sort of libertarians' "prime directive," stressing the wisdom of nonintervention in *all* sociopolitical affairs? Carroll Quigley and his decades of elite students undoubtedly had one view of the question. But to properly begin the debate, we turn to the cautious and somewhat pessimistic masterpieces that revolutionized American art.

Part One:

Theory

1

Art as Ideas:
Thomas Cole's The Course
of Empire *(1836)*

In 1836, New York City was already well along its way to wresting national political and cultural preeminence from Boston. Boston was the nation's "Cradle of Liberty," widely recognized at the time as the American cultural heartland. Throughout the Jacksonian period—propelled by the generation of Whiggish, conservative, antiquarian Knickerbocker writers like Washington Irving and continuing through a new generation of artists and intellectuals calling themselves the "Young Americans"—New York assumed the position as the cultural capital of the United States.

Publisher and *literatus* Evert Duyckinck's literary circle, the Tetractys group, purposively created the Young America movement in the mid 1830s with the specific goal of birthing an authentically American national culture. The Loco-Foco movement (ca. 1820s–70s) provided radical ideological fuel to the Young American artists' nationalistic, romantic fire.[20] The Loco-Focos revived the revolutionary legacy of Paine and Jefferson, aiming to destroy all vestiges of Old World feudalism remaining in the United States. The confluence of New York Knickerbockerism and locofocoism launched Young America as a full-fledged, generational movement of its own. Fine artist Thomas Cole's work stands as the best visual representation of the ideas and the romantic fury that drove Young Americans.[21]

Born in Lancashire, England, in 1801, the young Cole spent short periods in Steubenville, Ohio, and Philadelphia before he settled permanently in New York City. To supplement his family's meager income, Thomas taught himself to paint landscapes, quickly excelled at his new craft, and caught the attentions of wealthy New York patrons. Personally of a conservative, somewhat Whiggish political temperament, Cole was skeptical of Democrats' claims to moral supremacy. He saw their appeals to the "voice of the people" as simple demagogy. Despite this somewhat "Older American" politics, Cole was also lifelong friends with the rather radical locofoco Democrat William Cullen Bryant.

No mere friendship, the two men's connection represents the reciprocal effects of the locofoco politics and Young American art. When fused, the two produced explosive results, ranging from Cole's authentically American form of landscape painting to Bryant's own lifelong struggle for political abolitionism. Bryant's generation of Knickerbocker literati and the new locofoco intelligentsia provided Young American artists with imagery and subject matter; new techniques; structural support for their paintings, including publicity and exposure; and a constant stream of radical republican ideology that both learned from and positively informed Young American art.

Landscape painters generally used their genre as a method of critiquing historical development and humanity's moral and spiritual position in the world. Through depictions of the land, artists like Cole juxtaposed humanity's constant transience and restless pursuits against the relatively constant state of the natural world. As such, landscapes provided artists an opportunity to advance their own visions of spiritual life, ethics, and politics; they were able to present their own theories of psychological, social, and historical development.[22]

Few places on the planet could provide daily evidence of revolutionary change better than Cole's own New York City in the 1830s. The emergent cultural capital buzzed with locofoco radicalism, incipient concepts of manifest destiny, and a heady atmosphere of constant and bewildering technological and economic progress. Political pessimists like Cole, however, harbored deep suspicions of democratic virtue and popular power. Classical liberal theories of history—including the romantic republican version advanced by the New York locofocos—stressed that historical change was the result of inevitable and relatively constant individual and social battles for liberty against the forces of power. The dualistic dynamic described not only humanity's progression through the individual life cycle but the development, culmination, and decline of civilizations.

Cole translated the romantic model of historical progression and the radical liberal values permeating his city into landscapes of transfixing beauty, thus carrying powerful moral instructions to the viewer. His paintings did not merely reflect the ideas of philosophers and locofoco theorists, but Cole made positive contributions through visual media. His masterful series of paintings, *The Course of Empire* (1833–36), is without equal for its explorations of historical theory and themes. It presents a stadialist interpretation of the liberal theory of history, showing stage by stage the timeless and cyclical conflict between liberty and power.

The Savage State is dominated by a vast and swirling wilderness. It is the perfect image of liberty: the lone individual, nakedly braving the world on his own, hunting his game across the land unhindered wherever it might go. There exist only the barest indications of civilization or complex society, including a clustered handful of teepees, some of which emit thin wisps of smoke from their roofs. At the center of the painting stands

Stage One: *The Savage State*. Credit: New-York Historical Society Museum and Library, New York City.

a true natural monument, the towering height and power of this particular natural world: a great rocky mountain and its cloud-shrouded summit scratching the skies. The *Savage State* of civilization represents preagricultural hunter-gatherer societies, especially reminiscent of premodern Native American life. When humanity's power over nature (and, consequently, other people), was at its lowest point, humans correspondingly enjoyed their greatest amount of liberty. Virtually unencumbered by the innumerable desiderata of settled society, our subject civilization is practically indistinguishable from nature.

For the second piece in the series, Cole shifts the tone of color from dark, brooding, and lonely to light, effervescent, and hopeful. Closely resembling Homeric Greece, the *Arcadian or Pastoral State* of civilization has tamed the savage wilderness, exercised

Stage Two: *The Arcadian or Pastoral State*. Credit: New-York Historical Society Museum and Library, New York City.

humanity's own faculties for power, and in turn lessened humanity's enjoyment of perfect liberty. Having come far from chasing a single deer through an endless forest, humans now herd their own small flocks of animals, cultivate small gardens, and even improve their environment by constructing roads, boats, clothing, simple farming implements, and what appears to be a small town of wooden houses.

Most obviously, our subject civilization has introduced social hierarchies along with increasing amounts of power and wealth. In the center stands a lone temple, built of great stone slabs, the smoke of recent offerings pouring from the rooftop. All of humanity's creations—exercises of power over nature—remain, however, well below the heights of the rocky mountaintop. In fact,

Stage Three: *The Consummation of Empire*. Credit: New-York Historical Society Museum and Library, New York City.

yet another mountain even more towering and imposing than the last has appeared in the farthest reaches of the background as if to remind the viewer that the subject society remained yet extremely young compared with nature's timelessness.

At the height of our subject civilization's power and glory, the trappings of Empire are on full public display. Nature has sunk to relative insignificance and virtually faded from the scene. What remains has been thoroughly incorporated into urban life: a fully navigable harbor replete with bridges and vessels of all kinds, a hillside paved over with constructed mountains of granite and polished marble temples and manses, no trace of the original forest whatsoever, no wildlife in sight, and our once-high mountain now paling in comparison to the vast heights achieved by advanced humanity's own buildings and monuments. As humans increased their power over nature, they clearly expanded on Arcadian organized religious and social life. With the *Consummation of Empire* comes also the consummation of social hierarchy—abundant visible distinctions between rulers and ruled, masters and slaves, priests and laity, rich and poor. Although the tone of the painting is unquestionably bright and hopeful, close observers must be uncomfortably aware that the young Empire's foundations are far from secure.

Cole believed that history operated cyclically. Although knowledge could advance in fits and spurts, revolutionizing the world from time to time, virtue tended to lag significantly. We are, therefore, virtually condemned to repeat the mistakes of the past just as we attempt to learn from them. In our endless attempts to improve our world—to expand both our power over the forces of nature and to protect our equally natural liberty—we set in motion a series of dialectical conflicts, both generative and destructive. Humans have learned and accomplished a great deal since their time as a "savage," but their rise in this particular civilization has been marked by conquest and exploitation stretching beyond the mere felling of trees. They have, through the projection of power abroad, exploited and constrained the liberty of their neighbors. History simply did not allow for actions without equal and opposite reactions.

Just as no individual human may escape the life cycle, *Destruction* suggests that no civilization that has chosen to abandon perfect liberty to exercise power may escape the judgment of history. Here is an absolute orgy of death as the Empire's enemies destroy our subjects. Wholesale slaughter reigns in the streets, makeshift siege

Stage Four: *Destruction*. Credit: New-York Historical Society Museum and Library, New York City.

engines take the place of crumbling infrastructure, the mansions and temples once rising to the highest peaks of the visible world now burn to cinders. Whether the destroyers are rebellious slaves, a subjugated neighbor, or a still more powerful empire invading from abroad, we cannot be sure. Regardless, the viewer cannot but feel that the Empire has in some significant sense earned its fate. Nature, for her part, prepares to reclaim the scene, once again gathering her own forces from the swirls of flame, sea, and smoke. Humanity's monuments to war still provide the highest visual cues, but the solitary mountain peak has risen once again above the hillside palaces and captured the center of the frame.

The *Desolation* of Cole's subject civilization is now complete, and the historical cycle turns into its final phase. The mountain summit has retired to the edge, and nature has begun her

Stage Five: *Desolation*. Credit: New-York Historical Society Museum and Library, New York City.

long, slow reconquest of the land and sea. The sky is still; the clouds are thin, nonthreatening wisps; and innumerable hosts of flora steadily tear down humanity's surviving monuments to power. The lone, pale moon and its undisturbed reflection on the harbor surface control the center of the frame. There is barely a single stirring of life, not a single sign of creatures enjoying either liberty or power. For all its incredible strength and wealth during the *Consummation of Empire*, the subject society's power could not protect it from cyclical collapse. To Cole and his fellow Young Americans, this very process—the dialectical relationship between the liberty interest and the power interest—quite literally was history, and history was inescapable. Not merely inescapable, however, the historical process was necessary and even beneficial.

The tone of *Desolation*, while somber and lonesome, is undoubtedly peaceful. Humanity, after all, still exists apart from the life of any particular civilization, and as long as nature continues to provide the elements of life, history may begin anew atop the ruins of elder empires. With any luck, humanity may gradually learn the lessons of the past, imparted from cycle to cycle, lifetime to lifetime, generation to generation. As knowledge and virtue accumulate together, humanity may gradually advance through history with increasingly tangible improvements in daily life. The message remains fundamentally pessimistic, however, warning audiences that they themselves stood at the peak of another historical cycle. What they did in their lifetime—the course Young America steered for the United States and much of the world—would determine whether they approached the point of consummation or whether destruction and desolation lay immediately ahead.

Politics held forth no hope to those who wished to break the cycle of history forever, but Cole saw in the land timeless, cautious lessons of inestimable value. In his work, North America is a frontier in history more so than a geographical expression; it is nature holding a mirror to humanity, showing humanity's unquenchable desires for both liberty and power. On the frontier, humans battled endlessly for power over nature and a wide variety of other enemies, each in turn barely scratching out a living from the earth. As the world rapidly transformed from early modern to decidedly modern, Cole challenged his fellow Young Americans to remain knowledgeable and wise in their exercise of previously unimaginable power. Without sufficient virtue maintaining the moral integrity of the Republic, the Empire would surely rise to take its place.

Thomas Cole's importance and influence as an American artist exploded during the mid 1830s, and his career flourished in the early 1840s. He deeply influenced his immediate peers and successive generations of American artists. He transformed the landscape genre from a reflective art to a medium of expressing historical, social, and political theory. In a speech to the American Art-Union, Joel Headley once implored his audience: "Give me the control of the art of a country, and you may have the management of its administration. . . . The tariff, internal improvements, banks, political speeches and party measures . . . all together do not so educate the soul of the nation."[23] By producing titanic icons of classical liberal, romantic, locofoco historical and social theory, Thomas Cole stands as one of the most influential fine artists in the history of liberal thought.

John Ponet, A Short Treatise on Political Power (1556)

When Martin Luther nailed his 95 theses to the door of Wittenberg's Castle Church in 1517, he inaugurated a movement that transformed European civilization. During the ensuing "Century of Iron" (ca. 1520s–1650s), Europeans slaughtered one another in wholesale orgies of religious violence throughout the entire continent. Beginning with the German peasant rebellions, Protestants seized Switzerland and fought Roman Catholic forces; Catholic armies under the Holy Roman Emperor attempted to crush the Lutheran Schmalkaldic League; Dutch Protestants revolted against the Catholic Austrian and Spanish Hapsburgs for 80 years; as many as four million French died as a result of their own 36 years of religious civil war; eight million Europeans (including roughly 10 percent of all German-speaking people) expired during the Thirty Years' War (1618–48); and the English Civil War—especially the brutal and bloody conquest of Ireland—remains the most costly war in British history when the dead are counted as a percentage of the population. Through it all—and the foregoing list is far from exhaustive—the people suffered and states grew immensely powerful. Empire fueled war, war fueled empire, and by the end of the Century of Iron, massive nation-state militaries and navies battled each other on a global scale for the first time in human history.

It was in this context of intense intellectual, political, and social upheaval that the Anglican bishop of Winchester in England began his theological studies. John Ponet earned his BA from Queens' College, Cambridge, in 1533 and his MA in 1535. From Queens', Ponet joined the Anglican priesthood, inaugurating a somewhat short, although fabulously storied, career in the church. Always the renegade, Ponet defied Parliament's standing ban on clerical marriage and wed in 1548. He was arrested in 1549 for his involvement in court intrigue but emerged from the affair being elected bishop. He failed, however, to escape the Roman Catholic reconquest of England during the reign of Mary I (1553–58). Fleeing with roughly 800 fellow Protestant elites, Ponet spent the last years of his life exiled in Strasbourg. Seething, stuck in Germany, and fuming with hatred for the Roman Catholic queen of

England, Ponet published his *Short Treatise on Political Power* shortly before his death in 1556.[24]

In his 1787 *Defence of the Constitutions of Government of the United States of America*, John Adams reflected that "there have been three periods in the history of England, in which the principles of government have been anxiously studied, and very valuable productions published." Although many of these venerable tomes were by Adams's day "wholly forgotten in their native country," the best of them were "perhaps more frequently read abroad." Included among these great political treatises, Adams asserted, was John Ponet's *On Political Power*. Ponet's tract "contains all the essential principles of liberty," rediscovered during the Interregnum period (ca. 1640–60). In the 17th and 18th centuries, "Sidney, Locke, Hoadley, Trenchard, Gordon, Plato Redivivus," and others revived Ponet's ideas. Post-Revolutionary Americans, John Adams argued, "should make collections of all these speculations, to be preserved as the most precious relics of antiquity both for curiosity and use."[25] To Ponet, the commonwealth remained the prince's overriding and proper interest. The good prince existed on a meager taxation and ruled wisely, purely for the good of his charges. Should worldly rulers exceed their natural and moral authorities, however, the people may go so far as executing kings. No longer should the English labor under the false feudal idea that the king's body was a sacred instrument. Men—that is to say all men—were by nature corrupt and fallen. He and his contemporaries only had to glance around them to see the results of evil, self-interested rulers. The bishop concluded that "kings, princes, and other governors, although they are the heads of a political body, yet they are not the whole body," and that sometimes even decapitation could be justified. Yet if the people refused to replace wicked leaders with new heads of state, they had only themselves to blame should God demolish their evil society, perhaps sprouting a new one in its wretched place.

Chapter I. From Where Political Power Grows, for what purpose it was ordained, and the right use and duties of the same: & etc.

As oxen, sheep, goats, and other such unreasonable creatures cannot for lack of reason rule themselves, but must be ruled by a more excellent creature, that is man: so man, although he has reason, yet because through the fall of the first man, his reason is radically corrupt, and sensuality has gotten the upper hand, he is not able by himself to rule himself, but must have a more excellent governor. Those of this world thought that this governor was their own reason. They thought that they by their own reason might do the things they lusted for, not only in private matters, but also in public. They thought reason to be the only cause that men first assembled themselves together in companies, that commonwealths were designed, that policies were well governed and long continued: but those of that mind were utterly blinded and deceived in their imaginations, their works and inventions (though they never seemed so wise) were so easily and so soon (contrary to their expectations) overthrown.

Where is the wisdom of the Greeks? Where is the fortitude of the Iberians? Where is both the wisdom and the force of the Romans gone? All have vanished away, nothing almost left to testify that they were, but that which declares well, that their reason was not able to govern them. Therefore, such were desirous to know the perfect and the only governor of all, constrained to seek further than themselves, and so at length to confess, that it was one God that ruled all. By Him we live, we move, and we have our being. He made us, and not we ourselves. We are His people, and the sheep of His pasture. He made all things for man: and man He made for Himself, to serve and Glorify Him. He has taken upon Himself the order and government of man, His chief creature, and prescribed a rule to him, how he should behave himself, what he should do, and what he may not do.

This rule is the law of nature, first planted and grafted only in the mind of man, then after that his mind was defiled by sin, filled with darkness, and encumbered with many doubts. God set this rule forth in writing in the Decalogue, or the Ten Commandments: and after that, reduced by Christ our Savior to just two commands: You will love the Lord your God above all things, and your neighbor as yourself. The latter part He also expounded on: Whatever you would want done unto yourself, do that unto others.

In this law is compiled all justice, the perfect way to serve and glorify God, and the right means to rule each and every man: and the only stay to maintain every commonwealth. This is the touchstone to try every man's works, whether he is king or beggar, whether he be good or evil. By this all men's laws will be discerned, whether they be just or unjust, godly or wicked. For example; those that have authority to make laws in a commonwealth, make this law, that no punishment be imposed, but in their own country. This seems to be a trifling matter. Yet is by this means the people may be kept from idleness, it is a good and just law and pleases God. For idleness is a vice by which God is offended: and the way to offend Him in breach of the commandments: you shall not steal, you shall not kill, you shall not commit adultery, etc. For all these evils come from idleness. On the other side, if the people are well occupied in other things, and the people of another country live by pin making, and uttering them: if there should be a law made, that they may not sell them to their neighboring country, which is otherwise well occupied, it is a wicked and an unjust law. For taking away the means, whereby they live, a course is devised to kill them with famine, and so not only is this commandment broken, you shall not kill, but also the general law, which says: You shall love your neighbor as yourself; And, whatever you would want done unto yourself, do that unto others, for you yourselves would not be killed with hunger.

Likewise, if there is a law made, utterly prohibiting that any man can remain chaste, and cannot marry, this is an unjust, an ungodly, and a wicked law. For it is an occasion, that with marriage, he might avoid sinning: But if he does not marry, he commits fornication and adultery in act or thought contrary to God's will and commandment; You shall not commit adultery.

Again, a prince forces his subjects (under the name of request) to lend him what they have, which they do unwillingly: and yet for fear of a worse turn, they must seem to be content with the action. Afterwards, he causes a Parliament to be assembled as if he had been lent nothing at all, and they dare not displease him. To please him, they remit this general debt. This is a wicked and an unjust law. For they are not acting as they would want acted upon, but be an occasion, that a great number of people are undone, their children perish by famine for lack of sustenance, and their servants are forced to steal, and even possibly commit murder. So if men will weigh this order and law that God has proscribed to man—thou shalt love the Lord God above all things, and your neighbor as yourself. And, what ever you will have men do to you, do the same to them: they may soon learn to discern good from evil, godliness from ungodliness, right from wrong.

And it is so plain and easy to be understood, that any plea of ignorance can or will excuse him that causes offense in this manner. . . .

By [the Ten Commandments] He instituted political power and gave authority to men to make more laws. For He that gave man authority over the body and life of man, because He would have man to live quietly with man, that all might serve Him quietly in holiness and righteousness all the days of his life, it cannot be denied, but He gave him authority over goods, lands, possessions, and all such things that may breed controversy and discord, and so hinder the service and worship that He requires. . . . But whether this authority to make laws, or the power to execute the same, shall be and remain in one person alone, or in many, it is not expressed, but left to the discretion of the people to make so many and so few, as they think necessary for the maintenance of the state. . . .

And these diverse kinds of states or policies have distinct names, as where one ruled, a Monarchy: where many of the best, Aristocracy: where the multitude, Democracy: and where all together, that is, a king, the nobility, and commoners, a mixed state: which men by long continuance have judged to be the best sort of all. For where that mixed state was exercised, there did the commonwealth longest continue. But yet every kind of these states tended to one end, that is, to the maintenance of justice, to the wealth and benefit of the whole multitude, and not of the superior and governors alone. And when they saw that the governors abused their authority, they altered the state. . . . The rich would oppress the poor, and the poor seek the destruction of the rich, to have what the rich had: the mighty would destroy the weak, and as Theodoretus says, "the great fish eats up the small," and the weak seeks revenge on the mighty: and so one seeking the others destruction, all at length should be undone and come to destruction. . . .

And the wonderful providence of God is herein to be well noted and considered, of all such as love and fear God, that in all places and counties where God's word has been received and embraced, there for the time the people followed God, no tyranny could enter, but all the members of the body sought the prosperity and wealth of one another, for God's word taught them to do this. You shall love the Lord your God (it says) above all things, and your neighbor as yourself. And, what you will have men do unto you, do you also to them. The fruits of His word is love one another, whatever state or degree in this world they be in. And the state of the policies and commonwealths have been disposed and ordained by God, that the heads could not (if they would) oppress the other members. . . .

If he ought to be sharply used, who deceives one poor man, how much more sharply ought he to be punished, and of all men to be abhorred (yes, and even cast unto the dogs) that deceives the whole of the realm of ten or twenty hundred thousand persons? If he is thus to be punished and abhorred who is required to do another man's business, and deceives him, how much more ought they to be abhorred and hated, that takes upon them to do for others, not desired but sung for it: not called thereto, but trusting in themselves: not praying, but paying, giving many liveries, procuring and making friends to give them their voice, obtaining great men's letters, and ladies tokens, feasting freeholders, and making great bankletting cheer: not by the consent of the party, but by force and strength, with troops of horsemen, bills, bows, pikes, guns, and such of like kind and quality.

If this opinion be held, and judgment given against a man that seeks his own gain with the loss of his friends in small things: what opinions men have, what judgment shall be given of those that, intending to make themselves noble and rich, cuts the throats of those that committed themselves, their wives, their children, their goods, yes, and even their lives upon trust in to their hands?

If this judgment is given for worldly things, what judgment shall be given to those that willfully go about to destroy men's souls, and to make them a present to the devil, so that they for a time may be his deputies here on earth? If men abhor and punish such that are unfaithful and dishonest persons, how much more will the Almighty God abhor, condemn, and exercise His severe judgment upon them that abuse the authority given to them by Him, and deceive and undo those poor sheep of His, in whom (as His ministers) they put their trust?

Listen, listen (while there is time for repentance) to the sentence of God, pronounced by the mouth of his servant Isaiah; "Wo be unto you that make unrighteous laws, and devise things which are hard to be kept, whereby the poor are oppressed on every side, and the innocent of my people are robbed of judgment, that widows may be your prey, and that you may rob the fatherless. What will you do in the time of the visitation and destruction that shall come from afar? To whom will you run to for help? Or to whom will you give your honor, that he may keep you from becoming prisoners, or lie among the dead?

This terrible woe of everlasting damnation was spoken not only to Jerusalem, but to Germany, Italy, France, Spain, England, Scotland, and all other countries and nations, where the like vices shall be committed. For God is just, and hates sin, that be never leaves it in any place unpunished: but the more common it is, the greater plagues and force does He use to repress it: as we may learn from the examples of the cities of Sodom and Gomorrah, and Jerusalem, His own city. And besides the general plague, he whips the authors of it with some special scourge, that they may be a spectacle, not only to those that are present, but also a remembrance to all that are to come.

But some, who are put in trust and authority to make the laws and statutes, will say that they would not do anything willingly against God's honor, or the wealth of our country, or deceive any that put their trust in us.

If any such thing follows, it is by reason that we were ignorant. . . .

Do you think that this bald excuse will serve? Is it not written, that if the blind leads the blind, both shall fall into the pit? Did the plea that Eve made for offending in eating the forbidden fruit (when she said that the serpent had deceived her) excuse her? Nothing less. She was not only herself punished with pains (none greater than death could be devised) but also all her posterity.

Perhaps others of you will say that you do not dare to do otherwise. If you did, you should be taken for enemies of the governor, running into indignation, and so lose your bodies and goods, and undo your children. O you that are faint of heart, do you think that your parents would have left you as you were found, if they were so faint of heart? Or do you think that you will serve your turn? Was it enough for Adam, our first father, when he fell with his wife in eating the forbidden fruit, to say, "I dare not displease my wife." Or to say as he said, "The woman that you gave me, gave the fruit to me?" No, it did not avail, but he and all his posterity were plagued for his disobedience, as we and all that shall follow us will do, if we have any fear of God before our eyes. . . .

Thus you have heard not only from where political power grows, and of the true use and duty thereof, but also what will be laid to their charge, those that do not do their duty in making laws. Now see, what is said by God to the executors of the laws: "See what you do, for you execute not the judgment of man, but of God. And whatever you judge, it shall be rebounded to yourselves." Let the fear of God be before your eyes, and do all things with diligence. For with the Lord our God there is no iniquity, neither difference among persons, nor does He have pleasure in rewards or bribes.

But of the ministers of the laws and governors of realms and countries, more shall be said hereafter.

Chapter II. Whether Kings, Princes, and other Governors have absolute power and authority over their subjects

For as much as those that be the rulers in the world, and would be taken for gods (that is, the ministers and images of God here in earth, the examples and mirrors of all godliness, justice, equity, and other virtues) claim and exercise an absolute power, which also they call a fullness of power, or prerogative to do what they lust, and none may contradict them: to dispense with the laws as it pleases them, freely and without correction or offense do contrary to the law of nature, and other god's laws, and the positive laws and customs of their countries, or break them: and use their subjects as men do their animals, and as lords do their villains and bondsmen, getting their goods from them by hook and crook, with *sic volo, sic jubeo*, and spending it to the destruction of their subjects: the misery of this time requires us to examine whether they do it rightfully or wrongfully, that if it be rightful, the people may the more willingly obey and receive the same: if it be wrongful, then those that use it may leave it for fear of God. For (no doubt) God will come and judge the world with equity, and revenge the cause of the oppressed. Of the popes power (who believes himself one, yes, the chief of these kind of gods, yes, above them all, and fellow to the God of God's) we mind not now to treat: no other is a requisite. For all men, yes half women and babes can well judge, that his power is worthy to be laughed at: and were it not bolstered and propped up with the sword and faggot, it would (as it will notwithstanding) shortly lie in the mire, for it is not built on the Rock, but on sand, not planted by the Father of Heaven, but by the devil of hell, as the fruits manifestly declare. But we will speak of the power of kings and princes, and such potentates, rulers, and governors of commonwealths.

Before you have heard how for a great long time, that is until after the general flood, there was no civil or political power, and how it was then first ordained by God Himself, and for what purpose He ordained it: that is (to comprehend all briefly) to maintain justice: for everyone doing his duty to God, and one to another, is but justice. You have heard also how states, political bodies, and commonwealths have authority to make laws for the maintenance of the policy, so that they are not contrary to God's law and the laws of nature: which, if you note well the question before propounded whether kings and princes have absolute power, shall appear not doubtful, or if any world affirms it, that he shall not be able to maintain it. First with God's laws (by which name also the laws of nature are comprehended) kings and princes are not joined makers here with God, so that thereby of themselves they might claim any interest or authority to dissolve them or dispense with them, by this maxim or principal, that He that may knit together, may loose asunder: and He that may make, may marry: for before magistrates were, God's laws were. Neither can it be proved that by God's word they have any authority to dispense or break them: but that they are still commanded to do right, to minister justice, and not to swerve, neither on the right hand or on the left. . . .

If we will not submit ourselves to God's judgment expressed by His word, as Christians should, let us mark the result: and thereby gather God's judgment, as Ethnarcs do. For when we have wrought our wits out, and devised and done what we can, we can not exclude God, but He will have a word with us.

God's word, will and commandment is, that he that willfully kills a man, shall also be killed by man: that is, the magistrate. But this law has not been observed and all ways executed, but kings and princes upon affection have dispensed and broken it, granting life and liberty to traitors, robbers, murderers, and etc.

But what has followed as a result of it? Have they (whose offenses have been so pardoned) afterwards shown themselves penitent to God, and thankfully profitable to the commonwealth? No, God and the commonwealth have had no greater enemies. They have added murder to murder, mischief to mischief, and of private malefactors, have become public, and of men killers, they have at length grown to be destroyers of their country, yes and many times those that have been saved from hanging and other just pains of the law. And this is no marvel: for God does not only punish the principals and authors of such mischief, but also those that are accessories and maintainers of it, and plagues iniquity with iniquity. You may likewise see what fruits have followed, were popes have dispensed, that marriages might be made contrary to God's laws. We shall not need to rehearse any? The end will declare all. But let us leave to reason that, wherein something may be said: that is, whether kings and princes may do things contrary to the positive laws of their country. For example:

It is a positive law that a mean kind of apparel, or a mean kind of diet should be used in a commonwealth, to the intent that men leaning the excess thereof, where many occasions both to destroy nature and to offend God follow, they might convert that they spent evil, to the relief of the poverty, or defense of their country.

Answer this question, this divisions ought to be made, that there be two kinds of kings, princes, and governors.

The one, who alone may make positive laws, because the whole state and body of their country have given, and resigned to them their authority to do so: which nevertheless is rather to be thought a tyranny than a king, as Dionisius, Philippus, and Alexander were, who saved whom they would and plundered whom they desired. And the other be such, unto whom the people have not given such authority, but keep it themselves: as we have before said concerning the mixed state.

It is true that in indifferent matters, that is of themselves be neither good nor evil, hurtful, or profitable, but for a decent order: kings and princes (to whom the people have given their authority) may make such laws, and dispense with them. But in matters that are not indifferent, but godly and profitably ordained for the commonwealth, they can not (for all their authority) break them or dispense with them. . . .

If this were tolerable, then is it in vain to make solemn assemblies of the whole state and long parliaments? Yes (I beseech you) what certainty should there be in anything, where all should depend on one's will and affection? But it will be said that although kings and princes cannot make laws, but with the consent of the people, they may dispense with any positive law, by reason that a long time ago they used to, and prescribed so to do: for long custom makes a law.

To this it may be answered that evil customs (be they never so old) are not to be suffered, but to be utterly abolished: and none may prescribe to do evil, whether king or subject. If the laws appoint you to the term of thirty or forty years to claim a sure and perfect interest in what you enjoy, yet if you know that either yourself or those by whom you claim came wrongfully by it, you are not in deed a perfect owner of it, but are bound to restore it. Although the laws of man do excuse and defend you from outward trouble and punishment, yet they do not quiet the conscience, but when your conscience remembers that [which] you enjoy what is not yours, it will convict you that you have done wrong: it will accuse you before the judgment of God, and condemn you. And if princes and governors would show themselves to be half as wise as they would have men take them to be, and by the example of others learn what mischief might happen to themselves, they would not (if they might) claim, much less execute any such absolute authority. No, neither would their counselors (if they loved them) maintain them in it: nor would the subjects suffer their prince to do what he lusted for.

For the one purchases for themselves a perpetual uncertainty of life and goods: and the other procures the hatred of all, although it be colored and dissembled for a season, yet it does not at length burst out, and works the revenge with extremity. . . .

He is a good citizen that does not do evil (so said a noble wise man) but he is better who does not allow others to hurt or do injustice to the innocent. For the blood of the innocent shall be demanded not only from those that shed blood, but also of those that make or consent to wicked laws, to condemn the innocent, or suffer their head to kill them contrary to just laws, or to spoil then of what they justly enjoy be the order of law.

Now kings, princes, and governors of commonwealths have not, can justly [not] claim, an absolute authority, but the end of their authority is the maintenance of justice, to defend the innocent, and to punish evil. And that so many evil and mischiefs may follow, where such absolute and, indeed, tyrannical power is usurped: let us pray that they may know their duty, and discharge themselves to God and to the world, or else that those which have the authority to reform them, may know and do their duty, that the people finding and acknowledging the benefit of good rulers, may thank God for them, and everyone labors to do their duty: and that saying—the head is not spared, but evil sin is punished— they may be more willing to abstain from tyranny and other evil doings, and do their duties, and all glorify God.

Chapter III. Whether Kings, and other Governors are subject to God's laws, and the positive laws of their country

One who observes the proceedings of princes and governors in these days will note how ambitious they are to usurp the dominions of others, and how negligent they are to see their own well governed, might think that wither there is no God, or that He has no care for the things of this world: or they think themselves exempt from God's laws and power. But the wonderful overthrow of their devices (when they think themselves most sure and certain) is so manifest, that it is not possible to deny that there is a God, and that He cares for the things of this world. And His word is so plain that none can contradict that they are to be subject and obedient to God's laws and word. For the whole Decalogue and every part thereof is written as well to kings, princes, and other public persons, as it is to private persons. A king may no more commit idolatry than a private man: he may not take the name of God in vain, he may not break the Sabbath, no more than any private man. It is not lawful for him to disobey his parents, to kill any person contrary to God's laws, to be a whoremonger, to steal, to lie and bear false witness, to desire and covet any man's house, wife, servant, maid, ox, ass, or anything that belongs to another, more than any other private man. No, he is bound and charged under great pains to keep them more than any other, because he is both a private man in respect of his own person, and a public figure in respect to his office, which may appear in a great many places which I will recite. The Holy Ghost said by the mouth of a king and a prophet: "And now you kings understand, and be learned you that judge the earth. Serve the Lord in fear, and rejoice with trembling. Kiss the Son (that is, receive with honor), lest the Lord become angry, and you lose the way, when His wrath shall in a moment be kindled." And in another place: "The Lord upon your right hand shall smite and break into pieces even kings in the day of His wrath." Isaiah, the prophet, also says: "The Lord shall come to judgment against the princes and elders of the people." Likewise, the Prophet Micah speaks to all princes and governors under the heads of the house of Jacob, and the leaders of the house of Israel: "Hear all you princes and governors. Should you not know what was lawful and right? But you hate the good, and love evil, you pluck off men's skin, and the flesh from their bones: you chop them into pieces, as it were in to a caldron, and as flesh in to a pot. Now the time shall come that when you call unto the Lord, He shall not hear you, but hide His face from you, because through your own imaginations you have dealt wickedly." And again he says: "O hear all you rulers and governors, you that abhor the thing that is lawful, and waste aside the thing that is straight: you that build up Zion with blood, your majesty and tyranny with wrong doing." So may Zion and Jerusalem be well expounded: "O you judges, you give sentence for gifts: O you priests, you teach for lucre: O you prophets, you prophesy for money: yet they will be taken as those that hold upon God and say, 'Is not the Lord among us? How can any misfortune happen to us?' But Zion (that is, your cities) for your sakes shall be plowed like a field: and Jerusalem (that is, your palaces) shall become a heap of stones, and the hill of the Temple (that is, your monasteries, friaries, and chantrys) shall become a high forest." The Holy Ghost also speaks by the mouth of King Solomon: "Hear, O you kings, and understand. O learn you that be judges of the ends of the earth. Give ear, you that rule the multitudes, and delight in many people. For the power is given unto you is from the Lord, and the strength from the high heavens, who shall try you works, and search out your imaginations, how you being officers of His kingdom have not kept the law of righteousness, nor walked in His will. Horribly and soon He shall appear to you, for upon the highest among you, He will execute a most severe judgment. Mercy is granted unto the simple, but those that are in authority shall be punished. For God, who is Lord over all, shall not regard any man's person, neither shall He regard any man's greatness, for He cares alike for all. But the mighty shall have a sorer punishment. To you therefore (O princes) do I speak, that you may learn wisdom, and not offend. . . .

Therefore, seeing no king or governor is exempted from the laws, hand, and power of God, but that he ought to fear and tremble at it, we may proceed to the other part of the question: that is, whether kings, princes, and other governors ought to be obedient to the positive laws of their country. To discuss this question, the right way and means is as in all other things, to resort to the fountains and roots, and not to depend on the rivers and branches. For if men should admit that the church of Rome were the catholic church, and the pope the head of it, and God's only vicar on earth, and not seek further how he comes by that authority: then no man could say that all his doings (were they never so wicked) should seem just: so if men should build upon the authority that kings and princes usurp over their subjects, and not seek from whence they have their authority, not whether that which they use, be just, there could be nothing produced to let their cruel tyranny. But as we see from whence all political power and authority comes, that is, from God: and why it was ordained, that is, to maintain justice: we ought (if we will judge rightly) by God's word examine and try this matter.

Saint Paul, treating the subject of who should be obedient, and to whom obedience is due, says: "Let every soul be subject to the powers that rule, for there is no power but from God." There are some who would have this word, soul, taken to be man, not as he consists of soul and body both together, but only of the flesh: and by that word, soul, should be understood only as a worldly man, that is, a lay man or temporal man (as we term it) and not a spiritual man and a minister of the church. Where upon Antichrist, the bishop of Rome, seeking for subjects to be under his kingdom, has taken the clergy to be his subjects, along with everything that belongs to them: and he has made laws that they should be his subjects, obedient to him and not to the political power and authority, where he leaves subjects only the temporal. . . .

But here it may be asked, who handed out this justice to kings and princes before that time, since it was only then committed to the bishop of Rome? We need not answer that at this time, for we do not seek presently to know who should be judge, but only to declare and prove that kings and princes ought, both by God's law, the law of nature, man's law, and good reason, to be obedient and subject to the positive laws of their country, and may not break them, and that they are not exempt from them, nor may dispense with them, unless the makers of the laws give them express authority to do so.

Who shall be the king's judge, you will hear later.

Chapter V. Whether All The Subject's Goods Be The Kaisers and Kings Own, And That They May Lawfully Take Them As Their Own

The Anabaptists wresting Scripture to serve their madness, among other foul errors, have this: that all things ought to be common, they imagine man to be of that purity that he was before the Fall, that is, clean without sin, or that (if he will) he may so be: and that as when there was no sin, all things were common, so they ought to be now.

But this mingling of the state of man before the Fall, and of him after the Fall deceives them much. For by the Fall, and ever after the Fall, this corruptible flesh of man is clogged with sin, and shall never be rid of sin, as long as it is in this corrupt world, but shall be always disposed and prone to do that which is evil. Therefore, as one means to be uncombered of the heap of sin, God ordained that man should get his living by the sweat of the brow: and that he should be the more forced to labor, the distinction of things and property (mine, and yours) was (contrary to Plato's opinion) ordained, being apparent by these two laws: Thou shall not steal: Thou shall not covet your neighbor's wife, not his servant, nor his maid, nor his ox, nor his ass, nor anything that is his. Afterward, in deed, Scripture speaks of communion of things, not that they ought so to be (for so Scripture should be directly against Scripture) but that there was such charity among people, that of their own free will, they gave and sold all they had, to relieve the misery of their poor brethren: who for impotency, or for multitude of children, were not with their labor able to get sufficient to relieve their necessity. Nor of this so given might every man take as much as lusted for, but to everyone (according to his necessity) sufficient was distributed. So that it stood in the liberality of the giver, and not in the liberty of the taker.

But there are some in these days, not of the meanest or poorest sort, but of the chief and rich: that is, many wicked governors and rulers, who in this error excel the common Anabaptists.

For the common Anabaptists do not only take other men's goods as common, but are content to let their own also be common, which smacks of some charity: for they themselves do not to others, but as they themselves are content to suffer.

But the evil governors and rulers will have all that their subjects have, common to themselves, but they themselves will depart with nothing, but where they ought not: no, not so much as pay for those things, that in words they pretend to buy of their subjects, not pay those poor men their wages, whom they force to labor and toil in their works. But the manner of coming thereby is so divers, that it makes the justness of their doings much suspect. For some do it under pretense to do the people good: some by crafty and subtle means, color their doings: and some of right (but without right) claim them for their own.

Of the first sort are those, that put great taxes and impositions on drink, for as much as the people with overmuch drinking become drunkards (and so sin against God) they would seem by making them pay as much or more to them as the drink is worth, they should force them the rather to abstain from too much drinking, and so from sin. But in this it may appear they seek not abstinence from sin, and the wealth of the people, but their own private profit. . . .

The second sort be those that rob the people indeed, yet would not have their doings known. They walk in nets, and think no man sees them. And of this kind be those, that contrary to all laws (both of God and man) and contrary to their other, changing the coin that is ordained to run between man to man, turning the substance from gold to copper, from silver to worse than pewter, and advancing and diminishing the price at their pleasure. . . .

The third sort of these evil princes are those that claim all their subjects goods for their own, who allege for them this common saying: All things are the Kaisers, all things be the kings, all things be the princes. And as the devil brought forth Scripture to serve his purpose against Christ, so they abhorring all other parts of Scripture, that teach them their office or Christian duty, pike out only a piece that may maintain their tyranny. . . .

But let us imagine an untruth, that all the subjects goods were the princes, and that he might take them at his pleasure. Let us imagine, that the subjects were only carnal men without knowledge and fear of God. Yes, and let it be granted also, that they were spoiled of all their armor, and great garrisons set in every place to keep them in office, so that they had not wherewith to address their injuries, as nature would counsel them: were this a way to make the people labor, when others should take the bread out of their mouths? Would they desire to increase the world with children, when they knew that they should be left in the worst estate, than unreasonable beasts? No surely, and that you may see by the work of nature in the people of the West Indies, now called New Spain: who knew of Christ nothing at all, and of God no more that nature taught them. The people of that country when the Catholic Spaniards came to them, were simple and plain men, and lived without great labor, the land was naturally so plentiful of all things, and continually the trees had ripe fruit on them. When the Spaniards had by flattery put in their foot, and little by little made themselves strong, building forts in various places, they to get the fold that was there, forced the people (that were not used to labor) to stand all the day in the hot sun gathering gold in the sand of the rivers. By this means a great number of them (not used to such pains) died, and a great number of them (seeing themselves brought from so quiet a life to such misery and slavery) of depression killed themselves. And many would not marry, because they would not have their children slaves to the Spaniards. The women when they felt themselves with child, would eat a certain herb to destroy the child in the womb. So that where at the coming of the Spaniards, there were believed to be in that country nine hundred thousand persons, there were in short time by this means so few left, as Peter Martyr (who was one of the Emperor Charles the fifth's counsel there, and wrote this history to the Emperor) says, it was a shame for him to name.

This is the fruit, where princes take all their subjects things as their own. And where at length will it come, but that either they must be no kings, or else kings without people, which is all one. But you will say: where comes this common saying: all things be the kaisers, all things be the kings? It cannot come from nothing. But with that already said, you see that every man may keep his own, and none may take it from him, so that it cannot be interpreted, that all things be the kaisers or kings, as his own property, or that they may take them from their subjects at their pleasure, but thus it is to be expounded, that they ought to defend what every man has, that he may quietly enjoy his own, and to see that they be not robbed or spoiled thereof. . . . The princes watch ought to defend the poor man's house, his labor the subject's ease, his diligence the subject's pleasure, his trouble the subject's quietness. And as the sun never stood still but continually goes about the world, doing his office: with his heat refreshing and comforting

all natural things in the world: so ought a good prince to be continually occupied in his ministry, not seeking his own profit, but
the wealth of those that are committed to his charge. . . .

Chapter VI. Whether It Be Lawful To Depose An Evil Governor, And Kill A Tyrant

As there is no better nor happier commonwealth nor no greater
blessing of God, than where one rules, if he is a good, just, and
godly man: so there is no worse nor none more miserable, nor
greater plague of God, than where one rules, that is evil, unjust
and ungodly. A good man knowing that he or those by whom he
claims was to such office called for his virtue, to see the whole
state well governed, and the people defended from injuries:
neglecting utterly his own pleasure and profit, and bestows all his
study and labor to see his office well discharged. And as a good
physician earnestly seeks the health of his patient and a shipmas-
ter the wealth and safeguard of those he has in his ship, so does
a good governor seek the wealth of those he rules. And therefore
the people feeling the benefit coming by good governors, used in
times past to call such good governors, fathers: and gave them
no less honor than children owe to their parents. And evil person coming to the government of any state, either by usurpation,
or by election or by succession, utterly neglecting the cause why
kings, princes, and other governors in commonwealths be made
(that is, the wealth of the people) seeks only or chiefly his own
profit and pleasure. And as a sow coming into a fair garden, roots
up all the fair and sweet flowers and wholesome simples, leaving
nothing behind, but her own filthy dirt: so does an evil governor

subvert the laws and orders, or makes them to be wrenched or racked to serve his affections, that they can no longer do their office. He spoils the people of their goods, either by open violence, making his ministers to take it from them without payment therefore, or promising and never paying: or craftily under the mane of loans, benevolences, contributions, and such gay painted words, or forbear he gets out of their possession that they have, and never restores it. And when he has it, consumes it, not to the benefit and profit of the commonwealth, but on whores, whoremongers, dice games, cards, bankletting, unjust wars, and such evils and mischiefs, wherein he delights. He spoils and takes away from them their armor and harness, that they shall not be able to use any force to defend their right. And not content to have brought them in to such misery (to be sure of his state) seeks and takes all occasions to dispatch them of their lives. If a man keeps his house, and nothing in metal, than shall it be said that he frets at the state. If he comes abroad and speaks to any other, further with it is taken for a just conspiracy. If he says nothing, and shows a merry countenance, it is a token, that he despises the government. If he look sorrowful, than he laments the state of his country, how many so ever be for any cause committed to prison, are not only asked, but are racked also to show whether he is privy of their doings. If he departs, because he would live quietly, then he is proclaimed an open enemy. To be short, there in no doing, no gesture, no behavior, no place can preserve or defend innocence against such a governor's cruelty: but as a hunter makes wild beasts his prey, and uses toils, nets, snares, traps, dogs, ferrets, mining and digging the ground, guns, bows, spears, and all other instruments, engines, subtle devises and means, whereby he may come by his prey: so does a wicked governor make the people his game and prey, and uses all kinds of subtleties, deceits, crafts, policies, force, violence, cruelty, and such devilish ways, to spoil and destroy the people, that be committed to his charge. And when he is not able without most manifest cruelty to do by himself that which he desires, then fain unjust causes to cast them into prison, where like as the bearwards muzzle the bears, and tie them to the stakes, while they are baited and killed by mastiffs and curies, so he keeps them in chains, while the bishops and his other tormentors and heretical inquisitors do tear and devour them. Finally, he says and denies, he promises and breaks promises, he swears and forswears, and no other passes on God nor the devil (as the common saying is) so he may bring to pass that which he desires. Such an evil governor men properly call a tyrant.

Now for as much as there is no express positive law for punishment of a tyrant among Christian men, the question is, whether it is lawful to kill such a monster and cruel beast covered with the shape of a man.

And first for the better and more plain prose of this matter, the manifold and continual examples that have been from time to time of the deposing of kings, and killing of tyrants, do most certainly confirm it to be most true, just and constant to God's judgment. The history of kings in the Old Testament is full of it. . . .

But here you see the body of every state may (if it will) yea and ought to redress and correct the vices and heads of their governors. And for as much as you have already seen, whereof political power and government grows, and the end where unto it was ordained: and seeing it is before manifestly and sufficiently proved, that kings and princes have not an absolute power over their subjects: that they are and ought to be subject to the law of God, and the wholesome positive laws of their country: and that they may not lawfully take or use their subjects goods at their pleasure: the reasons, arguments, and law that serve for the deposing and displacing of an evil governor, will do as much for the proof, that it is lawful to kill a tyrant, if they may be indifferently heard. As God has ordained magistrates to hear and determine private men's matters, and to punish their vices: so also will He, that the magistrates doings be called into account and reckoning, and their vices corrected and punished by the body of the whole congregation or commonwealth. . . .

For in some places and countries they have more and greater authority, in some places less. And in some the people have not given this authority to any other, but retain and exercise it themselves. And is any man so unreasonable to deny, that the whole may do as much as they have permitted one member to do? Or those that have appointed an office upon trust, have not authority upon just occasion (as the abuse of it) to take away that they gave? All laws do agree, that men may revoke their proxies and letters of Attorney, when it pleased them: much more when they see their proctors and attorneys abuse it. . . .

For it is no private law to a few or certain people, but common to all: not written in books, but grafted in the hearts of men: not made by man, but ordained of God: which we have not learned, received or read, but have taken, sucked, and drown it out of nature: where unto we are not taught, but made: not instructed, but seasoned: and (as St. Paul says) man's conscience bearing witness of it.

This law testifies to every man's conscience, that it is natural to cut away an incurable member, which (being suffered) would destroy the whole body.

Kings, princes, and other governors, although they are the heads of a political body, yet they are not the whole body. And though they be the chief members, yet they are but members: no other are the people ordained for them, but they are ordained for the people. . . .

Good kings, governors, and states in time past took it to be the greatest honor that could be, not to take cities and realms to their own use (when they were called to aid and relieve the oppressed) as princes do now a days: but to rescue and deliver the people and countries from the tyranny of the governors, and to restore them to their liberties. . . .

If a prince robs and spoils his subjects, it is theft, and as a thief ought to be punished. If he kills and murders them contrary or without the laws of his country, it is murder, and a murderer he ought to be punished. If he commits adultery, he is an adulterer and ought to be punished with the same pains that others be. If he violently ravish men's wives, daughters, or maidens, the laws that are made against ravishers, ought to be executed on him. If he goes about to betray his country, and to bring the people under a foreign power: he is a traitor, and as a traitor he ought to suffer. And those that be judges in commonwealths, ought (upon complaint) to summon and cite them to answer to their crimes, and so to proceed, as they do with others. . . .

And where this justice is not executed, but the prince and the people play together, and one winks and bears with the others faults, there cannot be, but a most corrupt, ungodly, and vicious state, which although it prosper for a season, yet no doubt at length they may be sure, that unto them shall come that came to Sodom, Gomorrah, Jerusalem, and such other, that were utterly destroyed.

And on the other side, where the nobility and people look diligently and earnestly upon their authorities, and do see the same executed on their heads and governors, making them to yield account of their doings: than without fail will the princes and governors be as diligent to see the people do their duty. And so shall the commonwealth be godly, and prosper, and God shall be glorified in all. But you will say, that if the nobility, and those that be called to common Councils, and should be the defenders of the people, will not or dare not execute their authority: what is then to be done? The people be not so destitute of remedy, but God has provided another means, that is, to complain to some minister of the word of God, to whom the keys be given to excommunicate not only common people for all notorious and open evils: but also kaisers, kings, princes, and all other governors, when they spoil, rob, undo and kill their subjects without justice and good laws. . . .

3

Anonymous to Thomas Jefferson, November 30, 1808

According to the liberal theory of history, as states and other institutions centralize and use their power, they are met in historical battle with opposite-class formation from below. The accumulation and exercise of political power encouraged the elite's victims to form themselves according to class interest, namely, the interest of destroying elite privileges and leaving each individual a self-governor. When this popular "liberty interest" manifested in the formation of "plebeian" class identities, the people's antithesis battled the aristocracy's thesis. Through an unending series of social conflicts, synthetic settlements, and generative spurts of change, human beings advanced their history as a species—the story we tell ourselves about why the world is the way it is. In the following selection of sources from chapters 3 through 8, a variety of writers in the liberal tradition explain the class foundations of historical conflict.

* * *

When an anonymous slave demanded that President Thomas Jefferson abolish slavery, the slave did so with reference to the Declaration of Independence, centuries of liberal thought, and an intimate personal knowledge of the class tensions born when government established "a mere monopoly of men."[26] It is not known whether the author was a former or current slave; nor do we know the author's gender. From start to finish, the writer maintains a singular focus on the moral and practical necessity of abolition, especially given Jefferson's own world-famous philosophy of universal, equal human rights. The author apparently wrote in response to recent speeches and writings by William Duane of Philadelphia, former editor of the Democratic-Republican *Aurora* and an important figure in the Jeffersonian political coalition of southern yeomen and northern workingmen.

The slave desecrated the idols of "American exceptionalism," and the moral supremacy of American democracy, arguing that from the slave's perspective, whites had merely democratized the institution of aristocracy. Although the Revolution indeed threw off the Old World's shackles on countless white men, the American project for liberty ended with Washington's victory at Yorktown. From that day in 1781, the newly freed white population prosecuted a deliberate counterrevolution to curtail the slave population's ability to achieve their freedom in turn.

Most ominously, the slave calls upon Jefferson's naturalistic, rationalistic philosophy to convince him that American slave owners must either renounce their iniquitous claims on their fellow human beings, pay them back wages to November 1781, and recognize them as moral and political equals or face devastating (though decidedly natural) wars of servile insurrection. The slave threatened Jefferson's life in particular, although by the end of his two terms, the president was assuredly used to this sort of rhetoric. Our author argues, ultimately, that the physical and political power of the slaveholders cannot stand against the fact of universal human rights and individual liberty. The author concludes with a final plea that Jefferson embrace the truths of human nature that he himself had become so famous for articulating and begin a movement of all Americans to abolish tyrants and tyranny of all kinds.

Sir,

Our burdens are heavy & call loud for justice! Call loud for mercy! I Therefore, take the liberty Sir, to address you myself upon the subject of slavery, and ask you a few questions respecting Mr. Duane's politicks. What does he mean by this? Young as our country is, in the political world, says he, it has furnish'd a world of useful experience; and that we are, thank Providence, the only nation that has yet profited by our education. If to spit in the face, cudgel in the streets, fight dewils, quarrel in the law, make laws & violate them, oppress & enslave mankind, take away all the honest labours & genius of one part of the community to riot upon, and to aggrandize the rest, gamble, drink to excess, wallow in debauchery, violate the chastity of women, betray publick trust, waist the funds, deceive the people, bely other nations, enslave their citizens, & your own, aggrandize one part of the citizens at the expence of the others, nurse, educate, & exercise children in tyranny and oppression, support a knot of idle hypocritical priests & rapacious lawyers, to lounge & strut about the country, divide the people into supersticious hostile sectaries; then setting these poor ignorant people to quarrel in the law one with the other, that they may fall an easy prey to their rapacity; and many more vices of a like heinous nature; can be said to be a world of useful experience, & a profitable education, America can vie with any nation on earth.

Yet, with all these vices staring him bold in the face, he has the vanity to say, that we are, thank Providence, the only nation that has yet improved by our education; & the impiety to call out to God to save his country from the afflictions of war; but above all from the example of England.—

What is this mighty uproar about England? Was there ever any thing in her example, more inhuman, irreligious, or damning, than slavery? Is any nation capable of committing a more heinous crime in the sight of God, or more insulting to fellow-man?

What said Mr. Wilkinson respecting slavery in '95? why, believing, said he, that a faithful history of slavery with all its consequences, would be of all others, the darkest pages in the annals of mankind. What said you sir, in '81? see notes on Virginia. Well then, if as Wm. asserts, Britain has got three thousand American citizens in slavery on board her ships of war: Has not America, likewise, got in slavery 2,000000 of the former citizens of Africa? If 1,000000 of the subjects of Britain are starving in her work-houses; are not 2,000000 of the citizens of America, running almost naked, starved and abused in a most inhuman and brutal manner, in her fields & kitchens. If Britain takes away one fifth of the labour of her subjects for taxes: Does not the tyrants of America take away the whole of the labour of 2,000000 of the most industrious citizens to riot upon?

I cannot give you a fairer picture of our unfortunate condition sir, then in the words of Esqr. Pigott. Among men, says he, you see the ninety and nine toiling to git a heap of superfluities for One; gitting nothing for themselves all this while, but a little of the coarsest of the provisions which their own labour produces; and this One too, oftentimes is the worst of the whole set; a child, a woman, a madman or a fool; looking quiettly on while they see the fruits of all their labours spent on spoiled; and if one of them take a single particle of it, the others join against, and hang him for the theft. What say you sir, to this? can you plead ignorance in these vices and follies; and in this inhuman slavery? If not, what can be your reasons (since you have been rais'd to the highest office in the government) for suffering us to be used in this brutal manner? Can any man who is not over-aw'd by a tyrant, sway'd by prejudice, in love with slavery & oppression, or who lives him self in idleness, drunkenness & debauchery, say, that there is either, honour, honesty, humanity, piety, charity, virtue, or religion in such conduct? O! merciful God, is this humanity? . . . To prove our human-nature, sir, and our rights as citizens of these states, we have only to appeal to the Declaration of Independence, which says . . . that all men, (not all white men) are created equal . . . with inherent & unalienable rights. . . . What think you now sir, are we men, or are we beasts? If this is not sufficient to prove our human-nature; our right and our citizenship, take another section from the original draft of the same authority: In speaking of the outrages committed by the king of England you say, He has waged cruel war against human-nature itself, violating its most sacred rights of life & liberty in the persons of a distant people, who never offended him, captuating and carrying them into slavery in another hemisphere or incur miserable death in their transportation thither: this piratical warfare, the approbum of infidel powers, in the warfare of the Christian king of Great Britain— Determined to keep open a market where MAN shall be bought and sold. This is sufficient one would suppose, to convince any unprejudiced mind; but it seem that it has not carried conviction into the flinty hearts of the sainted pilgrims in America, & I fear nothing will but the sword.

Whatever may be the mode of any government, either civil or religious, says the friend of justice & mercy, if it cannot exist and prosper without affecting the peace & harmony of a neighbouring nation, is unjust: Much more must that government be unjust, which aggrandizes one half, or less, of a community, at the expence of the other. The monarchies & aristocracies which have been so often decried by polititions, as oppressive and violent, are states of independence in comparison of that state of bondage in which the American black-man is kept. . . .

Again, in the midst of all these complicated horrors, Wm. has the affrontry to call upon the farmers of this land, and upon all the simple honest labouring classes of people, to look at this happy country, and be proud that there is no lord or lordlings to put them from their path of industry, nor to tare from them the fruits of their honest labour and genius.

In the name of God! what does Wm. mean by this? Where has he spent his time? In what cellar has he been shut since the year '76? Does he not know nor did he never hear, that the greatest part of all the manual labour that is done in the southern states is performed by slaves, and that they in general git nothing for it (except kicks and curses) and that their haughty lordling masters live in idleness, drunkenness and debauchery, and aggrandize themselves and families at the expense of the honest labours of the unfortunate people? Can he plead ignorance in all this? If not, by what name does he call such men, who have got four of five hundred slaves at their heels? whom they beat, scourge and abuse in a most inhuman manner, and take away all their honest labours and industry to riot upon? . . .

Slavery is unjust, because it destroys the rights of women & children. It is a mere state of barbarism, in which neither the delicacy and chastity of sex, nor the debility & ignorance of little children are regarded. The situation of the female slave is more deplorable & degrading than that of the untutored savage. For little as savages respect the rights of women & children, their women have exemption from labour, & protection from insult during those delicate & painful periods which are peculiar to their sex; & their children are instructed in all the knowledge which is by them deem either useful or ornamental. The degree of servitude to which savage women are bound, is trifling in comparison with the task of a female slave; and inasmuch as their husbands & children reap the fruits of their labour, & in some measure repay it by acquiring a superior skill in hunting & war, their labour becomes rather a pleasure than a burden. But what is to mitigate the labour of the poor female slave, with the precious burden of her affections at her breast? Slavery is unjust, as it destroys all the physical & commercial distinctions of labour & property. It is a mere monopoly of men, and all their abilities and services.

He who contributes by manual labour to the great stock of wealth, must in justice be entitled to some reward; but in vain does the wretched slave fell the forests, clear the grounds, prepare them for seed; watch & cultivate the tender plant, reap down & gather in the harvest, & bear it to the market.— . . .

This sufficiently proves my assertions, and justifies me in saying, that a majority of the American agents in the Southern States, are a set of inhuman scoundrils, and ought to be tar'd and feather'd and tyed to the tail end of a dung cart, and horse-whipt throughout the country, from state to state, and forever after banished from human society.

If slavery has become so firmly established in this country, as not to be avoided or guarded against, or is such a pleasing object, as to be no longer odious and irreligious, but a source of happiness and prosperity, its high time for America to give up all pretentions to liberty & freedom, & acknowledge herself at once, a joint heir with Jon Bull.

But we have not lost all hopes; we can't yet believe, sir, that you have become so deprav'd as to be in love with slavery, or have done reflecting upon the wrath of a just God, or that his justice cannot sleep forever. Yet there appears to me something in your administration, sir, very mysterious. What your reasons can be for keeping open that execrable market where MAN shall be bought and sold, which you wrote so warmly against in the year '76, and condemn'd as a mark of disgrace, of the deepest dye in the Christian king of G. Britain, I cannot conceive. Is a crime of this execrable nature any more criminal in the Christian Crown of Britain, than in the Christian Executive of America? If not, what are your reasons, sir, for suffering us since 30th. Nov. '81 to be trodden under foot & abused in such an inhuman & brutal manner? Are not Our rites as well secured to us by every law of nature's God as any man's in the universe? we think so; therefore, sir, we consider ourselves, entitled to our yearly wages from that very hour, and no man in the government (except a tyrant) can dispute our demand a single moment. And you may depend on this sir, that we shall never be reconciled to this government till we git it, & our freedom with it.—I think sir, you can't do yourself & your country a greater honour, nor your unfortunate country men a greater piece of justice and mercy, then by freeing your slaves & paying them their yearly wages from '81 to this day. And then, if any slave-holder in America shall here after refuse or neglect so to do, let him or them be made an example of, and their heads be hung in gibbets for an everlasting monument; & a terror to tyrants & evil doers. O! Thomas, you have had a long nap, and spent a great number of years in ease & plenty, upon our hard earned property, while we have been in the mean time, smarting under the cow-hide and sweating in the fields to raise provision to nurse tyrants to cut your throat and perpetuate our own bonds.

Why you should wish, in a free republic, to nurse, educate and exercise your children in such a tyrannical manner, I cannot conceive; since you so early saw, and confes'd the error; and must long ere this most severely have felt the effects of your folly. If not, fold your arms, and lull yourself into a slumber a little longer, and then see how the pig will eat the grapes.— . . .

Its high time for you sir, to decide, whether or not you will any longer use us in this brutal manner, or adopt us as brethren, for, in our opinion; on this single circumstance alone, depends the future prosperity, or destruction of these states, and the safety of your own life in particular. . . .

Yea, it has come to this, that our lives are no longer safe, for our inhuman masters and over-seers, publickly say that they would as soon take away our lives as that of a dog's, and that they will do it, if we should happen to offend them again, even in the most trifling offence. And the right of our wives, during those delicate & painful periods which are peculiar to their sex, and which the most savage nations respect, are disregarded by our cruel masters, over-seers, & even by our mistresses, & are driven like cattle from their beds in the morning at early dawn, & forced into the fields almost naked, & there obliged to labour in the heat of the scorching sun during the whole live long day, and many times, even in these painful moment, when eight or nine months gone in pregnancy, they are beaten down & trodden under foot in a most inhuman manner.

These are painful truths which no person can deny, who has ever lived three months among slave-holders. This being our unhappy condition, we humbly beseech you, sir, to lay our cause before the agents of this government, & request them to interpose between us & our inhuman tyrants, or other-wise, necessity will ere long oblige us to seek our own safety, by taking away the lives of our tyrants, & freeing ourselves at once from such inhuman monsters. . . .

Let me once more request you sir, to lay our grievances before the sovereign people of these states—Don't neglect it sir, unless you take delight in tyranny & oppression, or are thirsting after blood—if you be, your appetite may ere long git glutted. God forbid that I should have such a thought; or should live to see another drop of human blood unjustly spilt in America.

O! rouse up the brave sons of '76, and the children of those heroes who bleed & died to free their country from foreign foes, & from bondage, that we & our children might live free from foreign, as well as domestick tyrants—Don't let their labours be lost—Don't let so much blood be spilt in vain, and so much treasure be bartered for a whistle—for Spanish folly, or for British knavery and pride. O! rouse, rouse quickly, and snatch your weapons, & unite your strength, & let us banish all tyrants, tyranny and oppression from North America, and let us who surv[ive] the fatal shock, "form but one society, one great family." "And since human-nature has but one constitution, let there in future (at least in America) exist but one law; that of nature; but one code; that of reason; but one throne; that of justice and but one alter; that of union. Then might the sons and daughters of America set under their vines and fruit-trees, and enjoy the fruits of their labour, and the friendship of the whole human family.

4

Levi Slamm, Daily Plebeian, *July 2, 1842*

New York newspaper editor and radical liberal activist Levi Slamm was of the generation that inherited Thomas Jefferson's America. Building upon the Enlightenment liberals' theories of state and class, Slamm and his fellow locofoco "Young Americans" proudly embraced their position as "plebeians" in the ongoing historical class war. Slamm was one of the most important radical Democratic activists and public intellectuals in antebellum New York City. As one of the first members of the "Loco-Foco" or Equal Rights Party (1835–37), Slamm represented Jeffersonian, Paineite radical republican Democrats and the Working Men's faction alike. His newspapers, the *Democratic-Republican New Era* (1839–42) and the *Daily Plebeian* (1842–45), were among the most widely circulated, syndicated, and influential of all locofoco, Democratic outlets in the country. He used his talents for writing and activism to translate radical ideology into a politically relevant movement, although his penchant for partisan unity and compromise often raised the eyebrows of his more curmudgeonly contemporaries. Friends and enemies alike charged him with demagogy and desperate office seeking, whereas many others looked to his work as a guide for effective radical activism.

In the first issues of his New York newspaper, *Daily Plebeian*, Slamm introduced the audience to his paper, his purpose, and the position he intended to occupy in American political life. Following the introduction, Slamm commented on the choice of his paper's name. He cast American political life as a battle between the great mass of common people (the plebeians) with an interest in maintaining their liberty and those few who would rule over the people through the paper mysteries of bank credit and corporate personhood. He argued here and in many, many other places in his body of work, that human cultures virtually all develop social classes on the basis of the conflicting interests between liberty and power. In most cases, power concentrated in the hands of an elite few while the herded majority either meekly accepted their fetters or revolted to acquire their natural liberty. Slamm concluded by unapologetically and uncompromisingly declaring his allegiances in the grandest of all historical struggles.[27]

"Introductory"

To enter into an explanation of the plan on which this paper will be conducted, and the principles we intend to advocate, would seem almost like the repetition of a thrice-told tale. To those who have known us, it is hardly necessary to say, that we are willing that our past course shall be considered an earnest—at least in part—of our future career, and that under more favorable circumstances than it has hitherto been our fortune to enjoy, we promise ourselves a more extended sphere of usefulness. To those who know us not, we will sum up our political code in the briefest form. We are the supporters of the principles of Democratic liberty, the opposers of every scheme or device by which that liberty is sought to be abridged, the unyielding opponents of all partial legislation, the denouncers of monopoly in every form, the friends of free trade, the antagonists of all protection—so called—that adds to the wealth of the wealthy and the poverty of the poor, the favorer of that "credit" which is best regulated by the non-interference of government, and, in a word, the advocate of those equal rights bestowed upon man by his Maker. Such is our creed, comprehensive enough to embrace the interests of all.

Regarding party organization as a *means* of securing the triumph of great principles, we deem the strictest adherence to its usages as essential to success. We believe that in nine cases out of ten, conciliation of feeling and interest may be effected without a compromise of principle.—Though no abject slaves to party, our journal is in the strictest sense, a party paper.

So much for the political character of the Plebeian. In other respects, we intend it shall be in the best sense, a *newspaper*, addressing itself to all interests, catering for all sound tastes, giving all information of a local or general nature that the most extended arrangements can secure, agreeable for its variety, useful for its business character, and the welcome inmate in all circles—everywhere.

A word or two upon an important point. It is our wish to regard each and all of our newspaper contemporaries as *impersonalities*. Whether we can carry those wishes into effect, depends upon their treatment of us. If it be charged that in our past career, we have been somewhat neglectful on this point, we might plead that if personal attack can justify personal replies, our justification is perfect, for in the history of the press, no editor has been more the subject of contumely, vilification and slander, than ourselves. The very climax of the political wit of our opponents was comprised in those cabalistic words "SLAMM, BANG, MING & CO." It was a ready argument when all other arguments failed, a suit of complete mail with which the veriest pot-house brawler was duly armed and equipped, a piece of sounding slang ready set to music, and chaunted in full chorus by the sweet-voice Whig minstrels throughout the land. It seemed to be a sort of political nursery song, the "fee faw fum" by which timid Whigs of tender years were frightened into good behavior. Surely, if personalities could justify a retaliation in kind, we were justified. But as to all that, we have only to say "let by-gones be by-gones." We have no heart-burnings, no resentments. If to our expositions of the principles to which our life is pledged, we are to be answered by the stereo-type, argument of "SLAMM, BANG, MING & CO.," why let the matter stand before the court of public opinion on its merits.

We are not *very* fearful of the verdict. We shall in our intercourse with our contemporaries guard ourselves against any breach of editorial courtesy, but if attacked by unmanly weapons we shall defend ourselves in our own way.

In good humor with our friends, in good humor with ourselves, with the assistance of most able contributors, with youth, health, some portion of energy, and not a little experience, and with the brightest prospect of enduring success and usefulness, we make our best bow to the public. *Jacta est aleo* ["The die is cast."]

"The Plebeian"

Not a few of our best-natured friends, personal and political, have caviled at the adoption of the name which stands at the head of our paper. We might answer, and our answer would be a good one, that it was our humor to adopt it; that if we prove true to the principles we profess, we can as well advocate them under that title as under any other; and that he who supports or repudiates our doctrines because our name does or does not suit his fastidious taste, must in our opinion be an indifferent democrat, a very shadow-hunter, a gentleman of the expediency school to whom the form of keeping up appearances in almost everything, and the substance of sticking to principles, next to nothing. We have been told too, that we should have adopted a title which would not conflict with the prejudices of any class, and thereby obtain admission into circles from which our unfortunate name is certain to exclude us. In a word, we have had good advice enough to make our paper the best ever published, and—in the way of small draw-backs—doubts enough suggested by the best of friends, to make us question whether by possibility, we could in our proposed undertaking either advance the great cause to which we are pledged while our mind lasts, or in that attempt secure an honest allowance of bread for us and ours.

In adopting our name, we supposed it to be one identified with the interests of the mass—the people at large, the tillers of the earth, the "huge paws" of the land, the men of honest industry, whose every drop, in a word the producers of every thing that gives us national wealth and national character. Having brushed up our reading, we found we were not altogether at fault in our adoption of the name of PLEBEIAN. We are told by the highest authorities that the "common people," such as *merchants*, mechanics, farmers, indeed all the makers of wealth and the agents for its distribution, were comprised in this class. It included every interest save that of the hereditary drones, whose sole business it was to live on the labor of others, and, honest souls! Save them the trouble of making laws, and other trifles of the same character. The same authorities inform us, that the *Plebs Rustica*, meaning the common farmers of that day, were considered the most enlightened and respectable, or as Cicero expresses it, the richest and most praiseworthy. We quote this merely as a matter of history, not pretending to say whether in this point, the plebeians of that day differed from those of our own. In the course of our limited reading, we find, that from Harrington—the first originator among moderns of the famous idea so ably enlarged upon by Daniel Webster, that all government is founded on property, (and as a consequence that the possession of property can alone secure a political franchise,) down to Edmund Burke, the most eloquent tory that ever lived, our poor name has had but one meaning, a meaning so comprehensive that a child can understand it. It comprises every interest out of the pale of the privileged classes, whether such privileges be those of a titled hereditary aristocracy part and parcel of the government, or those of hereditary monopolies, neither part nor parcel of the government, but the excrescences of its rank luxuriance, the parasites that twine themselves around, and feed on its life-blood. We had armed ourselves with authorities, and entrenched ourselves within whole mounds of quotations, to prove how impregnably right we are in our construction of our name. But it seemed to us, after all, a waste of learning and of words, and we have concluded to spare our readers the infliction of our pedantry.

If it may be urged that in our free and happy country, where all are presumed to be equal, the distinction which our name implies, is unknown, our brief answer is this: To the term aristocrat the time honored name of Democrat has always been opposed. The latter is the supporter of the largest liberty of thought and action, under just and equal laws. The former is the abridger of man's rights, the doubter of his capacity of self-government, the supporter of the most odiously absurd doctrine that liberty is a pearl of so great value that its possession should be secured to a few, as it becomes cheap and priceless in the hands of the many. Such there are among us. Such are the principles of the party of which we are the undying antagonists. The political aristocrats of the day are but the inheritors of the principles of the patricians of elder ages. They both have claimed to belong to the "better" classes. They both have claimed a monopoly of all the talents and all the decency, though it has been reluctantly admitted that occasionally a stray brother has been found who rose superior to his condition and became, under proper training, a rather respectable member of society, and a fit associate of even the privileged magnates of the land.

But to be brief. If antiquity can hallow our name, ours is all hallowed. It took its rise at the very foundation of old Rome, and from that day to this has not lost its significance. The Chartists of old England are the present plebeians—God speed their efforts—of that land; the Democrats, the advocates of equal rights and equal laws, are the plebeians of our own. The name is one of honor, as it is synonymous with the name of Democrat, bound with the same associations, awakening and encouraging the same high hopes, pressing onward, and still onward, in its glorious and heaven-illumined progress of political emancipation.

To our friends—such we know we have—to our enemies—if such there be—let us say, that the name of PLEBEIAN, if it be honorable, shall meet no dishonor at our hands. To all, let us add, that the powers of usefulness can neither be increased nor impaired by the title we have assumed—that if we prove ourselves the honest expounders of Democratic truths, we know that we *must* secure the confidence and respect of those true hearts whose trust it is our highest hopes to win and to maintain. With every assurance of support from the best and truest of friends—with, we hope, a just appreciation of the rights, duties and responsibilities of the editorial career, and with every confidence of success, we unfurl to the breeze our banner having inscribed upon it THE PLEBEIAN.

5

"European Views of American Democracy," United States Magazine and Democratic Review, vol. 1, no. 1 (1837)

Alexis de Tocqueville has been considered one of the most important and insightful observers of American society virtually from the beginning of his nine-month tour of the country in 1831. His masterful two-volume work, *Democracy in America*, has been a staple source for social scientists studying the United States and democracy around the globe for nearly two centuries. Contemporary Americans, however, found much to criticize about the learned, aristocratic Frenchman's interpretation of their country. In the following article,

John L. O'Sullivan's hugely significant literary magazine, the *United States Magazine and Democratic Review*, surveys Tocqueville's first volume and counters its most glaring misinterpretations.[28]

At the heart of the *Democratic Review*'s critique lay the divisive concept of class. Not only did the *Democratic Review* charge that Tocqueville's views were necessarily tainted by his national and aristocratic backgrounds, but the nature of his American tour (essentially wining and dining his way through genteel circles) distorted his perceptions of how social classes formed from blocs of consenting and conflicting individuals.

Tocqueville remained unable to grasp the central force uniting the vast, diverse American public and polities— what the *Democratic Review* elsewhere refers to as the "voluntary principle," or what Tocqueville himself called "associationism." According to the *Democratic Review*, what Tocqueville thought was a careless disregard for law, order, and stability; what he assumed was the tyrannical, hegemonic power of the majority; what he saw as kowtowing, defeated, trampled minorities—they all were in fact evidence of the widespread *satisfaction* with democratic-republican governance in the United States and the relatively *limited* and *tame* expressions of social conflict. The class-conscious *Democratic Review* heartily agreed with contemporaries like Levi Slamm: history's internal dynamics destined that the United States act as the great plebeian nation-state. Historians of the past century have struggled to conclusively determine whether American history has been driven further through overwhelming and all-encompassing "consensus," or deeply divisive and revolutionary conflict.

In American reactions to Tocqueville similar to those from the *Democratic Review* as follows, we see some of the earliest attempts to recognize—in a systematic, scientifically historical way—the concepts of "American exceptionalism" and "manifest destiny." The beauty of the New World was that it allowed individuals from the Old to remake society in concert with natural law, preparing, in time, "an asylum for all Mankind." Although Tocqueville may have divined the eventual preponderance of democratic governments, the *Democratic Review* charged him with misunderstanding the fundamental forces, the spontaneously equilibrating factors, binding democratic-republican citizens together in common cause: the preservation of liberty against the encroachments of power.

M. de Tocqueville has been led into errors, not always unimportant, in part by the prejudices of some of the circles of society into which he naturally fell—in part by the mere effect of the imperfect observation and hasty generalization, which, to a certain extent, are almost unavoidable in this kind of writing. But there are no faults in his book which are not entirely consistent with great powers of thought and language, the most upright intentions, and an uncommon freedom from the class of prejudice to which the race of travellers are more particularly liable.

The general object of M. de Tocqueville is to ascertain the results of the principle of *democracy*, as applied to practice in the United States. . . . He remarks in his introduction that, on arriving in America, he was struck very forcibly with the general *equality* of conditions, and on farther observation and reflection, was fully satisfied that this is the substantial fact which lies at the bottom of our political institutions. Having come to this conclusion, he thought he could perceive, on turning his mind back to the state of things in the other hemisphere, a general tendency towards a similar equality of conditions. In illustration of this idea, he traces at considerable length the changes that have taken place in the structure of society within the last five or six centuries— all of them indicating the progress of the democratic principle, and the constantly increasing influence of the mass of the people, as compared with that of the hereditary privileged orders of the feudal times. This tendency he considers as *providential*—that is, as a result of general and not accidental causes, and as being consequently in a great measure beyond the control of any one generation. The ultimate ascendency of the democratic principle is inevitable: it is the part of wisdom, not to attempt to prevent it, but rather to facilitate it by anticipating and, as far as may be, providing for the changes which it will naturally bring about. To aid in this is the object of the present work. The mind of M. de Tocqueville expands with a feeling of sublimity under the contemplation of this glorious and inspiriting truth; and, to use his own phrase, he writes under the influence of a *religious awe*, inspired by the contemplation of this great revolution, the results of which, as of all great revolutions, the French philosopher gratuitously, and we think invidiously, presumes to be necessarily uncertain. He is not the panegyrist of the United States, as leading this mighty moral movement; nor is he a bigoted admirer of democratic principles and forms of government. . . . In the United States, therefore, he studies, not merely the institutions of the United States as such, but democracy itself—its nature, its inclinations, its passions, its prejudices. . . .

It is one of the remarkable features of the present state of the world, that it exhibits the two great principles of government—*liberty* and *despotism*—exemplified in practice, face to face with each other, in a purer form and on a more extensive scale than they have ever been before. While the free states of other times and countries have been mostly single cities, or confederacies of cities, inferior in power to the monarchies by which they were surrounded, the United States of America offer the splendid spectacle of a whole continent administered on the principle of pure, unadulterated *liberty*. In the great military empire of Russia, on the other hand, despotism, stretching her giant grasp over the vast extent of two continents, and developing the richness of resources and energy of action that belong to the youth of nations, wears perhaps a more imposing, and, to those within the sphere of her influence, a more dangerous aspect than she has ever worn before. But still, while we believe the principle of democracy to be established firmly and forever as the political faith of the whole western continent, and as destined, at no distant time, to obtain the ascendency in the west of Europe, we cannot but cherish the hope that it is destined also to conquer to itself, with a certain, though slow and toilsome progress, the eastern half of that continent. . . .

M. de Tocqueville, although, in applying his observations on this country to the state of things in Europe, he keeps his eye chiefly on France, where the tendency is strong towards democracy, does not lose sight of the opposite tendency in another quarter, and expresses In the closing paragraphs of his work substantially the same opinions as those here stated. . . .

M. de Tocqueville traces the *equality*, which he remarked as the principal result of our institution, to its origin in the *point of departure* of our people; that is, in the character and habits of the first settlers. . . .

His tone is, on the whole, decidedly favorable to the cause of democracy. It is evident, however, that his views of persons and things were in some respects unfavorably modified by influences of which he was himself unconscious, and from which few European travellers among us can escape. In speaking of the character of political parties, M. de Tocqueville correctly remarks, that however various may be their origin, and apparent or immediate objects, they all resolve themselves ultimately into one or the other of the two great divisions of society, which have always existed in free countries, and which labor respectively to extend and diminish the influence of the government; in other words, the *aristocracy* and the *democracy*. Now, in this country, the nucleus of the aristocratic party, by whatever name it may be temporarily known, will always be found in the monied men of the commercial cities. But this is precisely the class of persons among whom a well recommended traveller is naturally thrown on his first arrival in the country, and from whom he receives his first impressions, which cannot but give a general bias to his future observations. . . . In this way we account in part for the tone of disparagement in which our public functionaries and institutions are spoken of by most travellers, substantially liberal in their sentiments, and even to a certain extent by M. de Tocqueville. This gentleman, in fact, hints significantly that he has received important revelations of this description, in the confidence of private intercourse, which the persons making them would not like to proclaim upon the house-top, or even publicly in conversation;—but which they trust without reflection to the passing stranger! The weakness of the evidence, upon which M. de Tocqueville professes to found some of these unfavorable opinions, forms a singular contrast with the gravity of the charges, and serves of itself to prove that they rest substantially on such authority as we have just referred to—that is, that they are the opinions, not of M. de Tocqueville, but of the *aristocracy* among ourselves upon *Democracy in the United States*. We shall briefly notice some of these charges.

"*Many Americans*, says M. de Tocqueville, *consider the instability of the laws as a necessary consequence of a system of which the general results are good. But there is nobody, I believe, in the United States, who pretends to deny that this instability exists, and who does not regard it as a great evil. . . .*"

Far from admitting the justice of the charge, of a too great proneness to frequent change in the laws, we have always considered the *stability* of our political institutions, in the midst of the wreck of matter and the crush of worlds that has been

constantly going on around them ever since their establishment, as one of their most remarkable characteristics, and the
strongest proof that could possibly be given of their substantial
goodness. . . . Wo to the impious reformer who would lay sac-
rilegious hand on venerable evils, consecrated by time, and by
the vested interests which never fail to vegetate most luxuri-
ously from the most corrupt soil—Wo to him, we repeat; he
will be denounced as a visionary theorist, a raving madman,
an agrarian, a destructive, a *sans culottes*, and, the English language (beautifully rich as is the vocabulary of abuse which it
can furnish at need) being exhausted, a new word,—fearfully
compounded,—of uncouth sight and sound,—redolent of fire
and brimstone,—and pregnant with monstrous but mysterious
meaning, will be invented and fastened upon him, to frighten
the whole community out of its propriety, as at the cry of
"mad dog."

That a Frenchman, of all persons, should consider our laws and
institutions as obnoxious to the charge of instability, is really curious. . . . If M. de Tocqueville will compare the history of our
government, during the fifty years of its existence, with the history of any which he may choose, for any fifty years in the whole
tide of time, and will produce an example of one that has suffered
so little change of any kind, except in the tranquil and gradual
growth of prosperity in the course of half a century, we will admit
the correctness of his stricture. The fact undoubtedly is, that from
the adoption of the constitution to the present day, the Government has suffered no change whatever, in any essential point—
although the period has, in our opinion, *unquestionably arrived*,

when the slow development, during the course of half a century, of the different elements combined together as ingredients at the formation of the system, some for good and some for evil, requires some modifications in its forms, to adapt it to the evident progress of public opinion within that period. In points of minor importance, our laws are no doubt occasionally altered, though not more frequently than those of other nations. . . .

But what are alterations in the duties on imports, in the charter of a bank, in the mode of collecting the revenue, needed by an economical Government, in comparison with the tremendous convulsions that constantly agitate the kingdoms of the old world? Let M. de Tocqueville go back to the spring of 1789, when the first written constitution of France and the present constitution of the United States both went into operation. Let him then trace the successive reorganizations of the whole frame of the government that have since taken place in his own country. . . .

Let M. de Tocqueville recollect what has happened during the same time in the other parts of Europe—in Spain, Portugal, Italy, Holland, Germany; let him observe the boasted constitution of England herself, after breasting triumphantly the attack of the continent in arms for a quarter of a century, breaking down at last under the results of its own internal vices; let him look especially at the Spanish colonies on our continent, placed, as nearly as possible, in the same situation with the United States, yet thus far, as M. de Tocqueville himself correctly remarks, utterly unable to reach any solid basis, and floundering along from one revolution to another through a chaos of anarchy and wild uproar; let him go back, if he will, to the past history of the most celebrated nations of ancient or modern times, such as Rome, France, modern Italy, or England—at their brightest periods—and produce any one of fifty years, in the history of any of them, so free from internal change or convulsion as that of the United States for the last half century. If this comparative tranquillity on our side proves nothing more, it at least absolves our institutions from the charge of "*instability*."...

[Tocqueville further stated that:]

> The only historical documents in the United States are the newspapers. If a single paper is missing in a file of one of these, the chain of events is, as it were, broken—the present and the past cannot again be united. I am quite sure that fifty years hence it will be more difficult to collect materials for the history of the United States, during the present time, than for that of France during the middle ages. This instability, in every thing relating to the administration, has begun to extend itself to the habits of the people. I might almost say that it has already become a pretty general trait of character. No one troubles himself about what was done before him—no method is adopted—no collections are made—no documents are brought together, even when it might be done most easily—no value is set upon such papers by those who happen to possess them. I have myself original documents which were given me in some of the public offices, in answer to my inquiries for information.

As we cannot suspect the good faith of M. de Tocqueville, we are rather at a loss to conjecture on what ground he can have conceived views so entirely at variance with the truth as these. . . . We need hardly say that in this country public records are kept in nearly, if not quite all, the cases in which they are kept in Europe, and with equal regularity, particularly in the courts of justice, and in the various departments of the General and State Governments. Even the towns have their public records, as we are told by M. de Tocqueville himself; who, in speaking of the constitution of the municipalities, enumerates, among the other authorities, the town clerk, who keeps a record of the proceedings at town meetings, and of other public acts. Some of these town records have been kept very regularly from the first settlement of the country, and are habitually consulted, with great profit, by those who are engaged in historical researches. It is scarcely necessary for us to advert to the numerous and valuable collections of papers, by eminent public men, known to exist, such as the Jefferson papers . . . the Washington papers . . . the Madison papers . . . the papers of the two Adams . . . the immense diplomatic correspondence of the Government . . . the papers of Franklin. . . . Nor will we make more than a passing allusion to the historical societies of the different States, which make it their precise object to collect, arrange, and, as far as their means permit, publish every thing which they can find of interest, respecting the country at large, and especially the State and vicinity in which they are seated. Some of these societies have been very active and successful in their researches. . . . To this vast mass of documents, must be added the newspapers and other journals, which form a most valuable body of contemporary materials, and which, we need not say, exist in this country to an extent unknown in any other. . . . The historian will be much more likely to find himself laboring under the *embarrass de richesses*. It will require indeed, we apprehend, the most untiring industry to master those multifarious treasures, and the highest talent and taste to digest their essence into a compact form. . . .

Another trait in the political aspect of our community, which M. de Tocqueville signalises as one of the most injurious, is the supposed . . . tyranny of the majority. . . .

"The most absolute monarchs," he remarks,

> cannot prevent the circulation of works, inculcating democratic doctrines, among their subjects, even at their courts—In the United States there is nothing published, either openly or secretly, in support of aristocratic and arbitrary principles of government. The inquisition has never been able to suppress the circulation, in Spain, of works opposed to religion. In the United States no such books are written. The governments of Europe are often compelled to punish severely the authors and publishers of immoral works. In the United States no such punishment takes place, because no one dreams of publishing a work of this description.

"Now," continues M. de Tocqueville,

> it cannot be supposed that there are no persons in the United States who prefer the aristocratic or monarchical theory of government to the democratic; who are destitute of religious faith; who are inclined, by character, to licentiousness and immorality. There must be a certain

number of persons of this description; who constitute, of course, a minority of the people. There is nothing to prevent them from expressing their opinions but their respect for the contrary opinion of the majority. *Done*, consequently, the majority in the United States wield a power more absolute, more tyrannical, than all the inquisitions and despots of Europe a power which is fatal to all freedom, not merely of action and speech, but even of thought. There is no liberty of mind in America. I know no country where there is less freedom of discussion, less real independence of mind, than in the United States. . . .

M. de Tocqueville has not stated his facts quite correctly. The difference between the expression of public opinion on the subjects alluded to, in this country and in Europe, is not so great as he supposes it to be; and so far as it is real, it is easily accounted for by the difference in the state of society.

It is far from being correct, to say that there is no expression of opinion among us against religion, against morals, or against the republican theory of Government. Irreligious and immoral books circulate to a certain extent and are occasionally made the subjects of public prosecution. This, however, we rejoice to say, takes place to a much less extent than in Europe, and the difference is readily accounted for by a real difference in the state of society, which M. de Tocqueville himself is the first to acknowledge and even to insist upon as the basis of his reasoning on the subject of our political institutions. The almost universal respect for religion and purity of private morals are largely dwelt upon throughout the work, and justly described as the great security of our liberty. . . .

In the same way we account for the absence, to a great extent, of any demonstration of opinion in opposition to republican theories of government. To say that no such opinion is ever expressed, would not be true. We might mention, as an example to the contrary, Fisher Ames, one of the finest writers our country has produced, who had contracted, from the peculiar circumstances in which he was placed, a strong distaste for democratic principles of Government, and expressed it, not only without hesitation, but with extraordinary power of eloquence. Governeur Morris took no pains to conceal his dislike of democracy. In fact, the political school to which both these gentlemen belonged, and of which Hamilton was the leader, considered *democracy* not, as M. de Tocqueville correctly represents it, as the *principle*, but as the *disease* of our political institutions. Far from concealing this opinion, they filled the newspapers with it for years, in discussion. And even at the present day, the number of respectable journals which openly avow strongly anti-democratic opinions, to an extent implying fully a preference for the "strong" forms of Government of aristocracy or monarchy, is not inconsiderable. . . . The general satisfaction of the people with the existing form of government—their conviction of its superiority over all others—their self-complacency at being able to reduce to practice so beautiful a theory, which had been previously regarded as visionary and impracticable, are pointed out by our author as remarkable traits in the national character. Miss Martineau describes the universal *contentment* of the people with the existing political institutions, as *sublime*. What wonder, then, that there should be but little expression of opinion to the contrary? If the people are all, not affectedly, but sincerely, enthusiastic in their attachment to republican principles, why resort to forced suppositions to account for the fact that they do not declare themselves openly in favor of aristocracy and monarchy? . . .

The absence of any open opposition to religion, good morals, and republican government, is not owing, as our author supposes, to the omnipotence and tyranny of the majority, but correctly indicates the almost universal sentiment of the people on those subjects. Upon other matters on which opinion is divided, our minorities certainly express themselves with at least as much freedom as majorities, and not unfrequently with a violence in direct proportion to their weakness.

6

John L. O'Sullivan, "Political Tolerance," United States Magazine and Democratic Review, vol. 3, no. 9 (1838)

In 1838, the two great American political parties were the relatively young spawn of dueling efforts surrounding the Jackson campaign. Jackson and his supporters felt robbed by Adams's and Clay's "corrupt bargain" in 1824. Political machinists like Martin Van Buren saw the opportunity to construct new partisan establishments atop Jackson's persona and cause. By 1828, the Democratic Party was not exactly the creature we know today, but in significant ways it was awfully close, and the following decade was its formative period.

Jackson's conservative and Hamiltonian opponents, however, constructed their own partisan apparatus for the specific purpose of unseating the hero of New Orleans. Although undoubtedly *generative*, the culture surrounding the Second Party System was hardly genteel. In the following article, John L. O'Sullivan pleaded with his readership for "political tolerance."[29]

O'Sullivan begins by observing the bewildering display of variety and difference proliferating throughout both the natural world and the mental composition of individuals. Recognition of *difference* as a fact of nature implied "the duty of the widest tolerance of opinion," and yet political institutions arrayed human beings in veritable battle lines against one another. Through the prism of democratic politics, "men enter into conflict, armed . . . with invective," and as long as such conditions persisted, O'Sullivan believed that society would remain fundamentally medieval. His primary target, therefore, was the system of "special" or "partial" legislation that empowered the state and private sectors to mutually reinforce one another and manipulate the population into fighting among themselves with their (purely symbolic) ballots. Politics thus became a game for partisan and corporate spoils rather than an honest servant of the people.

The infinite variety of nature furnishes an unfailing source of admiration to all who contemplate her works. The boundless affluence of creative wisdom, is signally and beautifully illustrated in this interminable diversity. . . . Her excelling hand fashions no two objects alike. Not only does kind differ from kind, and species from species, but one individual differs from another. . . .

Mind differs from mind, not less than feature from feature. In tastes, habits, modes of thinking, and degrees of intelligence; in memory, imagination, and the power of comparison and inference; and in every separate faculty of intellect, each human being is marked by qualities exclusively his own. Boundless as is the field of knowledge and speculation, there is perhaps scarcely a subject that employs the thoughts of men, on which the opinions of any two wholly coincide. They worship at the same altar from similarity, not identity of creed: they support the same system of government, not because it fully accords with the political theory of either, but approaches more nearly than the counter systems which the others maintain; and they draw their swords in the same cause, influenced by general correspondence of motive, not by precisely coincident views of national honor and right.

A consideration of this inevitable and all pervading difference in the constitution of intellect would seem sufficient, in itself, to teach mankind the duty of the widest tolerance of opinion. Yet, strange anomaly! Difference of opinion has ever been regarded as an occasion for the most vehement persecution. For this, martyrs innumerable have been immolated at the stake, and the whole earth has been incarnadined with the blood of human victims. . . . There are still left, in the hands of intolerance, other weapons of coercion, by the free use of which she strives, though with efforts of comparative impotence, to retard the march of truth. Abuse is now substituted in place of force. Opprobrious terms and epithets of derision are the racks and pincers of the modern question. On the gravest subjects which affect the happiness of their kind, men enter into conflict, armed, not with arguments, but with invective. They address themselves not to reason and justice, but to passion and prejudice. They impugn the motives of their antagonists, instead of combatting their opinions; and exercise all the arts of a perverted logic to heap ridicule and contempt on their persons and characters, instead of temperately demonstrating, by the irrefragable methods of dialectic proof, the unsoundness of their positions, and the inherent badness of their cause.

This modified form in which the spirit of the dark ages still lingers among men displays itself nowhere so grossly as in the field of political discussion. The controversialists here . . . assail each other with the rancor of mortal hostility, rather than the generous rivalry of champions alike zealous in the cause of truth. They contend as if their aim were to exterminate, not to convince; as if obloquy were a more powerful weapon than reason, and to defame an opponent a prouder achievement, than to refute the errors of his creed. In this respect, political controversy is behind the improved temper of the age. . . . No longer do arrogant synods proclaim arbitrary standards of faith, to which men must conform their worship on pain of anathemas and persecution. No longer need the astronomer fear, while directing his tube to the stars, that the discoveries he may make will subject him to derision and reproach. No Galileo is now summoned before an inquisitorial tribunal to recant his sublime theory of the mechanism of the heavens; and no Bacon is maligned with the imputation of a league with the powers of darkness for the fruits he derives from a patient investigation of the mysteries of nature.

Happily for mankind, in religion and science, a wide and continually extending spirit of tolerance prevails. Their votaries seem at last to have discovered that the utmost liberty of inquiry furnishes the surest means for the ascertainment of truth, the only object worthy of pursuit; that all truth is single, and consistent with itself; and that it is its grand and peculiar characteristic ever to come forth from the alembic of discussion unchanged, and purified from the adulterations of error, with which passion and ignorance may have blended it. . . .

Politics are a branch of morals. All the duties of life are embraced under the three heads of religion, politics, and private ethics. The object of religion is the regulation of human conduct with reference to happiness in a future state of being. The object of politics is to regulate conduct with reference to happiness in communities. The object of private ethics is to regulate conduct with reference to individual happiness. Happiness, then, is the single aim of these three great and comprehensive branches of duty; and it may be questioned whether the obligations imposed. Importance of a higher scale of political morality by either can be fully performed by him who neglects those which the others enjoin. If we believe in the divinity of that precept which teaches us to love our neighbour as ourselves, in what mode can we more effectually show its authority over our minds, than by taking a firm and temperate part in political affairs? The right ordering of a State directly promotes the welfare of multitudes of human beings; and it is therefore not only the private interest, but the christian duty, of every individual of those multitudes, strenuously to exert his just influence in accomplishing so important a result. . . .

They who call themselves politicians, not having this as their cardinal object, are not politicians, but demagogues; and, on the contrary, they only deserve the name, no matter what the anomalies and contradictions of their several creeds, who are truly governed by this high and generous purpose. That mind should differ from mind, in its estimate of the relative adequacy of opposite systems of politics to accomplish the same result, is a necessary consequence of the infinite variety which is displayed in the constitution of intellect. But that they should differ from each other in the end proposed, can only be accounted for, not by inherent diversity of understanding, but by depravity of heart. To which of these causes must be ascribed the wild intemperance and asperity which distinguish our political controversies? . . .

There are none so ignorant as not to know, that our party strifes are conducted with intemperance wholly unsuited to the conflicts of reason, and decided, in a great measure, not by the preponderance of honest opinion, but by the influence of the worst motives, operating on the worst class of people. . . . By *the worst class of people*, in our sense of the expression, all those are included—whether sons of idleness or of toil, whether rolling in affluence or pinched with want, whether dressed in furred gowns or in tatters who enter into the strife of party without paramount regard to the inherent dignity and true end of politics; without due reference to the interests of their country and of mankind; without singly and solely aiming to advance the greatest happiness of society; but actuated by private and unworthy motives; by personal preferences and dislikes; by lust of office, or the hope of achieving, directly or indirectly, some sinister object through the means of party pre-dominance. These are, indeed, *the lower orders*, if we measure things by the sound standard of the moral scale. These are *the dregs of society*, often, it is true, cast to the surface by the agitation of the political elements, but infallibly doomed to sink to the bottom when the fierce ebullition of passion, ignorance, and selfishness shall subside.

It is from the undue influences of causes such as these, that elections come to be regarded by many as a mere game of mingled hazard and calculation, on the issue of which depends, as matters of absorbing importance, the division of party spoils, the distribution of chartered privileges, and the allotment, in various forms, of distinctions and pecuniary rewards. The antagonist principles of government, which should constitute the sole ground of controversy, are lost sight of in the eagerness of sordid motives, or only viewed as supplying an opportunity for inflammatory invective; and the struggle, which should be one of reason and opinion, with no aim less noble than the achievement of political truth, and the promotion thereby of the greatest good of the greatest number, sinks into a wretched brawl, in which passion, avarice, and profligacy, act the chief parts on the desecrated scene. . . .

Whence, let us inquire, chiefly arises the harsh and vindictive tone of our party disputations? Do we place ourselves in the opposition of mortal foes . . . because our theoretic views of the best means of promoting national welfare do not entirely coincide? Or is this rancor aggravated by causes not necessarily connected with politics. . . . Is not the fierce and intolerant temper of our political controversy largely owing to the fact, that government, instead of being conducted exclusively for the protection of the equal rights, and promotion of the general happiness of the community, has been extended to embrace the control of a thousand objects, which might safely, and with far greater advantage, be left to the regulation of social morals, and to the unrestrained efforts of individual enterprise and competition. Are our elections, in truth, the means of deciding mere questions of government, or does not upon them depend, to a much greater extent than the cardinal principles of politics, the decision of numerous questions affecting private and peculiar interests, schemes of selfishness, rapacity, and fraud, and artful projects of men who, under illusory pretexts of seeking to advance the public good, aim only to make the many tributary to the few? . . .

The true end of government is the equal protection of its citizens in life, liberty, and the pursuit of happiness, leaving them to think, speak, and act, in whatever way their ideas of happiness may suggest, with no limit to unbounded freedom, save that which restrains them from mutual injury. But widely have we departed, in practice, from this principle of our political faith. We have fallen into the besetting sin of mankind of governing too much. We have undertaken to regulate, by political interference, the pursuits of industry and improvement; we have connected government with the speculations of trade; we have imposed burdens on the whole people in order to afford peculiar advantages to certain branches of traffic; and worse than all, we have endowed with exclusive privileges, and hedged and guarded round with all the cunning devices of the law, an order of chartered money-changers, whose aggregate power is so tremendous, that it is yet an unsolved problem of fearful interest, whether, in the great struggle now waging, that or the democratic principle will finally prevail. This is the mode in which we have complicated the functions of government; and hence the maddening elements which give such violence and acrimony to party strife. We have perverted legislation from its high and holy office of equal protection, and debased it into an almoner of special advantages and immunities to a few. We have made our elections a contest for these favors—a vile scramble for crumbs cast from the tables of those whom we have lifted on our own shoulders into place. . . .

Can any truth in morals be more self-evident than the pernicious influence of special legislation? It degrades politics from its dignity as the most important branch of morals, to a system of trickery, artifice, and corruption. It changes the generous and ennobling rivalry of men for such improvements in government as should most effectually promote the happiness of their kind, into a low strife for doles and rewards, obtained by trampling on the equal rights of the people. It quenches the sentiment of patriotism; excites a feverish thirst for sudden wealth; provokes a spirit of wild and dishonest speculation; allures industry from its accustomed field of useful occupation; pampers the harmful appetites of luxury, and introduces intemperance and profligacy in a thousand hateful forms.

The remedy for these vast and continually increasing evils cannot be doubted, if the cause has been correctly assigned. It is to simplify government. It is to reduce it to its proper sphere. . . .

Twenty thousand churches are scattered over our land, and the number of their communicants probably exceeds two millions. Here then we see the happy fruits of applying to religion the principles of freedom; and what ground is there to doubt that equally happy would be the result of applying the same principles to trade? Why should trade, any more than religion, have its hierarchs, holding their powers from a political source? And why should tithes be imposed on the people, for the support of commercial, any more than ecclesiastical high priests and pontiffs?

It is no answer to these questions to call those who propose them agrarians, levellers, and visionaries. Abuse is not argument; and though it may retard, it cannot arrest, the progress of sound opinion. Well for mankind that this is so; since it has ever been the doom of reason to be assailed with scoff and clamor by ignorance and prejudice. . . . They who, in this age of the world . . . would attempt to obstruct the course of free, calm, fearless discussion by derisive epithets and paltry catch-words for folly to play upon, if they had lived three centuries ago, would have been incited by the same temper . . . to break their opponents on the wheel or burn them at the stake. Intolerance shows itself in many guises; but all impatience of the free, dispassionate exercise of reason—all hindrances to the utmost liberty of inquiry, whether consisting in physical resistance, or in the terrors of denunciation, and the arts of ridicule, are but various forms in which that bad spirit manifests itself. Discussion is the great means of eliciting truth. Truth is an ethereal light kindled by the attrition of opposite opinions. They who would quench it, if through fear of its effects, are despicable, if through any other motive, they are base.

7

François Pierre Guillaume Guizot, History of Civilization in Europe, *trans. William Hazlitt (New York: Colonial Press, 1846)*

At seven years old, François Guizot, who became the greatest French liberal historian of all time, had good reason to hate his country. During the revolutionary Reign of Terror, the Robespierre regime seized and executed Guizot's father, scarring the youth deeply and forcing early maturity. From a very early day in his life, the starkest facts of reality struck François with force and clarity. Guizot studied classical and postclassical history in Geneva, then diligently wrote and lectured his way to the Chair of Modern History at the Sorbonne.

By virtue of his intellectual celebrity, Guizot was also the de facto leader of liberal opposition to the ultraroyalists in the 1820s. In the elections of 1827, liberal forces acquired sufficient power to challenge King Charles X's royalists in the parliament, provoking a potential crisis of state and the possible dissolution of representative government. As a sop to the liberals, the government lifted its ban on unapproved university lectures. In response, Guizot began his immensely important series of lectures titled "History of Civilization in Europe."[30]

In his first lecture, Guizot defends and defines his subject. Civilization, he says, is an idea, and as such, is extremely difficult to specifically define and locate in the historical experience. But it is a fact, nonetheless. More than simply a fact, civilization is *the* historical fact—it is the sum total of an infinite complexity of human interactions, and histories of human civilization are the broadest and most widely encompassing of all possible histories. Civilization is the *process* through which societies improve themselves over time. For Guizot, however, the mechanisms producing change over time in and between civilizations were far more important than the mere fact of civilization's existence. As he promises to show throughout the course of his lectures, conflict drives history: man's dual nature as at once an atomized individual *and* a social creature produced an inherent

and unavoidable conflict between the liberty of the individual and the power of society. Warning his audience
against pride and vanity, he concludes by reminding us
all that we remain agents of history. Although we may
never be able to conquer the cycle of history, Guizot
suggests that we can indeed resolve ourselves to channel civilization's revolutionary energies toward accomplishing man's goals, individual *and* social.

In his second lecture, Guizot began by identifying the
key elements of Western civilization's historical fellows.
In the ancient world, each civilization clustered around
a single "great idea," or motivating force. In Egypt and
India, theocracy prevailed; in Greece and Asia Minor,
democracy; in Rome, the municipality provided cast and
character to all of Roman civilization. Modern Europe, by
contrast, grew out of a balanced multiplicity of "great
ideas" and institutions stitched together from a variety
of ancient antecedents. As a civilization of cities, Rome
proved incapable of maintaining a great empire and
dissolved in the fifth century, leaving a patchwork of
municipal corporations and sea of citizens behind.

The Christian church filled much of the political and
cultural void left by Western Rome's fall, dividing the
affairs of church and state while establishing the
moral fallibility of temporal rulers. Meanwhile, innumerable Germanic warlords claimed hereditary title to
Roman land, Roman legitimacy, and Roman privilege.
The Germans also contributed their unique love of

individual liberty, a creature unknown in the Roman world. Although Romans thought of liberty in purely civic, political terms, all "barbarians" thought of themselves as free by virtue of their individuality.

When combined, the Roman municipal and imperial traditions, new and powerful Christian institutions, and Germanic individualism produced a European culture capable of balancing interests, revitalizing itself, and avoiding the standard rise-decline-fall pattern of historical development. European history's endless conflicts between popes and emperors, scientists and clergymen, kings and vassals, rulers and peasants, Catholic sand heretics, all produced change from within. This internally produced drive for revitalization made European civilization an ever-changing project. Unlike the static ancient monuments to single ideas, European civilization by its very nature shifted and evolved according to its environment. Unable to evolve, the ancients disappeared. Guizot ultimately feared that the West might abandon its natural, difficult, although decidedly healthy pluralism and share the same dismal historical fate.

In his third lecture, therefore, Guizot pursued the long history of balancing conflict between "the various elements of our civilization[:] monarchy, theocracy, aristocracy, and democracy." He argues that behind each mode of governance and social order lay the ultimate authority of force. Because no one order prevailed over all, any particular group of rulers relied at base on their own personal power and authority only. As time wore on, new institutions emerged to solidify, codify, and justify existing concentrations of power.

Constant conflict from within and without entrenched rulers further and encouraged the formation of settled boundaries, personal kingdoms, and nascent nation-states. "Europe labored to emerge from this state," and in different corners of the continent, different models of Western civilization prevailed. Through it all, however, ancient civilization decidedly gave way to "barbarian" notions of individualism and liberty. As orders and interests balanced one another and ensured that no single component of Western life could dominate the whole, Germanic, feudal chaos proliferated throughout the continent.

After establishing the origins of European feudalism, the fourth lecture proceeds to explain exactly what feudalism was. Given that the French people and aristocracy had recently taken turns remaking history, Guizot urged his audience to look at feudalism with fresh perspectives attuned to analysis rather than simple criticism. Although there was (and remains) much to criticize about feudalism, Guizot argues that "in the tenth century the feudal system was necessary, and the only social system practicable."

Although his primary evidence for this controversial assertion remained "the universality of its adoption," Guizot maintains that in its own way, feudalism too was revolutionary. By fusing Germanic individualism, visions of Christian theocracy, and the corporate-imperial remnants of Western Rome, the earliest of European feudal lords created a new, dynamic, vibrant civilization of their own. Yes, the new feudal regimes were incredibly oppressive—all governments are founded on force and carry with them the seeds of social resentment and revolution. When stitched together, from generation to generation and over the centuries, such tensions became the historian's narrative of change over time.

Thus, to counteract the encroaching power of early feudal lords, innumerable barons, municipalities, bishops, and merchants petitioned legal authorities for the protection of person and property. Virtually all levels and components of early medieval society, therefore, incorporated themselves (or were forced) into the feudal patchwork of overlapping, interacting, and reciprocal legal, social, and economic obligations. The internal competition promoted stability and long-term deference to the forces of law and order. In Guizot's summation, therefore: "Feudalism, as a whole, was truly a confederation. It rested upon the same principles, for example, as those on which is based, in the present day, the federative system of the United States of America."

Lecture I. Civilization in General

I have used the term European civilization, because it is evident that there is an European civilization; that a certain unity pervades the civilization of the various European states; that, notwithstanding infinite diversities of time, place and circum-stance, this civilization takes its first rise in facts almost wholly similar, proceeds everywhere upon the same principles, and tends to produce well nigh everywhere analogous results. There is, then, an European civilization. . . .

Its history cannot be derived from the history of any single European state. If, on the one hand, it is manifestly characterized by brevity, on the other, its variety is no less prodigious; it has not developed itself with completeness, in any one particular country. The features of its physiognomy are wide-spread; we must seek the elements of its history, now in France, now in England, now in Germany, now in Spain.

We of France occupy a favorable position for pursuing the study of European civilization. . . . It is without vanity, I think, we may say that France has been the center, the focus of European civi-lization. . . . At different epochs, Italy has taken the lead of her, in the arts; England, in political institutions; and there may be other respects under which, at particular periods, other European nations have manifested a superiority to her; but it is impossible to deny, that whenever France has seen herself thus outstripped in the career of civilization, she has called up fresh vigor, has sprung forward with a new impulse, and has soon found herself abreast with, or in advance of all the rest. . . . There is scarcely any great idea, any great principle of civilization, which, prior to its diffu-sion, has not passed in this way through France.

And for this reason: there is in the French character something sociable, something sympathetic, something which makes its way with greater facility and effect than does the national genius of any other people; whether from our language, whether from the turn of our mind, of our manners, certain it is that our ideas are more popular than those of other people, present themselves more clearly and intelligibly to the masses and penetrate among them more readily; in a word, perspicuity, sociability, sympathy, are the peculiar characteristics of France, of her civilization, and it is these qualities which rendered her eminently fit to march at the very head of European civilization. . . .

The very portion of history which we are accustomed to call its philosophy, the relation of events to each other, the connection which unites them, their causes and their effects,—these are all facts, these are all history, just as much as the narratives of battles, and of other material and visible events. Facts of this class it is doubtless more difficult to disentangle and explain; we are more liable to error in giving an account of them, and it is no easy thing to give them life and animation, to exhibit them in clear and vivid colors; but this difficulty in no degree changes their nature; they are none the less an essential element of history.

Civilization is one of these facts; a general, hidden, complex fact; very difficult, I allow, to describe, to relate, but which none the less for that exists [and] has a right to be described and related. . . . It has been asked, whether it is a good or an evil? Some bitterly deplore it; others rejoice at it. We may ask, whether it is an universal fact, whether there is an universal civilization of the human species, a destiny of humanity; whether the nations have handed down from age to age, something which has never been lost, which must increase, from a larger and larger mass, and thus pass on to the end of time? For my own part, I am convinced that there is, in reality, a general destiny of humanity, a transmission of the aggregate of civilization; and, consequently, an universal history of civilization to be written. But without raising questions so great, so difficult to solve, if we restrict ourselves to a definite limit of time and space, if we confine ourselves to the history of a certain number of centuries, of a certain people, it is evident that within these bounds, civilization is a fact which can be described, related—which is history. I will at once add, that this history is the greatest of all, that it includes all.

And, indeed, does it not seem to yourselves that the fact civilization is the fact *par excellence*—the general and definitive fact, in which all the others terminate, into which they all resolve themselves? Take all the facts which compose the history of a nation, and which we are accustomed to regard as the elements of its life; take its institutions, its commerce, its industry, its wars, all the details of its government: when we would consider these facts in their aggregate, in their connection, when we would estimate them, judge them, we ask in what they have contributed to the civilization of that nation, what part they have taken in it, what influence they have exercised over it. It is in this way that we not only form a complete idea of them, but measure and appreciate their true value; they are, as it were, rivers, of which we ask what quantity of water it is they contribute to the ocean? For civilization is a sort of ocean, constituting the wealth of a people, and on whose bosom all the elements of the life of that people, all the powers supporting its existence, assemble and unite. This is so true, that even facts, which from their nature are odious, pernicious, which weigh painfully upon nations, despotism, for example, and anarchy, if they have contributed in some way to civilization, if they have enabled it to make an onward stride, up to a certain point we pardon them, we overlook their wrongs, their evil nature; in a word, wherever we recognize civilization, whatever the facts which have created it, we are tempted to forget the price it has cost. . . .

At all times, in all countries, religion has assumed the glory of having civilized the people; sciences, letters, arts, all the intellectual and moral pleasures, have claimed a share of this glory; and we have deemed it a praise and an honor to them, when we have recognized this claim on their part. Thus, facts the most important and sublime in themselves, independently of all external result, and simply in their relations with the soul of man, increase in importance, rise in sublimity from their affinity with civilization. Such is the value of this general fact, that it gives value to everything it touches. And not only does it give value; there are even occasions when the facts of which we speak, religious creeds, philosophical ideas, letters, arts, are especially considered and judged of with reference to their influence upon civilization; an influence which becomes, up to a certain point and during a certain time, the conclusive measure of their merit, of their value. . . .

For a long period, and in many countries, the word *civilization* has been in use; people have attached to the word ideas more or less clear, more or less comprehensive; but there it is in use, and those who use it attach some meaning or other to it. It is the general, human, popular meaning of this word that we must study. There is almost always in the usual acceptation of the most general terms more accuracy than in the definitions, apparently more strict, more precise, of science. It is common sense which gives to words their ordinary signification, and common sense is the characteristic of humanity. The ordinary signification of a word is formed by gradual progress and in the constant presence of facts; so that when a fact presents itself which seems to come within the meaning of a known term, it is received into it, as it were, naturally. . . .

When the meaning of a word, on the other hand, is determined by science, this determination, the work of one individual, or of a small number of individuals, takes place under the influence of some particular fact which has struck upon the mind. Thus, scientific definitions are, in general, much more narrow, and, hence, much less accurate, much less true at bottom, than the popular meanings of the terms. In studying as a fact the meaning of the word civilization, in investigating all the ideas which are comprised within it, according to the common sense of mankind, we shall make a much greater progress toward a knowledge of the fact itself than by attempting to give it ourselves a scientific definition, however more clear and precise the latter might appear at first. . . .

It appears to me that the first fact comprised in the word civilization . . . is the fact of progress, of development; it presents at once the idea of a people marching onward, not to change its place, but to change its condition; of a people whose culture is conditioning itself, and ameliorating itself. The idea of progress, of development, appears to me the fundamental idea contained in the word, *civilization*. . . .

The etymology of the word would seem to answer in a clear and satisfactory manner: it says that it is the perfecting of civil life, the development of society, properly so called, of the relations of men among themselves.

Such is, in fact, the first idea which presents itself to the understanding when the word civilization is pronounced; we at once figure forth to ourselves the extension, the greatest activity, the best organization of the social relations: on the one hand, an increasing production of the means of giving strength and happiness to society; on the other, a more equitable distribution, among individuals, of the strength.

Is this all? . . .

Our instinct at once feels repugnant to so narrow a definition of human destiny. It feels at the first glance that the word civilization comprehends something more extensive, more complex, something superior to the simple perfection of the social relations, of social power and happiness. . . .

We might point out [that in those] states in which the prosperity is greater, is of more rapid growth, is better distributed among individuals than elsewhere, and in which, nevertheless, by the spontaneous instinct, the general good sense of men, the civilization is judged inferior to that of countries not so well portioned out in a purely social sense.

What does this mean; what advantages do these latter countries possess? What is it gives them, in the character of civilized countries, this privilege; what so largely compensates in the opinion of mankind for what they so lack in other respects?

A development other than that of social life has been gloriously manifested by them; the development of the individual, internal life, the development of man himself, of his faculties, his sentiments, his ideas. If society with them be less perfect than elsewhere, humanity stands forth in more grandeur and power. There remain, no doubt, many social conquests to be made; but immense intellectual and moral conquests are accomplished; worldly goods, social rights, are wanting to many men; but many great men live and shine in the eyes of the world. Letters, sciences, the arts, display all their splendor. Wherever mankind beholds these great signs, these signs glorified by human nature, wherever it sees created these treasures of sublime enjoyment, it there recognizes and names civilization.

Two facts, then, are comprehended in this great fact; it subsists on two conditions, and manifests itself by two symptoms: the development of social activity, and that of individual activity; the progress of society and the progress of humanity. Wherever the external condition of man extends itself, vivifies, ameliorates itself; wherever the internal nature of man displays itself with lustre, with grandeur; at these two signs, and often despite the profound imperfection of the social state, mankind with loud applause proclaims civilization. . . .

When a great change is accomplished in the state of a country, when there is operated in it a large development of wealth and power, a revolution in the distribution of the social means, this new fact encounters adversaries, undergoes opposition: this is inevitable. What is the general cry of the adversaries of the change? They say that this progress of the social state does not ameliorate, does not regencrate in like manner, in a like degree, the moral, the internal state of man; that it is a false, delusive progress, the result of which is detrimental to morality, to man.

The friends of social development energetically repel this attack; they maintain, on the contrary, that the progress of society necessarily involves and carries with it the progress of morality; that when the external life is better regulated, the internal life is refined and purified. Thus stands the question between the adversaries and partisans of the new state. . . .

In the spontaneous, instinctive conviction of mankind, the two elements of civilization, the social development and the moral development, are closely connected together; that at sight of the one, man at once looks forward to the other. It is to this natural instinctive conviction that those who are maintaining or combating one or other of the two developments address themselves, when they affirm or deny their union. It is well understood, that if we can persuade mankind that the amelioration of the social state will be averse to the internal progress of individuals, we shall have succeeded in decrying and enfeebling the revolution in operation throughout society. On the other hand, when we promise mankind the amelioration of society by means of the amelioration of the individual, it is well understood that the tendency is to place faith in these promises, and it is accordingly made use of with success. It is evidently, therefore, the instinctive belief of humanity, that the movements of civilization are connected the one with the other, and reciprocally produce the one the other. . . .

If from history we extend our inquiries to the nature itself of the two facts which constitute civilization, we are infallibly led to the same result. There is no one who has not experienced this in his own case. When a moral change is operated in man, when he acquires an idea, or a virtue, or a faculty, more than he had before—in a word, when he develops himself individually, what is the desire, what the want, which at the same moment takes possession of him? It is the desire, the want, to communicate the new sentiment to the world about him, to give realization to his thoughts externally. As soon as a man acquires anything, as soon as his being takes in his own conviction a new development, assumes an additional value, forthwith he attaches to this new development, this fresh value, the idea of possession; he feels himself impelled, compelled by his instinct, by an inward voice, to extend to others the change, the amelioration, which has been accomplished in his own person. We owe the great reformers solely to this cause; the mighty men who have changed the face of the world, after having changed themselves, were urged onward, were guided on their course, by no other want than this. So much for the alteration which is operated in the internal man; now to the other. A revolution is accomplished in the state of society; it is better regulated, rights and property are more equitably distributed among its members—that is to say, the aspect of the world becomes purer and more beautiful, the action of government, the conduct of men in their mutual relations, more just, more benevolent. . . .

Of those two developments of which we have spoken, and which constitute the fact of civilization, the development of society on the one hand and of humanity on the other, which is the end, which is the means? . . . Is society made to serve the individual, or the individual to serve society? On the answer to this question inevitably depends that whether the destiny of man is purely social; whether society drains up and exhausts the whole man;

or whether he bears within him something intrinsic—something superior to his existence on earth. . . .

Royer-Collard, has solved this question according to his own conviction, at least, in his speech on the Sacrilege Bill. I find in that speech these two sentences: " Human societies are born, live and die, on the earth; it is there their destinies are accomplished. . . . But they contain not the whole man. After he has engaged himself to society, there remains to him the noblest part of himself, those high faculties by which he elevates himself to God, to a future life, to unknown felicity in an invisible world. . . . We, persons individual and identical, veritable beings endowed with immortality, we have a different destiny from that of states."

I will add nothing to this; I will not undertake to treat the question itself; I content myself with stating it. It is met with at the history of civilization: when the history of civilization is completed, when there is nothing more to say as to our present existence, man inevitably asks himself whether all is exhausted, whether he has reached the end of all things? This then is the last, the highest of all those problems to which history of civilization can lead. It is sufficient for me to have indicated its position and its grandeur. . . .

I believe that when we have got but a very little way into this study, we shall acquire the conviction that civilization is as yet very young; that the world has by no means as yet measured the whole of its career. Assuredly human thought is at this time very far from being all that it is capable of becoming; we are very far from comprehending the whole future of humanity: let each of us descend into his own mind, let him interrogate himself as to the utmost possible good he has formed a conception of and hopes for; let him then compare his idea with what actually exists in the world; he will be convinced that society and civilization are very young; that notwithstanding the length of the road they have come, they have incomparably further to go. This will lessen nothing of the pleasure that we shall take in the contemplation of our actual condition. . . .

Let us be careful, however, not to give ourselves up too much to the idea of our happiness and amelioration, or we may fall into two grave dangers, pride and indolence; we may conceive an over-confidence in the power and success of the human mind, in our own enlightenment, and, at the same time, suffer ourselves to become enervated by the luxurious ease of our condition. . . . Much has been given to us, much will be required of us; we must render to posterity a strict account of our conduct; the public, the government, all are now subjected to discussion, examination, responsibility. Let us attach ourselves firmly, faithfully, undeviatingly, to the principles of our civilization—justice, legality, publicity, liberty; and let us never forget, that while we ourselves require, and with reason, that all things shall be open to our inspection and inquiry, we ourselves are under the eye of the world, and shall, in our turn, be discussed, be judged.

Lecture II. Of European Civilization in Particular: Its Distinguishing Characteristics—Its Superiority— Its Elements

When we look at the civilizations which have preceded that of modern Europe, whether in Asia or elsewhere, including even those of Greece and Rome, it is impossible not to be struck with the unity of character which reigns among them. Each appears as though it had emanated from a single fact, from a single idea. One might almost assert that society was under the influence of one single principle, which universally prevailed and determined the character of its institutions, its manners, its opinions—in a word, all its developments.

In Egypt, for example, it was the theocratic principle that took possession of society, and showed itself in its manners, in its monuments, and in all that has come down to us of Egyptian civilization. In India the same phenomenon occurs. . . . In other regions a different organization may be observed—perhaps the domination of a conquering caste . . . imposing [its] laws and its character. In another place, perhaps, we discover society under the entire influence of the democratic principle; such was the case in the commercial republics which covered the coasts of Asia Minor and Syria. . . .

I do not mean to aver that this overpowering influence of one single principle, of one single form, prevailed without any exception in the civilization of those states. If we go back to their earliest history, we shall find that the various powers which dwelt in the bosom of these societies frequently struggled for mastery. . . . These struggles, however, mostly took place in periods beyond the reach of history, and no evidence of them is left beyond a vague tradition. . . .

The war always ended by the domination of some special principle, which, if not exclusive, at least greatly preponderated. The co-existence and strife of various principles among these nations were no more than a passing, an accidental circumstance.

From this cause a remarkable unity characterizes most of the civilizations of antiquity, the results of which, however, were very different. In one nation, as in Greece, the unity of the social principle led to a development of wonderful rapidity; no other people ever ran so brilliant a career in so short a time. But Greece had hardly become glorious, before she appeared worn out: her decline, if not quite so rapid as her rise, was strangely sudden. It seems as if the principle which called Greek civilization into life was exhausted. No other came to invigorate it, or supply its place. . . .

How different from all this is the case as respects the civilization of modern Europe! Take ever so rapid a glance at this, and it strikes you at once as diversified, confused, and stormy. All the principles of social organization are found existing together within it; powers temporal, powers spiritual, the theocratic, monarchic, aristocratic, and democratic elements, all classes of society, all the social situations, are jumbled together, and visible within it; as well as infinite gradations of liberty, of wealth, and of influence. These various powers, too, are found here in a state of continual struggle among themselves, without any one having sufficient force to master the others, and take sole possession of society. Among the ancients, at every great epoch, all communities seem cast in the same mould: it was now pure monarchy, now theocracy or democracy, that became the reigning principle, each in its turn reigning absolutely. . . .

In the moral character, in the notions and sentiments of Europe, we find the same variety, the same struggle. Theocratic opinions, monarchical opinions, aristocratic opinions, democratic opinions, cross and jostle, struggle, become interwoven, limit, and modify each other. . . .

In every part, then, we find this character of variety to prevail in modern civilization. . . . An unbounded career is open before it; and from day to day it presses forward to the race with increasing rapidity, because increased freedom attends upon all its movements. While in other civilizations the exclusive domination, or at least the excessive preponderance of a single principle, of a single form, led to tyranny, in modern Europe the diversity of the elements of social order, the incapability of any one to exclude the rest, gave birth to the liberty which now prevails. The inability of the various principles to exterminate one another compelled each to endure the others, made it necessary for them to live in common, for them to enter into a sort of mutual understanding. . . . The variety of elements of European civilization, and the constant warfare in which they have been engaged, have given birth in Europe to that liberty which we prize so dearly. . . .

Rome in its origin was a mere municipality, a corporation. The Roman government was nothing more than an assemblage of institutions suitable to a population enclosed within the walls of a city; that is to say, they were *municipal* institutions;—this was their distinctive character. . . .

At this time there were no country places, no villages; at least the country was nothing like what it is in the present day. It was cultivated, no doubt, but it was not peopled. The proprietors of lands and of country estates dwelt in cities; they left these occasionally to visit their rural property, where they usually kept a certain number of slaves; but that which we now call the country, that scattered population, sometimes in lone houses, sometimes in hamlets and villages, and which everywhere dots our land with agricultural dwellings, was altogether unknown in ancient Italy.

And what was the case when Rome extended her boundaries? If we follow her history, we shall find that she conquered or founded a host of cities. It was with cities she fought, it was with cities she treated, it was into cities she sent colonies. In short, the history of the conquest of the world by Rome is the history of the conquest and foundation of a vast number of cities. . . .

Examine the character of the monuments left us of ancient Rome—the old Roman roads. We find great roads extending from city to city; but the thousands of little by-paths, which now intersect every part of the country, were then unknown. Neither do we find any traces of that immense number of lesser objects—of churches, castles, country-seats, and villages, which were spread all over the country during the middle ages. Rome has left no traces of this kind; her only bequest consists of vast monuments impressed with a municipal character, destined for a numerous population, crowded into a single spot. In whatever point of view you consider the Roman world, you meet with this almost exclusive preponderance of cities, and an absence of country populations and dwellings. This municipal character of the Roman world evidently rendered the unity, the social tie of a great state, extremely difficult to establish and maintain.

A municipal corporation like Rome might be able to conquer the world, but it was a much more difficult task to govern it, to mould it into one compact body. Thus, when the work seemed done, when all the West, and a great part of the East, had submitted to the Roman yoke, we find an immense host of cities, of little states formed for separate existence and independence, breaking their chains, escaping on every side. This was one of the causes which made the establishment of the empire necessary; which called for a more concentrated form of government, one better able to hold together elements which had so few points of cohesion. The empire endeavored to unite and to bind together this extensive and scattered society; and to a certain point it succeeded. . . .

It was with this spirit, with this administrative organization, and with the military system connected with it, that the Roman empire struggled against the dissolution which was working within it, and against the barbarians who attacked it from without. But, though it struggled long, the day at length arrived when all the skill and power of despotism, when all the pliancy of servitude, was insufficient to prolong its fate. In the fourth century, all the ties which had held this immense body together seem to have been loosened or snapped; the barbarians broke in on every side; the provinces no longer resisted, no longer troubled themselves with the general destiny. At this crisis an extraordinary idea entered the minds of one or two of the emperors: they wished to try whether the hope of general liberty, whether a confederation, a system something like what we now call the representative system, would not better defend the Roman empire than the despotic administration which already existed. There is a mandate of Honorius and the younger Theodosius, addressed, in the year 418, to the prefect of Gaul, the object of which was to establish a sort of representative government in the south of Gaul, and by its aid still to preserve the unity of empire. . . .

Notwithstanding this call, the provinces and cities refused the proffered boon; nobody would name deputies, none would go to Arles. This centralization, this unity, was opposed to the primitive nature of this society. The spirit of locality, and of municipality, everywhere reappeared; the impossibility of reconstructing a general society, of building up the whole into one general state, became evident. The cities, confining themselves to the affairs of their own corporations, shut themselves up within their own walls, and the empire fell, because none would belong to the empire; because citizens wished but to belong to their city. Thus the Roman empire, at its fall, was resolved into the elements of which it had been composed, and the preponderance of municipal rule and government was again everywhere visible. The Roman world had been formed of cities, and to cities again it returned. . . .

It must be observed, then, that the two elements which passed from the Roman civilization into ours were, *first*, the system of municipal corporations, its habits, its regulations, its principle of liberty—a general civil legislation, common to all; *secondly*, the idea of absolute power;—the principle of order and the principle of servitude.

Meanwhile, within the very heart of Roman society, there had grown up another society of a very different nature, founded upon different principles, animated by different sentiments, and which has brought into European civilization elements of a widely different character: I speak of the *Christian Church*. . . . At the end of the fourth century, and the beginning of the fifth, Christianity was no longer a simple belief, it was an institution—it had formed itself into a corporate body. It had its government, a body of priests; a settled ecclesiastical polity for the regulation of their different functions; revenues; independent means of influence. It had the rallying points suitable to a great society, in its provincial, national, and general councils, in which were wont to be debated in common the affairs of society. . . .

And, first, it was of immense advantage to European civilization that a moral influence, a moral power—a power resting entirely upon moral convictions, upon moral opinions and sentiments—should have established itself in society, just at this period, when it seemed upon the point of being crushed by the overwhelming physical force which had taken possession of it. . . .

Finally, the Church commenced an undertaking of great importance to society—I mean the separation of temporal and spiritual authority . . . [which] rests solely upon the idea that physical, that brute force, has no right or authority over the mind, over convictions, over truth. It flows from the distinction established between the world of thought and the world of action, between our inward and intellectual nature and the outward world around us. . . .

Unfortunately, all its influences, even at this period, were not equally beneficial. . . . There already prevailed in the bosom of the Church a desire to separate the governing and the governed. The attempt was thus early made to render the government entirely independent of the people under its authority—to take possession of their mind and life, without the conviction of their reason or the consent of their will. The Church, moreover, endeavored with all her might to establish the principle of theocracy, to usurp temporal authority, to obtain universal dominion. And when she failed in this, when she found she could not obtain absolute power for herself, she did what was almost as bad: to obtain a share of it, she leagued herself with temporal rulers, and enforced, with all her might, their claim to absolute power at the expense of the liberty of the subject.

Such, then, I think, were the principal elements of civilization which Europe derived, in the fifth century, from the Church and from the Roman empire. Such was the state of the Roman world when the barbarians came to make it their prey; and we have now only to study the barbarians themselves, in order to be acquainted with the elements which were united and mixed together in the cradle of our civilization. . . .

There is one sentiment, one in particular, which it is necessary to understand before we can form a true picture of a barbarian; it is the pleasure of personal independence—the pleasure of enjoying, in full force and liberty, all his powers in the various ups and downs of fortune; the fondness for activity without labor; for a life of enterprise and adventure. Such was the prevailing character and disposition of the barbarians; such were the moral wants which put these immense masses of men into motion. It is extremely difficult for us, in the regulated society in which we move, to form anything like a correct idea of this feeling, and of the influence which it exercised upon the rude barbarians of the fourth and fifth centuries. . . .

This love of individual liberty . . . was unknown among the Romans, it was unknown in the Christian Church, it was unknown in nearly all the civilizations of antiquity. The liberty which we meet with in ancient civilizations is political liberty; it is the liberty of the citizen. It was not about his personal liberty that man troubled himself, it was about his liberty as a citizen. . . .

There is another, a second element of civilization, which we likewise inherit from the barbarians alone: I mean military patronage, the tie which became formed between individuals, between warriors, and which, without destroying the liberty of any, without even destroying in the commencement the equality up to a certain point which existed between them, laid the foundation of a graduated subordination, and was the origin of that aristocratical organization which, at a later period, grew into the feudal system. The germ of this connection was the attachment of man to man; the fidelity which united individuals, without apparent necessity, without any obligation arising from the general principles of society. In none of the ancient republics do you see any example of individuals particularly and freely attached to other individuals. They were all attached to the city. . . .

What we might call the hard fortune of European civilization—the trouble, the toil it has undergone—the violence it has suffered in its course—have been of infinitely more service to the progress of humanity than that tranquil, smooth simplicity, in which other civilizations have run their course. . . .

Lecture III. Of Political Legitimacy—Co-Existence of All the Systems of Government in the Fifth Century—Attempts to Reorganize Society

The various elements of our civilization . . . monarchy, theocracy, aristocracy, and democracy, each would have us believe that, originally, European society belonged to it alone, and that it has only lost the power it then possessed by the usurpation of the other elements. . . .

For what is political legitimacy? Evidently nothing more than a right founded upon antiquity, upon duration, which is obvious from the simple fact, that priority of time is pleaded as the source of right, as proof of legitimate power. . . . The Italian and Swiss aristocracies and democracies, the little republic of San Marino, as well as the most powerful monarchies, have considered themselves legitimate, and have been acknowledged as such; all founding their claim to this title upon the antiquity of their institutions; upon the historical priority and duration of their particular system of government. . . .

You will find that all power . . . owes its existence in the first place partly to force. I do not say that force alone has been, in all cases, the foundation of power, or that this, without any other title, could in every case have been established by force alone. Other claims undoubtedly are requisite. Certain powers become established in consequence of certain social expediencies, of certain relations with the state of society, with its customs or opinions. But it is impossible to close our eyes to the fact, that violence has sullied the birth of all the authorities in the world, whatever may have been their nature or their form.

This origin, however, no one will acknowledge. All authorities, whatever their nature, disclaim it. None of them will allow themselves to be considered as the offspring of force. Governments are warned by an invincible instinct that force is no title—that might is not right—and that, while they rest upon no other foundation than violence, they are entirely destitute of right. . . .

This fact alone proves that the idea of violence is not the foundation of political legitimacy,—that it rests upon some other basis.

This disavowal of violence made by every system, proclaims, as plainly as facts can speak, that there is another legitimacy, the true foundation of all the others, the legitimacy of reason, of justice, of right. It is to this origin that they seek to link themselves. As they feel scandalized at the very idea of being the offspring of force, they pretend to be invested, by virtue of their antiquity, with a different title. The first characteristic, then, of political legitimacy, is to disclaim violence as the source of authority, and to associate it with a moral notion, a moral force—with the notion of justice, of right, of reason. . . .

Violence presides at the birth of governments, at the birth of societies; but time rolls on. He changes the works of violence. He corrects them. He corrects them, simply because society endures, and because it is composed of men. Man bears within himself certain notions of order, of justice, of reason, with a certain desire to bring them into play—he wishes to see them predominate in the sphere in which he moves. For this he labors unceasingly; and if the social system in which he lives, continues, his labor is not in vain. Man naturally brings reason, morality, and legitimacy into the world in which he lives.

Independently of the labor of man, by a special law of Providence which it is impossible to mistake, a law analogous to that which rules the material world, there is a certain degree of order, of intelligence, of justice, indispensable to the duration of human society. From the simple fact of its duration we may argue, that a society is not completely irrational, savage, or iniquitous; that it is not altogether destitute of intelligence, truth, and justice, for without these, society cannot hold together. Again, as society develops itself, it becomes stronger, more powerful; if the social system is continually augmented by the increase of individuals who accept and approve its regulations, it is because the action of time gradually introduces into it more right, more intelligence, more justice; it is because a gradual approximation is made in its affairs to the principles of true legitimacy.

Thus forces itself into the world, and from the world into the mind of man, the notion of political legitimacy. Its foundation in the first place, at least to a certain extent, is moral legitimacy—is justice, intelligence, and truth; it next obtains the sanction of time, which gives reason to believe that affairs are conducted by reason, that the true legitimacy has been introduced. . . .

Political legitimacy is as much attached to liberty as to power; to the rights of individuals as to the forms under which are exercised the public functions. . . .

The dispute, then, that has arisen among the various systems which hold a part in European civilization, respecting which bore chief sway at its origin, proves that they all existed there together, without any one of them having prevailed so generally as to give to society its form or its name.

This is, indeed, the character of the dark age: it was a chaos of all the elements; the childhood of all the systems; a universal jumble, in which even strife itself was neither permanent nor systematic. By an examination of the social system of this period under its various forms, I could show you that in no part of them is there to be found anything like a general principle, anything like stability. . . .

Freemen were continually changing their condition, and becoming vassals to nobles, in consideration of some gift which these might have to bestow; while others were falling into the class of slaves or serfs. Vassals were continually struggling to shake off the yoke of patronage, to regain their independence, to return to the class of freemen. Every part of society was in motion. There was a continual passing and repassing from one class to the other. No man continued long in the same rank; no rank continued long the same.

Property was in much the same state. . . . There was nothing more settled, nothing more general, in the state of lands than in the state of persons. Everything shows the difficulties of the transition from the wandering life to the settled life; from the simple personal relations which existed among the barbarians as invading migratory hordes, to the mixed relations of persons and property. During this transition all was confused, local, and disordered.

In institutions we . . . find here three different systems at once before us:—first, Monarchy; second, Aristocracy, or the proprietorship of men and lands, as lord and vassal; and, [third], Free institutions, or assemblies of free men deliberating in common. No one of these systems entirely prevailed. Free institutions existed; but the men who should have formed part of these assemblies seldom troubled themselves to attend them. Baronial jurisdiction was not more regularly exercised. Monarchy, the most simple institution, the most easy to determine, here had no fixed character; at one time it was elective, at another hereditary—here the son succeeded to his father, there the election was confined to a family; in another place it was open to all, purely elective, and the choice fell on a distant relation, or perhaps a stranger. In none of these systems can we discover anything fixed; all the institutions, as well as the social conditions, dwelt together, continually confounded, continually changing.

The same unsettledness existed with regard to states; they were created, suppressed, united, and divided; no governments, no frontiers, no nations; a general jumble of situations, principles, events, races, languages; such was barbarian Europe. . . .

The material, or outward cause, was the continuance of invasion; for it must not be supposed that the invasions of the barbarian hordes stopped all at once in the fifth century. . . .

Such was the situation of Europe from the fifth to the ninth century. Pressed on the south by the Mohammedans, and on the north by the Germans and Slavonians, it could not be otherwise than that the reaction of this double invasion should keep the interior of Europe in a state of continual ferment. Populations were incessantly displaced, crowded one upon another; there was no regularity, nothing permanent or fixed. . . .

After all is said and done, whatever may be the course of external affairs, it is man himself who makes our world. It is according to the ideas, the sentiments, the moral and intellectual dispositions of man himself, that the world is regulated, and marches onward. It is upon the intellectual state of man that the visible form of society depends. . . .

It is clear that where men possess no ideas extending beyond their own existence, where their intellectual horizon is bounded in self, if they are still delivered up to their own passions, and their own wills,—if they have not among them a certain number of notions and sentiments common to them all, round which they may all rally, it is clear that they cannot form a society: without this each individual will be a principle of agitation and dissolution in the social system of which he forms a part.

Wherever individualism reigns nearly absolute, wherever man considers but himself, wherever his ideas extend not beyond himself, wherever he only yields obedience to his own passions, there society—that is to say, society in any degree extended or permanent—becomes almost impossible. . . .

Europe labored to emerge from this state. It is contrary to the nature of man, even when sunk into it by his own fault, to wish to remain in it. . . . In the midst of confusion and disorder, he is haunted and tormented by a taste for order and improvement. The claims of justice, of prudence, of development, disturb him, even under the yoke of the most brutish egotism. He feels himself impelled to improve the material world, society, and himself; he labors to do this, without attempting to account to himself for the want which urges him to the task. The barbarians aspired to civilization, while they were yet incapable of it—nay, more—while they even detested it whenever its laws restrained their selfish desires. . . .

Among the barbarians themselves, or their barbarian ancestors, many had witnessed the greatness of the Roman empire; they had served in its armies; they had conquered it. The image, the name of Roman civilization dazzled them; they felt a desire to imitate it; to bring it back again, to preserve some portion of it. This was another cause which ought to have forced them out of the state of barbarism. . . .

A third cause, and one which readily presents itself to every one was the Christian Church. The Christian Church was a regularly constituted society, having its maxims, its rules, its discipline, together with an ardent desire to extend its influence, to conquer its conquerors. . . . No society ever made greater efforts than the Christian Church did from the fifth to the tenth century, to influence the world around it, and to assimilate it to itself. When its history shall become the particular object of our examination, we shall more clearly see what it attempted—it attacked, in a manner, barbarism at every point, in order to civilize it and rule over it.

Finally, a fourth cause of the progress of civilization, a cause which it is impossible strictly to appreciate, but which is not therefore the less real, was the appearance of great men. . . .

These various causes, these various powers working together, led to several attempts, between the fifth and ninth centuries, to draw European society from the barbarous state into which it had fallen.

The first of these was the compilation of the barbarian laws. . . . This was evidently a commencement of civilization—an attempt to bring society under the authority of general and fixed principles.

In Italy and the south of Gaul, another attempt of a different character was made about this time. In these places Roman society had not been so completely rooted out as elsewhere; in the cities, especially, there still remained something of order and civil life; and in these civilization seemed to make a stand. . . .

In Spain, a different power, that of the Church, endeavored to restore the work of civilization . . . in short, each people had its separate laws, though united under the same government, and dwelling together in the same territory. This is what is called personal legislation, in contradistinction to real legislation, which is founded upon territory. . . . All the inhabitants of Spain, Romans, Visigoths, or what not, were compelled to yield obedience to one law. . . .

In France, the attempt was made by another power. It was the work of great men, and above all of Charlemagne. Examine his reign under its different aspects; and you will see that the darling object of his life was to civilize the nations he governed. . . . What he did sprang from necessity, and a desire to repress barbarism. From the beginning to the end of his reign he was occupied in staying the progress of a double invasion—that of the Mohammedans in the south, and that of the Germanic and Slavonic tribes in the north. This is what gave the reign of Charlemagne its military cast. . . . If we pass on from his wars to his government, we shall find the case much the same: his leading object was to introduce order and unity in every part of his extensive dominions. . . . He endeavored to do this . . . by the general assemblies or parliaments. . . . They were not assemblies formed for the preservation of the liberty of the subject, there was nothing in them bearing any likeness to the deliberations of our own days. But Charlemagne found them a means by which he could become well informed of facts and circumstances, and by which he could introduce some regulation, some unity, into the restless and disorganized populations he had to govern. . . .

An attempt of the same nature was made very soon afterwards in England, by Alfred the Great. . . .

At the commencement of the tenth century, there was no longer any visible appearance of the great empire of Charlemagne, nor of the glorious councils of Toledo, but barbarism was drawing nigh its end. Two great results were obtained:

1. The movement of the invading hordes had been stopped both in the north and in the south. . . .

2. In the interior of Europe we begin at this time to see the wandering life decline; populations became fixed; estates and landed possessions became settled; the relations between man and man no longer varied from day to day under the influence of force or chance. The interior and moral condition of man himself began to undergo a change; his ideas, his sentiments, began, like his life, to assume a more fixed character. He began to feel an attachment to the place in which he dwelt; to the connections and associations which he there formed; to those domains which he now calculated upon leaving to his children; to that dwelling which hereafter became his castle; to that miserable assemblage of serfs and slaves, which was one day to become a village. Little societies everywhere began to be formed; little states to be cut out according to the measure . . . of the capacities and prudence of men. There, societies gradually became connected by a tie, the origin of which is to be found in the manners of the German barbarians: the tie of a confederation which would not destroy individual freedom. On one

side we find every considerable proprietor settling himself in his domains, surrounded only by his family and retainers; on the other, a certain graduated subordination of services and rights existing among all these military proprietors scattered over the land. Here we have the feudal system oozing at last out of the bosom of barbarism. Of the various elements of our civilizations, it was natural enough that the Germanic element should first prevail. It was already in possession of power; it had conquered Europe: from it European civilization was to receive its first form—its first social organization.

Lecture IV: The Feudal System

We are now compelled to consider—science and reality—theory and practice—right and fact—and to make them move side by side. Down to the present time these two powers have lived apart. The world has been accustomed to see theory and practice following two different routes, unknown to each other, or at least never meeting. When doctrines, when general ideas, have wished to intermeddle in affairs, to influence the world, it has only been able to effect this under the appearance and by the aid of fanaticism. Up to the present time the government of human societies, the direction of their affairs, have been divided between two sorts of influences; on one side theorists, men who would rule all according to abstract notions—enthusiasts; on the other, men ignorant of all rational principle,—experimentalists, whose only guide is expediency. This state of things is now over. . . .

A great proof that in the tenth century the feudal system was necessary, and the only social system practicable, is the universality of its adoption. Wherever barbarism ceased, feudalism became general. This at first struck men as the triumph of chaos. All unity, all general civilization seemed gone; society on all sides seemed dismembered; a multitude of petty, obscure, isolated, incoherent societies arose. This appeared, to those who lived and saw it, universal anarchy—the dissolution of all things. Consult the poets and historians of the day: they all believed that the end of the world was at hand. Yet this was, in truth, a new and real social system which was forming: feudal society was so necessary, so inevitable, so altogether the only consequence that could flow from the previous state of things, that all entered into it, all adopted its form. Even elements the most foreign to this system, the church, the free communities, royalty, all were constrained to accommodate themselves to it. . . . All things were given in fief, not only estates, but rights and privileges: the right to cut wood in the forests, the privilege of fishing. The churches gave their surplice-fees in fief: the revenues of baptism—the fees for churching women. In the same manner, too, that all the great elements of society were drawn within the feudal enclosure, so even the smallest portions, the most trifling circumstances of common life, became subject to feudalism. . . .

The establishment of the feudal system wrought [a revolutionary change], which had a powerful and striking influence upon European civilization. It changed the distribution of the population. Hitherto the lords of the territory, the conquering population, had lived united in masses more or less numerous, either settled in

cities, or moving about the country in bands; but by the operation of the feudal system these men were brought to live isolated,
each in his own dwelling, at long distances apart. . . . The social
preponderance—the government of society, passed at once from
cities to the country; the baronial courts of the great landed proprietors took the place of the great national assemblies—the public
body was lost in the thousand little sovereignties into which every
kingdom was split. This was the first consequence—a consequence
purely physical, of the triumph of the feudal system. . . .

Having fixed upon an elevated solitary spot, strong by nature,
and which he takes care to render secure, the lordly proprietor
of the domain builds his castle. Here he settles himself, with his
wife and children, and perhaps some few freemen, who, not having obtained fiefs, not having themselves become proprietors,
have attached themselves to his fortunes, and continued to live
with him and form a part of his household. These are the inhabitants of the interior of the castle. At the foot of the hill on which
this castle stands we find huddled together a little population of
peasants, of serfs, who cultivate the lands of the possessor of the
fief. In the midst of this group of cottages religion soon planted a
church and a priest. A priest, in these early days of feudalism, was
generally the chaplain of the baron, and the curate of the village;
two offices which by and by became separated, and the village
had its pastor dwelling by the side of his church. . . .

A feeling of personal consequence, of individual liberty, was a
prevailing feature in the character of the barbarians. The feeling
here, however, was of a different nature; it was no longer simply
the liberty of the man, of the warrior, it was the importance of the

proprietor, of the head of the family, of the master. His situation, with regard to all around him, would naturally beget in him an idea of superiority—a superiority of a peculiar nature, and very different from that we meet with in other systems of civilization. . . . The greatness of [the Roman] aristocrats, associated with a religious and political character, belonged to the situation, to the corporation in general, rather than to the individual. That of the proprietor of a fief belonged to himself alone; he held nothing of any one; all his rights, all his power, centered in himself. He is no religious magistrate; he forms no part of a senate; it is in the individual, in his own person, that all his importance resides—all that he is, he is of himself, in his own name alone. What a vast influence must a situation like this have exercised over him who enjoyed it! What haughtiness, what pride, must it have engendered! Above him, no superior of whom he was but the representative and interpreter; near him no equals; no general and powerful law to restrain him— no exterior force to control him; his will suffered no check but from the limits of his power, and the presence of danger. . . .

[The] spirit of inheritance is a natural off-shoot of the spirit of family, but it nowhere took such deep root as in the feudal system, where it was nourished by the nature of the property with which the family was, as it were, incorporated. The fief differed from other possessions in this, that it constantly required a chief, or owner, who could defend it, manage it, discharge the obligations by which it was held, and thus maintain its rank in the general association of the great proprietors of the kingdom. There thus became a kind of identification of the possessor of the fief with the fief itself, and with all its future possessors. . . .

Quitting the baronial dwelling, let us now descend to the little population that surrounds it. Everything here wears a different aspect. The disposition of man is so kindly and good, that it is almost impossible for a number of individuals to be placed for any length of time in a social situation without giving birth to a certain moral tie between them: sentiments of protection, of benevolence, of affection, spring up naturally. Thus it happened in the feudal system. There can be no doubt, but that after a certain time, kind and friendly feelings would grow up between the feudal lord and his serfs. This, however, took place in spite of their relative situation, and by no means through its influence. Considered in itself, this situation was radically vicious. There was nothing morally common between the holder of the fief and his serfs. They formed part of his estate; they were his property; and under this word property are comprised, not only all the rights which we delegate to the public magistrate to exercise in the name of the state, but likewise all those which we possess over private property: the right of making laws, of levying taxes, of inflicting punishment, as well as that of disposing of them—or selling them. There existed not, in fact, between the lord of the domain and its cultivators, so far as we consider the latter as men, either rights, guarantee, or society.

From this I believe has arisen that almost universal, invincible hatred which country people have at all times borne to the feudal system, to every remnant of it—to its very name. We are not without examples of men having submitted to the heavy yoke of despotism, of their having become accustomed to it, nay more, of their having freely accepted it. Religious despotism, monarchical despotism, have more than once obtained the sanction, almost the love, of the population which they governed. But feudal despotism has always been repulsed, always hateful. It tyrannized over the destinies of men, without ruling in their hearts. Perhaps this may be partly accounted for by the fact, that, in religious and monarchical despotism, authority is always exercised by virtue of some belief or opinion common to both ruler and subjects; he is the representative, the minister, of another power superior to all human powers. He speaks or acts in the name of Divinity or of a common feeling, and not in the name of man himself, of man alone. Feudal despotism differed from this; it was the authority of man over man; the domination of the personal, capricious will of an individual. This perhaps is the only tyranny to which man, much to his honor, never will submit. Wherever in a ruler, or master, he sees but the individual man,—the moment that the authority which presses upon him is no more than an individual, a human will, one like his own, he feels mortified and indignant, and struggles against the yoke which he is compelled to bear. Such was the true, the distinctive character of the feudal power, and such was the origin of the hatred which it has never ceased to inspire.

The religious element which was associated with the feudal power was but little calculated to alleviate its yoke. . . . The church has exercised a very powerful influence in the civilization of Europe, but then it has been by proceeding in a general manner— by changing the general dispositions of mankind. When we enter intimately into the little feudal society, properly so called, we find the influence of the priest between the baron and his serfs to have been very slight. It most frequently happened that he was as rude and nearly as much under control as the serf himself; and there-fore not very well fitted, either by his position or talents, to enter into a contest with the lordly baron. . . .

This system, however, seemed naturally to pour into the mind of every possessor of a fief a certain number of ideas and moral sentiments—ideas of duty, sentiments of affection. . . .

The attempt was made to place all these rights under the pro-tection of institutions founded to ensure their respect. Thus the baronial jurisdictions were erected to administer justice between the possessors of fiefs, upon complaints duly laid before their common suzerain. Thus every baron of any consideration col-lected his vassals in parliament, to debate in common the affairs which required their consent or concurrence. There was, in short, a combination of political, judicial, and military means, which show the attempt to organize the feudal system—to convert the relations between the possessors of fiefs into laws and institutions.

But these laws, these institutions, had no stability—no guarantee. . . .

Without doubt the possessors of fiefs were not all equal among themselves. There were some much more powerful than others; and very many sufficiently powerful to oppress the weaker. But there was none, from the king, the first of the proprietors, down-ward, who was in a condition to impose law upon all the others; in a condition to make himself obeyed. Call to mind that none of the permanent means of power and influence at this time existed—no standing army—no regular taxes—no fixed tribunals. The social authorities—the institutions, had, in a manner, to be new formed every time they were wanted. A tribunal had to be formed for every trial—an army to be formed for every war—a revenue to be formed every time that money was needed. All was occasional—accidental—special; there was no central, permanent, independent means of government. It is evident that in such a system no individual had the power to enforce his will upon others; to compel all to respect and obey the general law.

On the other hand, resistance was easy, in proportion as repression was difficult. Shut up in his castle, with but a small number of enemies to cope with, and aware that other vassals in a like situation were ready to join and assist him, the possessor of a fief found but little difficulty in defending himself. . . .

The possessor of a fief, within his domain, was invested with all the rights and privileges of sovereignty; he inherited them with the territory; they were a matter of private property. What are now called public rights were then private rights; what are now called public authorities were then private authorities. When the possessor of a fief, after having exercised sovereign power in his own name, as proprietor over all the population which lived around him, attended an assembly, attended a parliament held by his sovereign—a parliament not in general very numerous, and composed of men of the same grade, or nearly so, as himself—he did not carry with him any notion of a public authority. This idea was in direct contradiction to all about him—to all his notions, to all that he had done within his own domains. All he saw in these assemblies were men invested with the same rights as himself, in the same situation as himself, acting as he had done by virtue of their own personal title. . . .

Force, indeed, was the true and usual guarantee of right under the feudal system, if force can be called a guarantee. Every law continually had recourse to force to make itself respected or acknowledged. No institution succeeded in doing this. This was so perfectly felt that institutions were scarcely ever applied to. If the agency of the baronial courts or parliaments of vassals had been of any importance, we should find them more generally employed than from history they appear to have been. Their rarity proves their insignificance. . . .

Feudalism, as a whole, was truly a confederation. It rested upon the same principles, for example, as those on which is based, in the present day, the federative system of the United States of America. It affected to leave in the hands of each great proprietor all that portion of the government, of sovereignty, which could be exercised there, and to carry to the suzerain, or to the general assembly of barons, the least possible portion of power, and only this in cases of absolute necessity. You will easily conceive the impossibility of establishing a system like this in a world of ignorance, of brute passions, or, in a word, where the moral condition of man was so imperfect as under the feudal system. The very nature of such a government was in opposition to the notions, the habits and manners of the very men to whom it was to be applied. How then can we be astonished at the bad success of this attempt at organization? . . .

These investigations, I think, bring us to this twofold conclusion:—

First. Feudalism seems to have exercised a great, and, upon the whole, a salutary influence upon the intellectual development of individuals. It gave birth to elevated ideas and feelings in the mind, to moral wants, to grand developments of character and passion.

[Second]. With regard to society, it was incapable of establishing either legal order or political guarantee. . . . Where can we open the history of this period, without discovering a crowd of noble sentiments, of splendid achievements, of beautiful developments of humanity, evidently generated in the bosom of feudal life. Chivalry, which in reality bears scarcely the least resemblance to feudalism, was nevertheless its offspring. It was feudalism which gave birth to that romantic thirst and fondness for all that is noble, generous, and faithful—for that sentiment of honor, which still raises its voice in favor of the system by which it was nursed. . . .

Here we see that the first sparks of European imagination, that the first attempts of poetry, of literature, that the first intellectual gratifications which Europe tasted in emerging from barbarism, sprung up under the protection, under the wings, of feudalism. It was in the baronial hall that they were born, and cherished, and protected. It is to the feudal times that we trace back the earliest literary monuments of England, France, and Germany, the earliest intellectual enjoyments of modern Europe. . . .

The very nature itself of feudality is opposed to order and legality. In the last century, some writers of talent attempted to dress out feudalism as a social system; they endeavored to make it appear a legitimate, well-ordered, progressive state of society, and represented it as a golden age. Ask them, however, where it existed: summon them to assign it a locality, and a time, and they will be found wanting. It is a Utopia without date, a drama, for which we find, in the past, neither theatre nor actors.

8

Levi Slamm and Michael Walsh, "Great Meeting of the Mechanics and Working Men at Tammany Hall!" Daily Plebeian, October 19, 1842

Libertarians and the labor movement have not always assumed hostile positions to one another in American political life. During the "golden age" of locofoco influence over the Democratic Party (ca. 1837–45), the most radical of libertarians joined with a host of reformist allies, from utopian socialists to the first national labor unions. The coalition produced a decades-long series of policy revolutions, cultural production, and ideological syncretism between individuals we now think of as occupying opposite corners of intellectual life. In the following two speeches, delivered in succession at a meeting of Democratic Working Men in Tammany Hall, locofoco editor of the *Daily Plebeian* Levi Slamm and populist editor of the *Subterranean* Michael Walsh argue for union among Democrats against the aristocratic Whiggery.[31]

One by one, Slamm addressed the planks of Henry Clay and the Whig Party's "American System," identifying protective tariffs, monopolistic bank and currency policies, and any other state interventions into economic affairs as decidedly harmful to the interests of average working people. To locofocos such as Slamm, Clay's policies represented one-half of the eternal struggle between liberty and power, the fundamental force that created historical change. Slamm, the Democratic Party, and his Working Men audience represented the other half of the battle.

Slamm "thickened" the standard "thin" liberal interpretation of history, which argued that social classes formed entirely on the basis of their access to political power. As he noted, those who controlled vast amounts of wealth were in fact more often than not indistinguishable from the overall political apparatus. Access to capital and access to power operated in tandem to curtail the liberties of the people and extract their substance, provoking in turn popular rebellions and revolutions—the long series of events called history. Walsh's speech continued Slamm's partisan and historical themes, emphasizing that ideas, in fact, drove events because ideas organized people according to their preferences for liberty or power. Americans, he argued, had only to recognize their individual roles as agents of history and warriors for liberty, and the powerful could not possibly stand against progress.

"Address to the Mechanics and Workingmen of the City and County of New York," by Levi D. Slamm

The duty devolved upon us of directing the attention of the laboring classes of the city and county of New York to the dangers by which labor is surrounded was never less difficult of execution. The cheering news which pours in upon us as State after State wheels into our ranks, has already done the work to our hands. The cheat of Whig protection to home industry, is already seen through and appreciated.

The history of the world is but the history of a struggle for capital and power. In every page of it we find capital resorting to every possible subterfuge, to enable it to suck up the hard earnings of labor. With the general spread of intelligence, a spirit of resistance has grown up to the extortionate demands of capital; and in Great Britain the unwieldy proportions of capital and the institution of white slavery, are at length both sustained only by a large standing army. And yet Great Britain, with all its affluence of the few, and its grinding poverty of the masses, is the model government of the friends of the restrictive system. The mechanics and workingmen who are filling the teeming cities and spreading over the broad fields of this fruitful country, have yet to resist the deleterious influence of the institutions of Great Britain upon our own—to restore the perfect equilibrium between capital and labor—to prevent labor from continuing in any degree a prey to the rich—to prevent labor from striking two blows for capital, and *one* for itself.

The first device of capital to obtain by indirection the earnings of labor, is the Banking System. We have seen the whole capital of this country concentrated in Banking Incorporations. We have seen them swelled up by a portion of the capital of Europe. We have seen issues of paper money creating artificial rise in prices—tempting labor to hazard in speculations the hard earnings of years. We have seen contractions of the paper circulation, causing periodical revulsions, in which the large estates have eaten up the smaller; and we have seen the breaking down of the banking system, its machinery, and its grand Regulator, before the progress of free opinion. With the downfall of the banking system, the notion is fast gaining ground, that capital is monopoly enough of itself, and that no other incorporation is needed, than an INCORPORATION of the intelligence of the mass, in order to enable it to stand up against wealth.

Having gone to the wall upon the banking system, the friends of capital have concluded to play a strong game upon the tariff. They yet hope that their siren cry of protection to domestic industry, will lure to their ranks the unthinking and the credulous—that the phrase of protection to home-labor, will prove a bait that will be greedily swallowed. In order to ascertain what protection to labor means, when put forth by the party which contains "all the respectability and all the wealth," we have only to look to that country where a kindred party has protected it to the utmost. In Great Britain the system works to admiration. After centuries of experiments, the problem of the capacity of capital to contrive, and labor to endure burdens, seems there about to be resolved. Lordly estates and princely pensions on the one hand, and fatigue and starvation upon the other. Mechanics and working men, shall we not resist at the threshold the efforts of capital, here to turn labor to its own account? Shall we not prevent the entering-wedge of a system which, under the garb of protection, would ultimately tax every article that enters into the consumption of the labor of the country? If the laboring classes of Great Britain had the power to legislate, would they not free themselves at once, from the grievous exactions of their wealthy capitalists; and shall we, the real laborers, and only true protectors of labor here, shall we be led hoodwinked to the support of a party, whose affinities are entirely with the moneyed classes of Great Britain, whose hypocritical cant about protection, is an insult to the true dignity of labor.

The doctrines of Free trade are more and more appreciated as conducing to the benefit of the labor of this great country; and the least departure from these doctrines consistent with the collection of adequate revenue, is all that can be yielded in its future legislation. An equal or horizontal tariff would afford sufficient revenue to the Government, and sufficient and equal protection to labor; but it would not suit the purposes of the capitalist, whose love for labor is extremely discriminating. He loves the manufacturer of iron, more than the builder, the rigger, the navigator of a ship—he loves the manufacturer of coarse wools, more than the grower of coarse wools. His love for the manufacturer is a dollar a yard, and for the wool grower, a mill per pound. He loves that branch of industry the most, the GAINS of which he can secure to himself the easiest. He loves any thing that is a corporation.

The temporary ascendancy of the Whig party, has enabled the capitalist, in addition to a Bank and High Tariff, to shadow forth their necessary adjunct, a National Debt. In order to bring labor into complete subjection, the whole *three* are necessary. The annual taxation of labor by the Government of Great Britain, is two hundred and forty millions of dollars; and of this sum one half goes to the *capitalist*, in the shape of interest upon the National Debt. The debt itself is viewed with indifference, but in the struggle to meet the interest, labor seems to have sunk into an entailed and grievous servitude. Shall we not, *mechanics* and *working men*, resist here, all debt, whether State or national, in its incipient stages? Shall we not work with all our might, against a party which sets no bound to debt and extravagant expenditure—opposes all taxation of capital, and shifts off upon labor, all the burdens of payment?

Our approaching State election again calls upon us to sustain the Democratic policy, the *true* working man's policy, with reference to State Debt and Internal Improvements. Shall we, through supineness, again allow a party to take the reins, which at the time of its arrest, was trafficking away at a most ruinous depreciation, the credit of the State—sinking us deeper and deeper in embarrassment and debt? The progress of Democratic principles is onward; but it must not be forgotten that "eternal vigilance is the price of liberty." The conviction that our principles are eternal, prevented our glorious Democracy from becoming disheartened when the cohorts of Whiggery triumphed in the memorable campaign of 1840. The general defection of the States from the Whig cause, and their return one after another to the Democratic fold, leaves the Whigs no other boast of 1840, but that it marks an epoch of their success in appealing to the passions, instead of the reason of the people. Shall we through divisions in our own ranks, neglect to secure at the coming election, members of Congress in favor of preserving the distinct rights—the cherished Institutions of the States; shall we from local or personal considerations, or from sectional jealousies, hazard our ascendancy in the State Legislature, and fail of sending back to his post, the distinguished Democrat, who now so ably represents us in the Senate of the Union? If any incentive to duty is needed, we have only to look at the heartless proscription, which our divisions among ourselves, have enabled the bitter enemies of the Democracy—though in a minority of thousands in this city—to inflict upon us. Let each one make some sacrifice for the common good. Let us present an undivided front in favor of regular nominations. Let us come out in our full strength, recollecting that we now have to whip the Federalists in their last stronghold, and in their very latest disguise. We have to whip them now as the PROTECTORS OF LABOR.

Speech by Michael Walsh

[After a series of resolutions,] MR. MICHAEL WALSH being called for with loud shouts from all sides of the room, rose and said:

Fellow citizens: It is rarely that I attempt to address an assemblage at Tammany Hall. About this time last year I opened one

Ball here, and now I appear before you to open another for the benefit of the working classes [loud cheerings]. I am opposed to anything like distinctions among the working classes [cheering]. There is but one class that I am disposed to recognize; not the merchants, traders or professional men, but the mechanics [cheers]. What constitutes a mechanic? Serving seven years to a craft did not constitute a mechanic; if so, on the same principle Peter the Great was a mechanic, because he learned ship-building. But I believe the mechanic to be one who was depending on his own labors for support, whom I would call the bone and sinew of the country. Not those who would go up to their marble palaces in the Fifteenth Ward, and throw cold water on the bone and sinew of the country, and see disqualification in their eyes. The fact is, there are certain men who would not show their face in favor of any measures introduced for the benefit of the working classes, and who never would have joined the Democratic ranks if it were not for their own advantage. What was Democracy? He would ask. Was it the elevation to power of this or that man, or of ten thousand men? No; but it was the elevation of principle [loud cheering]. It was the elevation of principle to elevate the man to that situation for which Nature and Nature's God intended him [loud and continued cheering]. What, he would ask, was it to him what was this man or that man, provided he was guided by principle? The Jews trampled on the cross to enrich themselves, and there were men who came into the Democratic ranks for the purpose of feeding on the party, and of blotting out the sprig of Democracy. He may stand where he was and flatter all of them, and tell them that they were all the most intelligent, the most honest, the most high-minded fellows under God's sun; but he would not tell them any such thing; he cared nothing for public opinion; he cared for principles. Public opinion was a fallacious test, as he had seen on the stand from which he spoke, men who had been lauded to the very skies, while in six months afterwards they may have been kicked and hooted through the streets.

He cared not what man came with the Democrats, provided he had principle and a good education, he would support him. If he had to acquire a profession, he had to work for it—first, by a good education, and next, when acquired, to labor for his bread. If he was to become a lawyer, he should work to get clients— if a physician, to get patients—and if a parson, to work for his congregation—though there were some who told them, that the best passport to Heaven was a bare back and a hungry belly. [Loud laughter.] The same men would sometimes tell them that they should bear with fortitude—[A band of music having here played loudly in the streets, and subsequently entered the room, made such a noise that several sentences were lost.]

Mr. Walsh continued. It was latterly a common trick to nominate committees for the express purpose of filling all the offices in the gift of the State, then neglecting their interest after they had selected them. Men had been selected as inspectors, who it was well known never thought of the interests of the working classes; and whenever a selection was made from the lower classes, it was some weak-minded individual, who as soon as he had got a little higher than he had been, felt so tickled and elevated when he got to Albany, that he soon forgot the interests of the people who had returned him. They wanted men in the halls of legislation—not such men as the Horace Greeleys, who were to be considered but a mere connecting link between the animal and vegetable kingdom—[roars of laughter;] men who, if they kicked a cockroach, would not be able to kill it; men who had not stamina enough in their body to keep their backs straight. [Roars of laughter.]

Mr. W. here, after urging the propriety of a judicious selection of Democratic candidates, apostrophized the . . . genius of American Democracy with able effort, and having taken a cursory view of the affairs of Rhode Island, and then made allusion to certain recent attacks that had been made upon him in some of the public journals, which he ably repelled, and went on to say that if they looked back to the remote ages of the world, they would find that those who had been elevated to the aristocratic ranks invariably rose to eminence upon the shoulders of the working classes; that as soon as they had elevated some tyrant king or aristocrat, they had invariably been kicked away like a dog. There were but two principles in the moral, social, physical, and material world, and between them they had to choose. They had to choose between heat and cold, light and shade, life and death, liberty or slavery; and which, he would ask them, would they choose? They should choose between Whiggery and Democracy [loud cheering].

In the magnificent temple of Minerva of old, where the productions of genius were judged according to their comparative merits, two rival artists who had been engaged, submitted the productions of their chisel to the judgment of the people. Being works of art, intended to be placed on a pedestal which had been prepared for their reception. The statues were submitted for inspection, and one being small and executed with great genius and ability, and breathing almost vitally, being beautifully moulded and chiseled, the voice was generally in favor of it. It was elevated gradually to the pedestal, until the beauty and harmony of its structure was so completely diminished in the distance as to make it appear a shapeless speck. The other statue, whose apparent deformities made it before appear without beauty in the eyes of the judges, when it was elevated and placed on the pedestal it was then that its beauties became obvious. Being forced into light by its position, it was then that the superior genius of the artist was made manifest, and the decision was given in favor of the larger statue.

Mr. W. spoke at considerable length in support of the Democratic principles, and concluded. The above is but a very meagre outline of his remarks.

The Hon. Mr. Davezac was here vehemently called for, and next addressed the meeting. In the course of his remarks he made forcible allusion to the address of the last speaker, and passed a glowing eulogy on General Jackson, after which he went very fully into the general policy of the Democratic party, and urged the judicious selection of candidates for Congress and the Legislature.

Mr. Alexander Ming next took the stand, and spoke at length on the subject matter introduced in the address as resolutions: in the course of his remarks, he made allusion to his steady and unalterable attachment to Loco Foco Democracy and urged the necessity of unity of action among all ranks of the Democratic party.

The Hon. Mr. Swackhamer was next vehemently called for, and made a powerful and eloquent appeal to the meeting. In the course of his remarks, he inflicted a severe castigation on the entire Whig party, showed up the fallacy of their doctrine, and interspersed his eloquent address with much humorous anecdote, which told with admirable effect upon his auditory. We very much regret that want of space obliges us to condense his speech as well as that of the other gentlemen who spoke on this occasion, as the crowded state of our columns will show the utter impossibility of our doing proper justice to the excellent speeches delivered in the course of the evening. The meeting was subsequently addressed by several gentlemen and separated at a late hour.

Part Two:

Practice

9

The Law of the Salian Franks (first compiled ca. 500)

As the Western Roman Empire dissolved through-out the fourth and fifth centuries, waves of Germanic ("barbarian") migrants established a slew of kingdoms along the old frontier. From Britain in the far north, to Iberia in the south, and across the central and eastern European plains, warlords and chieftains seized legiti-macy and power from Roman municipalities. In the empire's place, these budding feudal lords erected a new, vibrant, syncretic civilization.

In the early sixth century, Clovis, the first king of all the Frankish peoples, compiled the first written records of Germanic law.[32] The Salic law, or law of the Salian Franks, evolved over the centuries to reflect

changing circumstances, but perhaps most important, it was joined by a wide variety of competing
European legal orders. As the migratory Germanic
chiefdoms transformed into settled states of their
own, each kingdom established its own legal order.
As a result, Western civilization became marked by
a patchwork of interrelated, often-overlapping, and
competitive institutions, each reflecting the particu-
larity of specific sections of the European population.
For more than a millennium, Europeans interacted
with one another through a wide and overlapping
variety of socioeconomic, legal, political, and spiritual orders. Classical liberal historians like France's
Guizot and England's Lord Acton have long looked to
this grand diversity of orders to explain the particular vibrancy of Western civilization—the ability of the
West to meet new challenges with new organizations
and institutions without the process ending in a
Romanesque "decline and fall."

In the first of our investigations in early medieval legal
codes, we examine the law of the Salian Franks, which
established firm and incredibly specific rules for social
conduct and compensatory justice—a concept of prominent importance in early Germanic life. Virtually every
offense seems to have been assigned an appropriate
price for compensation, and the lawgiver legislates in
almost excruciating detail. The Salic law enshrines the
special social statuses of the king, freemen, men, and

Franks. Crimes committed (in any sense) against the king carried far larger fines than those committed against other Franks, and Franks themselves enjoyed similar privileges compared with Romans (or other "barbarians") living under Frankish rule. Significant, too, were the rules established for the generational transfer of property and title. Although the Salic law allowed women to inherit "moveable" property, the code specifically forbade female inheritance of land, reserving for the male sex an absolute monopoly and, therefore, distinct class advantages that have remained throughout Western history.

Title I. Concerning Summonses

If any one be summoned before the "Thing" by the king's law, and do not come, he shall be sentenced to 600 denars, which make 15 shillings (solidi).

But he who summons another, and does not come himself, shall, if a lawful impediment have not delayed him, be sentenced to 15 shillings, to be paid to him whom he summoned.

Title III. Concerning Thefts of Cattle

If any one steal that bull which rules the herd and never has been yoked, he shall be sentenced to 1,800 denars, which make 45 shillings.

But if that bull is used for the cows of three villages in common, he who stole him shall be sentenced to three times 45 shillings.

If any one steal a bull belonging to the king he shall be sentenced to 3,600 denars, which make 90 shillings.

Title XI. Concerning Thefts or Housebreakings of Freemen

If any freeman steal, outside of the house, something worth 2 denars, he shall be sentenced to 600 denars, which make 15 shillings.

But if he steal, outside of the house, something worth 40 denars, and it be proved on him, he shall be sentenced, besides the amount and the fines for delay, to 1,400 denars, which make 35 shillings.

If a freeman break into a house and steal something worth 2 denars, and it be proved on him, he shall be sentenced to 15 shillings.

But if he shall have stolen something worth more than 5 denars, and it have been proved on him, he shall be sentenced, besides the worth of the object and the fines for delay, to 1,400 denars, which make 35 shillings.

But if he have broken, or tampered with, the lock, and thus have entered the house and stolen anything from it, he shall be sentenced, besides the worth of the object and the fines for delay, to 1,800 denars, which make 45 shillings.

And if he have taken nothing, or have escaped by flight, he shall, for the housebreaking alone, be sentenced to 1,200 denars, which make 30 shillings.

Title XIII. Concerning Rape Committed by Freemen

If three men carry off a free born girl, they shall be compelled to pay 30 shillings.

If there are more than three, each one shall pay 5 shillings.

Those who shall have been present with boats shall be sentenced to 3 shillings.

But those who commit rape shall be compelled to pay 2,500 denars, which make 63 shillings.

But if they have carried off that girl from behind lock and key, or from the spinning room, they shall be sentenced to the above price and penalty.

But if the girl who is carried off be under the king's protection then the "firth" (peace-money) shall be 2,500 denars, which make 63 shillings.

Title XIV. Concerning Assault and Robbery

If any one have assaulted and plundered a freeman, and it be proved on him, he shall be sentenced to 2,500 denars, which make 63 shillings.

If a Roman have plundered a Salian Frank, the above law shall be ordered.

But if a Frank have plundered a Roman, he shall be sentenced to 35 shillings.

If any man should wish to migrate, and have permission from the king, and shall have shown this in the public "Thing": whoever, contrary to the decree of the king, shall presume to oppose him, shall be sentenced to 8,000 denars, which make 200 shillings.

Title XVII. Concerning Wounds

If any one have wished to kill another person, and the blow have missed, he on whom it was proved shall be sentenced to 2,500 denars, which make 63 shillings.

If any person have wished to strike another with a poisoned arrow, and the arrow have glanced aside, and it shall be proved on him: he shall be sentenced to 2,500 denars, which make 63 shillings.

If any person strike another on the head so that the brain appears, and the three bones which lie above the brain shall project, he shall be sentenced to 1,200 denars, which make 30 shillings.

But if it shall have been between the ribs or in the stomach, so that the wound appears and reaches to the entrails, he shall be sentenced to 1,200 denars—which make 30 shillings—besides 5 shillings for the physician's pay.

If any one shall have struck a man so that blood falls to the floor, and it be proved on him, he shall be sentenced to 600 denars, which make 15 shillings.

But if a freeman strike a freeman with his fist so that blood does not flow, he shall be sentenced for each blow-up to 3 blows, to 120 denars, which make 3 shillings.

Title XXIV. Concerning the Killing of Little Children and Women

If any one have slain a boy under 10 years—up to the end of the tenth—and it shall have been proved on him, he shall be sentenced to 24,000 denars, which make 600 shillings.

If any one have hit a free woman who is pregnant, and she dies, he shall be sentenced to 28,000 denars, which make 700 shillings.

If any one have killed a free woman after she has begun bearing children, he shall be sentenced to 24,000 denars, which make 600 shillings.

After she can have no more children, he who kills her shall be sentenced to 8,000 denars, which make 200 shillings.

Title XXX. Concerning Insults

If any one, man or woman, shall have called a woman harlot, and shall not have been able to prove it, he shall be sentenced to 1,800 denars, which make 45 shillings.

If any person shall have called another "fox," he shall be sentenced to 3 shillings.

If any man shall have called another "hare," he shall be sentenced to 3 shillings.

Title XLI. Concerning the Murder of Freemen

If any one shall have killed a free Frank, or a barbarian living under the Salic law, and it have been proved on him, he shall be sentenced to 8,000 denars.

But if he shall have thrown him into a well or into the water, or shall have covered him with branches or anything else, to conceal him, he shall be sentenced to 24,000 denars, which make 600 shillings.

But if any one has slain a man who is in the service of the king, he shall be sentenced to 24,000 denars, which make 600 shillings.

But if he have put him in the water or in a well, and covered him with anything to conceal him, he shall be sentenced to 72,000 denars, which make 1,800 shillings.

If any one have slain a Roman who eats in the king's palace, and it have been proved on him, he shall be sentenced to 12,000 denars, which make 300 shillings.

But if the Roman shall not have been a landed proprietor and table companion of the king, he who killed him shall be sentenced to 4,000 denars, which make 100 shillings.

Title LVII. Concerning the *Chrenecruda*

If any one have killed a man, and, having given up all his property, has not enough to comply with the full terms of the law, he shall present 12 sworn witnesses to the effect that, neither above the earth nor under it, has he any more property than he has already given, And he shall afterwards go into his house, and shall collect in his hand dust from the four corners of it, and shall afterwards stand upon the threshold, looking inwards into the house. And then, with his left hand, he shall throw over his shoulder some of that dust on the nearest relative that he has. But if his father and (his father's) brothers have already paid, he shall then throw that dust on their (the brothers') children—that is, over three (relatives) who are nearest on the father's and three on the mother's side. And after that, in his shirt, without girdle and without shoes, a staff in his hand, he shall spring over the hedge. And then those three shall pay half of what is lacking of the compounding money or the legal fine; that is, those others who are descended in the paternal line shall do this.

But if there be one of those relatives who has not enough to pay his whole indebtedness, he, the poorer one, shall in turn throw the *chrenecruda* on him of them who has the most, so that he shall pay the whole fine.

But if he also have not enough to pay the whole, then he who has charge of the murderer shall bring him before the "Thing," and afterwards to 4 Things, in order that they (his friends) may take him under their protection. And if no one have taken him under his protection—that is, so as to redeem him for what he can not pay—then he shall have to atone with his life.

Title LIX. Concerning Private Property

If any man die and leave no sons, if the father and mother survive, they shall inherit.

If the father and mother do not survive, and he leave brothers or sisters, they shall inherit.

But if there are none, the sisters of the father shall inherit.

But if there are no sisters of the father, the sisters of the mother shall claim the inheritance.

If there are none of these, the nearest relative on the father's side shall succeed to that inheritance.

But of Salic land no portion of the inheritance shall come to a woman: but the whole inheritance of the land shall come to the male sex.

Title LXII. Concerning Wergeld

If any one's father have been killed, the sons shall have half the compounding money (wergeld); and the other half the nearest relatives, as well on the mother's as on the father's side, shall divide among themselves.

But if there are no relatives, paternal or maternal, that portion shall go to the fisc.

10

The Visigothic Code:
(Forum judicum),
ed. S. P. Scott

Influenced by the Frankish example of compiling a written Germanic legal code, rival kingdoms throughout the continent codified their own laws likewise derived from ancient oral traditions and chiefly adjudications. Our second example, the Visigothic Code (or *Forum judicum*), was compiled in Germanic Iberia under orders from King Chindasuinth (ca. 642–43).[33] Most significantly, the Visigothic Code broke with the tradition of maintaining separate laws for Germanic and Roman peoples. Rather, the code asserts that all individuals, including the king, are subject to the law.

Although later kings expanded the code to include titles greatly extending royal power, the earliest version reflects the popular demand that leaders act not as an elevated and exalted class but as the common man's chieftains. Although this is all very well as a matter of theory, in practice the code granted tremendous powers and legal advantages to the king, which remained the basis for protecting and accumulating royal power over the centuries. The code dwells at length on the qualities of a good lawmaker and king, and although the later books contain as much specificity and detail regarding crimes and punishment as did the Salic law, we have here focused on legal ideas and the duties owed the people from the ruler.

Book I: Concerning Legal Agencies
Title I: The Lawmaker
I. What the Method of Making Laws Should Be

We, whose duty it is to afford suitable assistance in the formation of the laws, should, in the execution of this undertaking, improve upon the methods of the ancients, disclosing as well the excellence of the law to be framed, as the skill of its artificer. The proof of this art will be the more plainly evident, if it seems to draw its conclusions not from inference and imitation but from truth. Nor should it stamp the force of argument with the subtlety of syllogism, but it should, with moderation, and by the use of pure and honorable precepts, determine the provisions of the law. And, indeed, reason plainly demands that the work be performed in this manner. For, when the master holds in his hand the finished product, in vain is sought the reason for its having been impressed with that particular form. On subjects that are obscure, reason eagerly seeks to be informed by examination, in matters, however, that are well known and established, action alone is required. Therefore, when the matter in question is not clear because its form is unfamiliar, investigation is desirable; but it is otherwise in affairs known to all men, where not speculation, but performance, becomes essential. As we are more concerned with morals than with eloquence, it is not our province to introduce the personality of the orator, but to define the rights of the governor.

II. How the Lawmaker Should Act

The maker of laws should not practise disputation, but should administer justice. Nor is it fitting that he should appear to have framed the law by contention, but in an orderly manner. For the transaction of public affairs does not demand, as a reward of his labors, the clamor of theatrical applause, but the law destined for the salvation of the people.

III. What Should Be Required of the Lawmaker

First, it should be required that he make diligent inquiry as to the soundness of his opinions. Then, it should be evident that he has acted not for private gain but for the benefit of the people; so that it may conclusively appear that the law has not been made for any private or personal advantage, but for the protection and profit of the whole body of citizens.

IV. What the Conduct of the Lawmaker Should Be in His Daily Life

The framer of laws and the dispenser of justice should prefer morals to eloquence, that his speech may be characterized rather by virtuous sentiments, than by elegance of expression. He should be more eminent for deeds than for words; and should discharge his duties rather with alacrity than with reluctance, and not, as it were, under compulsion.

V. How the Lawmaker Should Impart Advice

He should be mindful of his duty only to God and to himself; be liberal of counsel to persons of high and low degree, and easy of access to the citizens and common people; so that, as the guardian of the public safety, exercising the government by universal consent, he may not, for personal motives, abuse the privileges of his judicial office.

VI. What Manner of Speech the Lawmaker Should Use

He should be energetic and clear of speech, certain in opinion; ready in weighing evidence, so that whatever proceeds from the source of the law may at once impress all hearers that it is characterized by neither doubt nor perplexity.

VII. How the Lawmaker Should Act in Rendering Judgment

The Judge should be quick of perception; firm of purpose, clear in judgment, lenient in the infliction of penalties; assiduous in the practice of mercy; expeditious in the vindication of the innocent: clement in his treatment of criminals; careful of the rights of the stranger; gentle toward his countrymen. He should be no respecter of persons, and should avoid all appearance of partiality.

VIII. How the Lawmaker Should Comport Himself in Private and Public Affairs

All public matters he should approach with patriotism and reverence; those concerning private individuals and domestic controversies he should determine according to his authority and power; so that the community may look up to him as a father, and the lower orders of the people may regard him as a master and a lord. He should be assiduous in the performance of his duties so that he may be feared by the commonalty to such a degree that none shall hesitate to obey him; and be so just that all would willingly sacrifice their lives in his service, from their attachment to his person and to his office.

IX. What Instruction It Is Fitting That the Lawmaker Should Give

Then, also, he should bear in mind that the glory and the majesty of the people consist in the proper interpretation of the laws, and in the manner of their administration. For, as the entire safety of the public depends upon the preservation of the law, he should attempt to amend the statutes of the country rather than the manners of the populace: and remember that there are some who, in controversies, apply the laws according to their will, and in pursuance of private advantage, to such an extent that what should be law to the public is to them private dishonor; so that, by perversion of the law, acts which are illegal are often perpetrated, which should obviously be abolished through the power of the law itself.

Title II: The Law

I. What the Lawmaker Should Observe in Framing the Laws

In all legislation the law should be fully and explicitly set forth, that perfection, and not partiality, may be secured. For, in the formation of the laws, not the sophisms of argument, but the virtue of justice should ever prevail. And here is required not what may be prompted by controversy, but what energy and vigor demand; for the violation of morals is not to be coerced by the forms of speech, but restrained by the moderation of virtue.

II. What the Law Is

The law is the rival of divinity; the oracle of religion; the source of instruction; the artificer of right; the guardian and promoter of good morals; the rudder of the state; the messenger of justice; the mistress of life; the soul of the body politic.

III. What the Law Does

The law rules every order of the state, and every condition of man; it governs wives and husbands; youth and age: the learned and the ignorant, the polished and the rude. It aims to provide the highest degree of safety for both prince and people, and, in renown and excellence, it is as conspicuous as the noon-day sun.

IV. What the Law Should Be

The law should be plain, and not lead any citizen to commit error or fraud. It should be suitable to the place and the time, according to the character and custom of the state; prescribing justice and equity; consistent, honorable, worthy, useful, and necessary; and it should be carefully noted whether its provisions are framed rather for the convenience, than for the injury, of the public; so that it may be determined whether it sufficiently provides for the administration of justice; whether or not it appears to be contrary to religion, and whether it defends the right, and may be observed without detriment to any one.

V. Why the Law Is Made

Laws are made for these reasons that human wickedness may be restrained through fear of their execution; that the lives of innocent men may be safe among criminals; and that the temptation to commit wrong may be restrained by the fear of punishment.

VI. How the Law Should Triumph over Enemies

Domestic peace having been once established and the plague of contention having been entirely removed from prince, citizen, and the populace, expeditions then may be made safely against the enemy and he may be attacked confidently and vigorously, in the certain hope of victory; when nothing is to be anticipated or feared from dissensions at home. The entire body of the people being prosperous and secure, through the influence of peace and order, they can set forth boldly against the enemy and become invincible, where salutary arts are aided by just laws. For men are better armed with equity than with weapons; and the prince should rather employ justice against an enemy than the soldier his javelin; and the success of the prince will be more conspicuous when a reputation for justice accompanies him, and soldiers who are well governed at home will be all the more formidable to a foe. It is a matter of common experience, that justice, which has protected the citizen, overwhelms the enemy; and that those prevail in foreign contests who enjoy domestic peace; and while the moderation of the prince insures temperance in the enforcement of the law, so the united support of the citizens promotes victory over the enemy. For the administration of the law is regulated by the disposition and character of the king; from the administration of the law proceeds the institution of morals, from the institution of morals, the concord of the citizens; from the concord of the citizens, the triumph over the enemy. So a good prince ruling well his kingdom, and making foreign conquests, maintaining peace at home, and overwhelming his foreign adversaries, is famed both as the ruler of his state and a victor over his enemies, and shall have for the future eternal renown, after terrestrial wealth, a celestial kingdom after the diadem and the purple, a crown of glory, nor shall lie then cease to be king; for when he relinquished his earthly kingdom, and conquered a celestial one, he did not diminish, but rather increased his glory.

Book II: Concerning the Conduct of Causes
Title I: Concerning Judges and Matters to Be Decided in Court
I. When Amended Laws Should Come in Force

In assigning their place to laws which have been amended, we have considered it proper to give them the most important rank, for, as clearness in the laws is useful in preventing the misdeeds of the people, so obscurity in their provisions interferes with the course of justice. For many salutary edicts are drawn up in obscure and contradictory language, and are instrumental in promoting the controversies of litigants; and, while they should put an end to chicanery, they, in fact, give rise to new sophisms and abuses. For this reason, therefore, litigation increases; disputes between parties are encouraged, the judges become undecided, so that, in attempting to dispose of false claims and charges, they are unable to form definite conclusions, as all seems perplexed and uncertain. And because all questions which arise in suits at law, cannot be disposed of in a few words, except those which have been determined in our presence; we have decided that certain laws should be amended in this book; that doubtful matters should be made clear; that profit should be extracted from those things that are evil; clemency from those that are mortal; clearness from those that are obscure; and that perfection should be given to those that are incomplete; whereby the people of our kingdom, whom our peaceful government alone restrains, may be checked and controlled, hereafter, by the aid of said amended laws. And therefore, these laws as amended, and approved by us, and our new decrees, as set forth in this book and its titles, as well as such as may be subsequently added, shall be enforced from the second year of our reign, and the twelfth Kalends of November, and shall be binding thereafter upon all persons subject to our empire, irrespective of rank. Those laws, however, which we have promulgated against the offences of the Jews, we decree shall be valid from the date when they were confirmed by us.

The Glorious Flavius Recesvintus, King

II. The Royal Power, as Well as the Entire Body of the People, Should Be Subject to the Majesty of the Law

The Omnipotent Lord of all, sole Founder and Provider of the means of human salvation, ordered the inhabitants of the earth to learn justice from the sacred precepts of the law. And, because the mandate of Divinity has been thus imposed upon the human race, it is fitting that all terrestrial creatures, of however exalted rank, should acknowledge the authority of Him whom even the celestial soldiery obey. Wherefore, if God should be obeyed, justice should be highly esteemed, which, if it were thus esteemed, would be constantly practiced, as every one loves justice more truly and ardently when a feeling of equity unites him with his neighbor. Willingly, therefore, carrying out the Divine commands, let us give temperate laws to ourselves and to our subjects; laws such as we and our successors, and the whole body of the people, may readily obey; so that no person of whatever rank or dignity may refuse to submit to the power of the law, which the necessity and will of the King has deemed it proper and salutary to inculcate.

Flavius Recesvintus, King

III. It Is Permitted to No One to Be Ignorant of the Law

All true science declares that ignorance should be detested. For while it has been written, "he need not understand who desires to act with propriety," it is certain that he who does not wish to know, despises an upright life. Therefore, let no one think that he can do what is unlawful because he was ignorant of the provisions of the laws, and what is sanctioned by them; for ignorance does not render him innocent, whom guilt has subjected to the penalties of the criminal.

Flavius Recesvintus, King

IV. The Business of the King Shall First Be Considered, then That of the People

God, the Creator of all things, in his arrangement of the human form, placed the head above the body, and caused all the different members of the latter to originate from it, and it is, therefore, called the head; there being formed the brightness of the eyes, by which all things that produce injury can be discerned; there being born also the power of intelligence, through which the members connected with, and subject to, the head, may be either controlled or protected. For this reason it is the especial care of skillful physicians to provide the remedies for the head before treating the other members of the body: which, indeed, may not be thought unreasonable, when properly explained; because, if the head should be healthy, it is reasonable to suppose that the other members can be readily cured For if disease attacks the head, health cannot be imparted by it to the members which are constantly being wasted by weakness. The most important duties of the prince are, therefore, the preservation of health and the defense of life; so that the proper method may be adopted in the conduct of the affairs of the people; and while the health of the king is cared for, the preservation of his subjects may be the better maintained.

11

The Canons of Adamnan, or the Law of Innocents (ca. 697)

In our final foray into the earliest of surviving medieval European legal codes, we turn to the farthest frontiers of Roman Britain and beyond. About the year 697, a monk and hagiographer named Adamnan delivered his Law of Innocents to a large and important assemblage of Irish clerics and noblemen celebrating the 100th anniversary of St. Columba's death. St. Columba was venerated for spreading Christianity to Scotland, and Adamnan intended to honor the saint's gift by enlarging the law's protective sphere. Adamnan's proposed Law of Innocents survives through a later copy that relates the law in the form of an epic story.[34] The new laws were among the first in Europe to dramatically limit the scope of violence in Christian societies. And although we have no records of any cases tried under Adamnan's law, the text offers valuable insight into the state's role as the former and shaper of social classes.

The laws note that before Adamnan, Irish women were kept as slaves, outside the protection of the law, discriminated against as a class of humans without rights as individuals. Women thus "had no share in bag or in basket" and existed at the sufferance of their husband-owners by virtue of a law that condemned them to exist outside of civil society. Through Adamnan's laws, kings agreed to no longer relegate women to the legal wilds, and many of the socioeconomic distinctions between men and women were thus dissolved.

We are told that the great lawgiver was inspired to act when he and his mother chanced upon a field of dead women and children. When one of them rose to life at Adamnan's touch, he devoted his remaining days to freeing women. As a result of his labors, the Irish nobility and clergy welcomed women into the sphere of state protection, but as ever, the state's gifts came at a cost. The Law of Innocents demands that women venerate Adamnan, that they subject themselves to the rule of his legal wardens (whatever their particular constituted forms), and proscribes an appropriate scheme of tithing and taxation to support the new legal framework. Although the new law accomplished great ends in protecting a new class of people, the more fundamental distinctions between those subject to the law and those executing the law remained—perhaps even strengthened now that the full population was complicit in promulgating a single legal order.

Five ages before the birth of Christ, to wit, from Adam to the Flood, from the Flood to Abraham, from Abraham to David, from David to the Captivity in Babylon, from the Babylonian Captivity to the birth of Christ. During that time women were in bondage and in slavery, until Adamnan . . . came.

Cumalach was a name for women till Adamnan come to free them. And this was the *cumalach*, a woman for whom a hole was dug at the end of the door so that it came over her nakedness. The end of the great spit was placed upon her till the cooking of the portion was ended. After she had come out of that earth-pit she had to dip a candle four man's hands in length in a plate of butter or lard; that candle to be on her palm until division of food and distribution of liquor and making of beds, in the houses of kings and chieftains, had ended. That woman had no share in bag or in basket, nor in the company of the house-master; but she dwelt in a hut outside the enclosure, lest bane from sea or land should come to her chief.

The work which the best women had to do, was to go to battle and battlefield, encounter and camping, fighting and hosting, wounding and slaying. On one side of her she would carry her bag of provisions, on the other her babe. Her wooden pole upon her back. Thirty feet long it was, and had on one end an iron hook, which she would thrust into the tress of some woman in the opposite battalion. Her husband behind her, carrying a fence-stake in his hand, and flogging her on to battle. For at that time it was the head of a woman, or her two breasts, which were taken as trophies.

Now after the coming of Adamnan no woman is deprived of her testimony, if it be bound in righteous deeds. For a mother is a venerable treasure, a mother is a goodly treasure, the mother of saints and bishops and righteous men, an increase in the Kingdom of Heaven, a propagation on earth.

Adamnan suffered much hardship for your sake, O women, so that ever since Adamnan's time one half of your house is yours, and there is a place for your chair in the other half; so that your contract and your safeguard are free; and the first law made in Heaven and on earth for women is Adamnan's Law.

This is the beginning of the story. Once Adamnan and his mother were wending their way by Ath Drochait. . . . [She said to Adamnan,] "I desire . . . that you should free women for me from encounter, from camping, from fighting, from hosting, from wounding, from slaying, from the bondage of the cauldron."

Then she went on her son's back until they chanced to come upon a battlefield. Such was the thickness of the slaughter into which they came to that the soles of one woman would touch the neck of another. Through they beheld the battlefield, they saw nothing more touching and pitiful than the head of a woman in one place and the body in another, and her little babe upon the breasts of the corpse, a stream of milk upon one of its cheeks, and a stream of blood upon the other. . . .

At the word of his mother Adamnan turned aside, adjusted the head on the neck, and made the sign of the cross with his staff across the breast of the woman. And the woman rose up.

"Alas! O my great Lord of the elements!" said she. "What makes you say alas?" said Adamnan, "My being put to the sword on the battlefield and thrown into the torments of Hell. I know no one here or yonder who would do a kindness or show mercy to me save Adamnan, the Virgin Mary urging him thereto on behalf of the host of Heaven." . . .

"Well now, Adamnan," [his mother said,] "to thee henceforth it is given to free the women of the western world. Neither drink or food shall go into thy mouth until women have been freed by thee." "No living creature can be without food," said Adamnan. "If my eyes see it, I shall stretch out may hands for it." "But thine eyes shall *not* see and thine hands shall *not* reach it."

[Adamnan confines himself to a pit and engages in a full fast until women be liberated. He dies, his mother buries him, and angels visit his tomb.]

At the end of four years God's angels came from Heaven to converse with him. And Adamnan was lifted out of his stone chest and taken to the plain of Birr at the confines of the Ui Neill and Munster. "Arise now out of thy hiding-place," said the angel to Adamnan. "I will not arise," said Adamnan, "until women are freed for me."

"It shall not be in my time if it is done," said Loingsech Bregban, native of Fanait he was, of the race of Conall. "An evil time when a man's sleep shall be murdered for a woman, that women should live, men should be slain. Put the deaf and dumb one to the sword, who asserts anything but that women shall be in everlasting bondage to the brink of Doom."

[The kings of Ireland] arose at the word of Loingsech to put Adamnan to the sword. . . . Adamnan took no sword with him to battle, but the Bell of Adamnan's Wrath, to wit, the little bell of Adamnan's alter-table. It is then Adamnan spoke these words:

> "I strike this little bell . . . [and] I shall sing my psalms to-day in the stone cave, may it not be without fame! . . .God's curse on Elodach, the chief of Femen of the Deissi, lest king or king's heir spring from him after him! My humble, gentle attendant, thou armed son of the rule, strike the bell against Cellach of Carman, that he may be in the earth before a year's end."

[Adamnan proceeds to strike his bell, levying curses against the Irish kings who refused to recognize the Law of Innocents.]

Adamnan did not rest satisfied until securities and bonds were given to him for the emancipation of women. . . .

Those guarantors gave three shouts of malediction on every male who would kill a woman with his right hand or left, by a kick, or by his tongue, so that his heirs are elder and nettle, and the corncrake. The same guarantors gave three shouts of blessing on every female who would do something for the community of Adamnan, however often his reliquaries would come. A horse to be given quarter to his reliquaries, (to be sent) to the coarb to the bath at Raphoe; but that this is from queens only, with whatever every other woman is able to give.

Woman have said and vowed that they would give one half of their household to Adamnan for having brought them out of the bondage and out of the slavery in which they had been. Adamnan accepted but a little from them, to wit, a white tunic with a black border from every penitent nun, a scruple of gold from every chieftain's wife, a linen cloth from every gentleman's wife, seven cakes from every unfree woman, a wether from every flock, the first lamb that was brought forth in a house, whether black or white, for God and for Adamnan. . . .

It is then that Adamnan spoke these words:

> "Unless ye women of this world do good to my community, the offspring ye will bear shall decay, or they shall die full of crimes. Scarcity shall fill your storehouses, the Kingdom of Heaven ye shall not obtain; ye shall not escape by niggardliness or falsehood from Adamnan of Hi [Iona].

"Adamnan of Hi [Iona] will help you, O women!
Give unto your prince all the good things that are you!"

Adamnan of Hi [Iona], beloved of all, has read the books of the Gael.

This is the enactment of the Law of Adamnan of Hi [Iona]. At Birr this enactment was enjoined by the men of Ireland and Britain as a perpetual law by order of their nobles, clerics and laymen, both their chiefs and ollaves [poet advisers] and bishops and sages and confessors, including [a list of several dozen names] . . . and the intercession of all the men of Ireland, both laymen and clerics.

All then, both laymen and clerics, have sworn to fulfill the whole Law of Adamnan till Doom. They have offered up the full *eric* of their female stock to Adamnan, and to every coarb who will be in his seat till Doom, nor does Adamnan take way fines from chieftain and church and family to whom they are due. . . .

Here begins the speech of the angel to Adamnan: —

After fourteen years Adamnan obtained this Law of God, and this is the cause. On Pentecost eve a holy angel of the Lord came to him, and again at Pentecost after a year, and seized a staff, and struck his side and said to him; "Go forth into Ireland, and make a law in it that women be not in any manner killed by men, through slaughter or any other death, either by poison, or in water, or in fire, or by any other beast, or in a pit, or by dogs, but that they shall die in their lawful bed. Thou shalt establish a law in Ireland and Britain for the sake of the mother of each one, because a mother has borne each one, and for the sake of Mary mother of Jesus Christ, through whom all are. Mary besought her Son on behalf of Adamnan about this Law. For whoever slays a woman shall be condemned to a twofold punsihment, that is, his right hand and his left foot shall be cut off before death, and then he shall die, and his kindred shall pay seven full *cumals*, and one-seventh part of the penance. If, instead of life and amputation, a fine has been imposed, the penance is fourteen years, and fourteen *cumals* shall be paid. But if a host has done it, every fifth man up to three hundred shall be condemned to that punishment; if few, they shall be divided into three parts. The first part of them shall be put to death by lot, hand and foot having been first cut off; the second part shall pay fourteen full *cumals*; the third shall be cast into exile beyond the sea, under the rule of a hard regimen; for the sin is great when any slays the mother and sister of Christ's mother and the mother of Christ, and her who carries a spindle and who clothes every one. But he who from this day forward shall put a woman to death and does not do penance according to the Law, shall not only perish in eternity, and be cursed for God and Adamnan, but all shall be cursed that have heard it and do not curse him, and do not chastise him according to the judgment of this Law."

This is the speech of the angel to Adamnan.—

This is the enactment of Adamnan's Law in Ireland and Britain: exemption of the Church of God with her people and her emblems and her sanctuaries and all her properties, live and dead, and her law-abiding laymen with their lawful wives who are obedient to Adamnan and to a lawful, wise and pious confessor. The enactment of this Law of Adamnan is a perpetual law on behalf of clerics and women and innocent children until they are capable of slaying a man, and until they take their place in the tribe, and their (first) expedition is known.

Whoever wounds or slays a young clerical student or an innocent child under the ordinance of Adamnan's Law, eight *cumals* for it for every hand (engaged), with eight years of penance, up to three hundred *cumals*; and one year of penance for it for each one from three hundred to three thousand or an indefinate number; and it is the same fine for him who commits the deed and for him who sees it and does not save to the best of his ability. If there is neglect or ignorance, half the fine for it, and (*arracuir*) that is neglect and that it is ignorance. . . .

These are the judges of Adamnan's Laws in every church and in every tribe, to wit, the clerics whom the community of Adamnan chooses and to whom they commit the enactment of the Law. . . .

Whatever violent death a woman dies, except it be (by) the hand of God, or (in consequence of) rightful lawful cohabitation, it is paid in full fines to Adamnan, both slaying and drowning and burning and poison and breaking and perishing in a quagmire and death by tame beasts and pigs and cattle. If, however, it is a first crime a *folath* (*foluth*?) or on the part of pigs or hounds, they shall be killed at once, and half due to the human hand for it; if it is not a first crime, full due is paid.

There shall be no cross-case or balancing of guilt in Adamnan's Law, but each one pays for his crimes for his own hand. Every trespass which is committed in Adamnan's Law, the communities of Adamnan are to a *forbach* of it, apart from women, whether it be innocents, or clerics, or anyone to whom they commit it, viz. a *cumal forbaich* to the community of Hi where seven *cumals* are paid, and half a *cumal* from seven half-*cumals*. Six *séts* on thirty *séts*, three *séts* on five *séts*.

One-eighth of everything small and great to the community of Adamnan from the slaying of clerics or innocent children. If it be a life-wound any one inflicts on a woman or a cleric or an innocent, seven half-*cumals* are due from him, fifteen *séts* upon the nearest and remoter kindred as being accomplices. Three *séts* for every white blow, five *séts* for every drawing of blood, seven *séts* for every wound requiring a tent, a *cumal* for every confinement to bed, and payment of the physician besides. If it be more than that, it goes upon half-dues for killing a person. If the blow with the palm of the hand or with the fist, one ounce of silver (is the fine) for it. If there be a green or red mark, or a swelling, an ounce and six scruples for it. For seizing women by the hair, five wethers. If there is a fight among women with outrage (?), three wethers.

Men and women are equally liable for large and small dues from this on to (any) fights of women, except outright death. For a woman deserves death for the killing of a man or woman, or for giving poison whereof death ensues, or for burning, or for digging under a church, that is to say, she is to be put in a boat of one paddle as a sea-waif (?) upon the ocean to go with the wind from the land. A vessel of meal and water to be given with her. Judgment on her as God deems it.

If it be charms from which death ensues that any one give to another, the fines of murder followed by concealment of the corpse (are to be paid) for it. Secret plunderings and *cnáim-chró* which are traced (?) to (one of) the four nearest lands, unless these four nearest lands can lay them on any one particularly, they swear by the *altbu* (?) of their soul that they do not to lay it upon any one and pay it themselves. If they suspect any one and prove it, it is he who shall be liable. If the probability lie between two or a greater number, let their names be written on leaves; each leaf arranged around a lot, and the lots are put into a chalice upon the altar. He on whom the lot falls is liable.

If the offenders who violate the Law do not pay, their kindred pay full fines according to the greatness of the crime, and after that (the offender) becomes forfeited, and is banished until the end of the law. One-half of seven *cumals* for accompliceship upon every direct and indirect kindred afterwards. If there be assistance and shelter and connivance, it is death for it; but such as the fine (of the principals) was such shall be that of accomplices.

A further enactment of the Law: they shall feed the stewards of Adamnan's Law, whatever their number, with the good food of their people, viz. five men as guarantors, and the feeding of every one who shall levy the dues of the Law shall be according to the wealth of every one, both chieftain and church and people. A *cumal* for leaving any one of them fasting, while fines are being levied, and offenders with regard to feeding, and they sustain a joint contract of debts unless they feed them. Two *cumals* to them from offenders.

This is the exemption of every guarantor who come to levy this tribute, viz. the guilt of their family does not come upon them so long as they support guarantors and while they are in possession and do not escape; but their own guilt (comes upon them) or the guilt of their offspring and their children and of their retainers.

If it be rape of a maiden, seven half-*cumals* (is the fine) for it. If a hand (is put) upon her or in her girdle, ten ounces for it. If a hand (is put) under her dress to defile her, three ounces and seven *cumals* for it. If there be a blemish or her head or her eyes or in the face or in the ear or nose or tooth or tongue or foot or hand, seven *cumals* are (to be paid) for it. If it be a blemish on any other part of her body, seven half-*cumals* are (to be paid) for it. If it be tearing of her dress, seven ounces and one *cumal* for it.

If it be making a gentlewoman blush by imputing unchastity to her or by denying her offspring, there are seven *cumals* (to be paid) for it until it comes to (the wife of) an *aire désa*. For her onwards to a *muiri*, seven ounces.

If women be employed in an assault or in a host or fight, seven *cumals* for every hand as far as seven, and beyond that it is to be accounted as the crime of one man. If a woman has been got with child by stealth, without contract, without full rights, without dowry, without betrothal, a full fine for it. . . .

Three guarantors for every chief church for the Law of Adamnan, viz. the prior and the cook and the steward; and a guarantor of the Law from (every) parent-family throughout all Ireland; and two guarantors of the Law from high chieftains, and hostages to be held for its payment, if there be the proof of a woman.

12

Privileges and Prerogatives Granted by Their Catholic Majesties to Christopher Columbus (1492) and the Charter to Sir Walter Raleigh (1584)

When the Black Death ravaged generations of Europeans throughout the late medieval period, no doubt many expected that the world was at an end. As it happened, the plagues spared most of the population, stopping short of absolute destruction. The dramatic decrease of readily available labor, however, resulted in higher wages, lower rents to landowners, and a very real financial crisis for the aristocracy as a whole class. When coupled with massive, long-lasting, and epochal conflicts between major powers (England and France's Hundred Years' War, Spain's *Reconquista*, and the Ottoman–Hapsburg Wars to name a few), the demographic crisis encouraged aristocrats to seek out new sources of revenue.

European rulers and their sponsored cliques of merchant-capitalists first turned their hungry gazes eastward to India. Finding the land and sea routes to the Far East lengthy and costly (made all the more so by Ottoman tariffs), the various crowns sponsored voyages of westward discovery and colonization. Monarchs exchanged royal rights and privileges for the wealth and talents of a new, burgeoning class of colonial aristocrats and venture capitalists. Christopher Columbus, to name the first among many New World aristocrats, was granted practically absolute rule over any and all conquered territories, and to him alone were the privileges of rule accorded.

A century later, Elizabeth I of England's "Charter to Sir Walter Raleigh" (1584) shows the development of charter-granting at the turn of the early modern era: Raleigh is granted the right not only to explore, conquer, and rule colonies in the name of the queen but also to go a-pirating against England's enemies. Importantly, however, should Raleigh ever entertain the notion of rebelling against his queen, he should immediately be banished from the English nation and removed from Elizabeth's royal protection. Monarchs thus relieved themselves of both burdensome rights and duties to their subjects and offset the cost of plagues. The royals shed their prerogatives, feathered their imperial executive beds, and constructed either absolutist or bourgeois mercantile nation-states to replace outdated medieval fiefdoms.[35]

Ferdinand and Elizabeth, by the Grace of God, King and Queen of Castile, of Leon, of Arragon . . .

For as much of you, Christopher Columbus, are going by our command, with some of our vessels and men, to discover and subdue some Islands and Continent in the ocean, and it is hoped that by God's assistance, some of the said Islands and Continent in the ocean will be discovered and conquered by your means and conduct, therefore it is but just and reasonable, that since you expose yourself to such danger to serve us, you should be rewarded for it. . . . Our will is, That you, Christopher Columbus . . . shall be our Admiral of the said Islands and Continent you shall so discover and conquer; and that you be our Admiral, Vice-Roy, and Governour in them, and that for the future, you may call and stile yourself, D. Christopher Columbus, and that your sons and successors in the said employment, may call themselves Dons, Admirals, Vice-Roys, and Governours of them; and that you may exercise the office of Admiral, with the charge of Vice-Roy and Governour of the said Islands and Continent, which you and your Lieutenants shall conquer, and freely decide all causes, civil and criminal . . . as you shall think fit in justice, and as the Admirals of our kingdoms use to do; and that you have power to punish offenders . . . and that you enjoy the perquisites and salaries belonging to the said employments, and to each of them, in the same manner as the High Admiral of our kingdoms does. . . . Concerning all which things, if it be requisite, and you shall desire it, We command our Chancellour, Notaries, and other Officers, to pass, seal, and deliver to you, our Letter of Privilege, in such form and legal manner, as you shall require or stand in need of. And that none of them presume to do any thing to the contrary, upon pain of our displeasure, and forfeiture of 30 ducats for each offence. . . . Under which same, we also command any Public Notary whatsoever, that he give to him that shows it him, a certificate under his seal, that we may know how our command is obeyed.

Given at Granada, on the 30th of April, in the year of our Lord, 1492.—

I, the King, I, the Queen
By their Majesties Command,

John Coloma
Secretary to the King and Queen

Elizabeth by the Grace of God of England, Fraunce and Ireland Queene, defender of the faith, &c. To all people to whome these presents shall come, greeting.

Knowe yee that of our especial grace, certaine science, and meere motion, we haue given and graunted, and by these presents for us, our heires and successors, we giue and graunt to our trustie and welbeloued seruant *Walter Ralegh*, Esquire, and to his heires assignes for euer, free libertie and licence from time to time, and at all times for ever hereafter, to discover, search, finde out, and view such remote, heathen and barbarous lands, countries, and territories, not actually possessed of any Christian Prince, nor inhabited by Christian People, as to him, his heires and assignes, and to every or any of them shall seeme good, and the same to haue, horle, occupie and enjoy to him, his heires and assignes for euer, with all prerogatives, commodities, jurisdictions, royalties, privileges, franchises, and preheminences, thereto or thereabouts both by sea and land, whatsoever we by our letters patents may graunt, and as we or any of our noble progenitors haue heretofore graunted to any person or persons, bodies politique or corporate: and the said *Walter Ralegh*, his heires and assignes, and all such as from time to time, by licence of us, our heires and successors, shall goe or trauaile thither to inhabite or remaine, there to build and fortifie, at the discretion of the said *Walter Ralegh*, his heires and assignes, the statutes or acte of Parliament made against fugitives, or against such as shall depart, remaine or continue out of our Realme of England without licence, or any other statute, acte, lawe, or any ordinance whatsoever to the contrary in anywise notwithstanding.

And we do likewise by these presents, of our especial grace, meere motion, and certain knowledge, for us, our heires and successors, giue and graunt full authoritie, libertie and power to the said *Walter Ralegh*, his heires and assignes, and every of them, that he and they, and euery or any of them, shall and may at all and euery time, and times hereafter, haue, take, and leade in the saide voyage, and trauaile thitherward, or to inhabit there with him, or them, and euery

211

or any of them, such and so many of our subjects as shall willingly accompanie him or them, and euery or any of them to whom also we doe by these presents, giue full libertie and authority in that behalfe, and also to haue, take, and employ, and vse sufficient shipping and furniture for the Transportations and Nauigations in that behalfe, so that none of the same persons or any of them, be such as hereafter shall be restrained by us, our heires, or successors.

And further that the said *Walter Ralegh*, his heires and assignes, and euery of them, shall haue holde, occupie, and enioye to him, his heires and assignes, and euery of them for euer, all the soile of all such lands, territories, and Countreis, so to bee discovered and possessed as aforesaide, and of all such Cities, castles, townes, villages, and places in the same, with the right, royalties, franchises, and iurisdictions, as well marine as other within the saide landes, or Countreis, or the seas thereunto adioyning, to be had, or used, with full power to dispose thereof, and of euery part in fee-simple or otherwise, according to the order of the lawes of England, as neere as the same conveniently may bee, at his, and their will and pleasure, to any persons then being, or that shall remaine within the allegiance of us, our heires, and successors: reseruing always to us our heires, and successors, for all services, duties, and demaundes, the fift part of all the oare of golde and siluer, that from time to time, and at all times after such discouerie, subduing and possessing, shal be there gotten and obtained: All which landes, Countreis, and territories, shall for ever be holden of the said *Walter Ralegh*, his heires and assignes, of us, our heirs and successors, by homage, and by the said paiment of the said fift part, reserued onely for all services.

And moreover, we doe by these presents, for us, our heires and. successors, giue and graunt licence to the said *Walter Ralegh*, his heirs, and assignes, and euery of them, that he, and they, and euery or any of them, shall and may from time to time, and at all times for euer hereafter, for his and their defence, encounter and expulse, repell and resist as well by sea as by lande, and by all other wayes whatsoever, all, and every such person and persons whatsoever, as without the especiall liking and licence of the saide *Walter Ralegh*, and of his heires and assignes, shall attempt to inhabite within the said Countreis, or any of them, or within the space of two hundreth leagues neere to the place or places within such Countreis as aforesaide (if they shall not bee before planted or inhabited within the limits as aforesaide with the subjects of any Christian Prince being in amitie with us) where the saide *Walter Ralegh*, his heires, or assignes, or any of them, or his, or their or any of their associates or company, shall within sixe yeeres (next ensuing) make their dwellings or abidings, or that shall enterprise or attempt at any time hereafter unlawfully to annoy, either by sea or lande, the saide *Walter Ralegh*, his heirs or assignes, or any of them, or his or their, or any of his or their companies giuing, and graunting by these presents further power and authoritie, to the said *Walter Ralegh*, his heirs and assignes, and euery of them from time to time, and at all times for euer hereafter, to take and surprise by all maner of meanes whatsoever, all and euery those person or persons, with their shippes, vessels, and other goods and furniture, which without the licence of the saide *Walter Ralegh*, or his heires, or assignes, as aforesaide, shall bee founde trafiquing into any harbour or harbors, creeke, or creekes, within the limits aforesaide, (the subjects of our Realms and Dominions, and all other persons in amitie with us, trading to the *Newfound lands* for fishing as heretofore they haue commonly used, or being driven by force of a tempest, or shipwracke onely excepted:) and those persons, and euery of them, with their shippes, vessels, goods and furniture to deteine and possesse as of good and lawfull prize, according to the discretion of him the saide *Walter Ralegh*, his heires, and assignes, and euery, or any of them. And for uniting in more perfect league and amitie, of such Countreis, landes, and territories so to bee possessed and inhabited as aforesaide with our Realmes of Englande, and Ireland, and the better incouragement of men to these enterprises: we do by these presents, graunt and declare that all such Countreis, so hereafter to be possessed and inhabited as is aforesaide, from thencefoorth shall bee of the allegiance of vs, our heires and successours. And wee doe graunt to the saide *Walter Ralegh*, his heires, and assignes, and to all, and euery of them, and to all and euery other person, and persons being of our allegiance, whose names shall be noted or entred in some of our Courtes of recorde within our Realme of Englande, that with the assent of the saide *Walter Ralegh*, his heires or assignes, shall in his journeis for discouerie, or in the iourneis for conquest, hereafter trauelle to such lands, countreis and territories, as aforesaide, and to their, and to euery of their heires, that they, and every or any of them, being either borne within our saide Realmes of Englande, or Irelande or in any other place within our allegiance, and which hereafter shall be inhabiting within any the lands, Countreis, and territories, with such licence (as aforesaide) shall and may haue all the priuiledges of free Denizens, and persons native of England, and within our allegiance in such like ample maner and fourme, as if they were borne and personally resident within our saide Realme of England, any lawe, custome, or vsage to the contrary notwithstanding.

And for as much as upon the finding out, discovering, or inhabiting of such remote lands, countreis, and territories as aforesaid, it shall be necessary for the safetie of al men, that shall aduenture them selues in those iournies or voyages, to determine to liue together in Christian peace, and ciuil quietnes ech with other, whereby euery one may with more pleasure and profit enjoy that whereunto they shall attaine with great paine and perill, we for vs, our heires and successors, are likewise pleased and contented, and by these presents do giue and graunt to the said *Walter Ralegh*, his heires and assignes for ever, that hee and they, and euery or any of them, shall and may from time to time for euer hereafter, within the said mentioned remote landes and Countreis in the way by the seas thither, and from thence, haue full and meere power and authoritie to correct, punish, pardon, gouerne, and rule by their and euery or any of their good discretions and pollicies, as well in causes capital, or criminall, as ciuil, both marine and other all such our subjects as shall from time to time aduenture themselves in the said iournies or voyages, or that shall at any time hereafter inhabite any such landes, countreis, or territories as aforesaide, or shall abide within 200. leagues of any of the saide place or places, where the saide *Walter Ralegh*, his heires or assignes, or any of them, or any of his or their associates or companies, shall inhabits within 6. yeeres next ensuing the date hereof, according to such statutes, lawes and ordinances, as shall bee by him the saide *Walter*

Ralegh his heires and assignes, and euery or any of them deuised, or established, for the better government of the said people as aforesaid. So always as the said statutes, lawes, and ordinances may be as neere as conveniently may be, agreeable to the forme of the lawes, statutes, governement, or pollicie of England, and also so as they be not against the true Christian faith, nowe professed in the Church of England, nor in any wise to withdrawe any of the subjects or people of those landes or places from the allegiance of vs, our heires and successours, as their immediate Soueraigne vnder God. . . .

Provided alwayes, and our will and pleasure is, and wee do hereby declare to all Christian kings, princes and states, that if the saide *Walter Ralegh*, his heires or assignes, or any of them, or any other lay their licence or appointment, shall at any time or times hereafter, robbe or spoile by sea or by lande, or do any acte of unjust or unlawful hostilitie, to any of the subjects of vs, our heires or successors, or to any of the subjects of any the kings, princes, rulers, governors, or estates, being then in perfect league and amitie with us, our heires and successors, and that upon such injury, or upon iust complaint of any such prince, ruler, governoir, or estate, or their subjects, wee, our heires and successours, shall make open proclamation within any the portes of our Realme of England, that the saide *Walter Ralegh*, his heires and assignes, and adherents, or any to whome these our letters patents may extende, shall within the termes to be limitted, by such procla-mation, make full restitution, and satisfaction of all such injuries done, so as both we and the said princes, or other so complayning, may holde vs and themselves fully contented. And that if the saide

Walter Ralegh, his heires and assignes, shall not make or cause to be made satisfaction accordingly, within such time so to be limitted, that then it shall be lawfull to us our heires and successors, to put the saide *Walter Ralegh*, his heires and assignes and adherents, and all the inhabitants of the said places to be discovered (as is aforesaide) or any of them out of our allegiance and protection, and that from and after such time of putting out of protection the said *Walter Ralegh*, his heires, assignes and adherents, and others so to be put out, and the said places within their habitation, possession and rule, shall be out of our allegeance and protection, and free for all princes and others, to pursue with hostilitie, as being not our subjects, nor by vs any way to be avouched, maintained or defended, nor to be holden as any of ours, nor to our protection or dominion, or allegiance any way belonging, for that expresse mention of the cleer yeerely value of the certaintie of the premisses, or any part thereof, or of any other gift, or grant by vs, or any our progenitors, or predecessors to the said *Walter Ralegh*, before this time made in these presents be not expressed, or any other grant, ordinance, provision, proclamation, or restraint to the contrarye thereof, before this time giuen, ordained, or provided, or any other thing, cause, or matter whatsoever, in any wise notwithstanding. In witness whereof, we haue caused these our letters to be made patents. Witnesse our selues, at *Westminster*, the 25. day of March, in the sixe and twentieth yeere of our Raigne.

13

Richard Frethorne, "Letters to Father and Mother" (March–April 1623)

Throughout the early modern era, nation-states and corporations surged in wealth and power. European monarchs and their merchant-capitalist financiers conquered much of the planet and shifted gigantic portions of the human population around the globe, subjecting them to forced labor of virtually every sort imaginable. The exploited masses from all continents emptied into the vast North American frontier zone, the aquatic republics condemned by authorities as "pirate ships," and shadowy, ungoverned spaces the world over. Wherever and whenever possible, individuals sought to live freely and place themselves permanently beyond the tandem reach of state and corporation. Chapters 13 through 20 will follow the stories of many such free peoples, forever struggling toward individual liberty in a world of empires.

* * *

Colonial Virginia was an almost unbelievably bad place for virtually everyone unfortunate enough to live there. From the beginning of the Jamestown settlement, Virginians long failed to produce enough food to feed themselves, failed to maintain any sort of peace with Native Americans, and failed to produce any profits for investors in what we often forget was a corporation more than it was a political extension of England.

By 1616, the Virginia Company faced bankruptcy and opted to allow settlers to own and operate private property, much of which must be devoted to producing the new cash crop, tobacco. The company began fervently importing indentured servants from English and continental city centers, often through illicit means, including kidnapping, impressment, fraud, and changes to the judicial system specifically designed to condemn convicts to plantation production in the New World.

Most of the new indentures were the "masterless men and women" displaced from traditional common fields in the English countryside by the long, grinding process of aristocratic land expropriation called "enclosure."

The "enclosure movement" fenced common lands tra-
ditionally farmed by landless peasants and tenant
farmers, forcing many to seek employment in cities.
Historian Alan Taylor describes London (ca. 1600) as
"a sprawling and frightening metropolis . . . notorious
for filth, poverty, plagues, fires, crime, and executions."
In an effort to prevent social revolution in London and
enrich themselves in the process, colonial companies
and their promoters advertised America as a place for
the "surplus poor" to improve their prospects, a new
frontier for social mobility, peace, and freedom. The
reality was starkly different.

Very few documents remain from common people for
the whole of the 17th century, especially so for those
in the early settler colonies, making documents like
Richard Frethorne's letters to his parents both rare
and precious. Frethorne was an indentured servant in
Virginia, whose parents contracted him into servitude
in the early 1620s. In these three letters, written in
March and April 1623, Frethorne desperately laments
his conditions and declares that he would rather sacrifice arms and legs than continue to live in Virginia.
Above all, he begs his parents to send cheese and
beef—anything he can trade to relieve his sufferings
and pay his indenture. It reminds us at once of the rav-
ages of the past compared with the relatively comfort-
able and pacific present while showing that people of
virtually all ages have dealt with similar struggles and

personal crises—from living with endless and crushing debt to battling against a variety of oppressive social and political forces in daily life.[36]

Note: The spelling and grammar will be easier to decipher if you read the letters aloud.

March 20, 1623

Loveing and kind father and mother my most humble duty remembred to you hopeing in God of yo[u]r good health. . . .I yor Child am in a most heavie Case by reason of the nature of the Country is such that it Causeth much sicknes, as the scurvie and the bloody flix [dysentery], and divers other diseases, wch maketh the bodie very poore, and Weake, and when wee are sicke there is nothing to Comfort us; for since I came out of the ship, I never at[e] anie thin but pease [porridge], and loblollie (that is water gruell) as for deare or venison I never saw anie since I came into this land, ther is indeed some foule, but Wee are not allowed to goe, and get [it], but must Worke hard both earelie, and late for a messe of water gruell, and a mouthful of breead, and beife, a mouthful of bread for a pennie loafe must serve for 4 men wch is most pitifull if you did know as much as I, when people crie out day, and night, Oh that they were in England without their lymbes and would not care to lose anie lymbe to bee in England againe, yea though they beg from doore to doore, for wee live in feare of the Enimy evrie hower [hour], yet wee have had a Combate with them on the Sunday before Shrovetyde, and wee tooke two alive, and make slaves of them, but it was by pollicie, for wee are in great danger, for o[u]r

Plantac[i]on is very weake, by reason of the dearth, and sicknes, of o[u]r Companie, for wee looke everie hower When two more should goe, yet there came some fo[u]r other mcn yet to lyve with us, of which ther is but one alive, and our L[ieutenant] is dead, and his ffather, and his brother, and there was some 5 or 6 of the last yeares 20 of wch there is but 3 left, so that wee are faine to get other men to plant with us, and yet wee are but 32 to fight against 3000 if they should Come, and the nighest helpe that Wee have is ten miles of us, and when the rogues overcame this place last, they slew 80 Persons how then shall wee doe for wee lye even in their teeth, they may easily take us but that God is merciful, and can save with few as well as with many; as he shewed to Gylead and like Gileads Souldiers if they lapt water, wee drinkee water wch is Weake [without alcohol], and I have nothing to Comfort me, nor ther is nothing to be gotten here but sicknes, and death, except that one had money to lay out in some thinges for profit; But I have nothing at all, no not a shirt to my backe, but two Ragges nor no Clothes, but one poore suite, nor but one paire of shooes, but one paire of stockins, but one Capp, but two bands [collars], my Cloke is stolen by one of my owne fellowes, and to his dying hower would not tell mee what he did with it but some of my fellows saw him have butter and beife out of a ship, wch my Cloke I doubt [not] paid for, so that I have not a penny, nor a penny Worth to helpe me to either spice, or sugar, or strong Waters, and strengthen them so water here doth wash and weaken the[se] here, onelie keepe life and soule togeather. but I am not halfe a quarter so strong as I was in England, and all is for want of victuals, ffor I doe protest unto you, that I have eaten more in [a] day at home th[a]n I have allowed me here for a Weeke. You have given more th[a]n my dayes allowance to a beggar at the doore; and if Mr Jackson had not relieved me, I should bee in a poore Case, but he like a ffather and shee like a loving mother doth still helpe me, for when wee goe up to James Towne that is 10 myles of us, there lie all the ships that Come to the land, and there they must deliver their goods, and when wee went up to Towne as it may bee on Moonedaye [Monday] . . . that Goodman Jackson pityed me & made me a Cabbin to lye in always when I come up, and he would give me some poor Jacks [fish] home with me wch Comforted mee more than pease, or water gruell. Oh they bee verie godlie folks, and love me verie well, and will doe anie thing for me, and he much marvailed that you would send me a servaunt to the [Virginia] Companie, he saith I had been better knockd on the head, and Indeede so I fynd it now to my greate greife and miserie, and saith, that if you love me you will redeeme me suddenlie, for wch I doe Intreate and beg, and if you cannot get the marchaunts to redeeme me for some little money then for Gods sake get a gathering or intreat some good folks to lay out some little Sum of moneye, in meale, and Cheese and butter, and beife, anie eating meate will yeald great profit, oile and vyniger is verie good, but ffather ther is greate losse in leaking, but for Gods sake send beife and Cheese and butter or the more of one sort and none of another, but if you send Cheese it must bee very old Cheese, and at the Chesmongers you may buy good Cheese for twopence farthing or halfepenny that will be liked verie well, but if you send Cheese you must have a Care how you packe it in barrels, and you must put Coopers chips between evrie Cheese, or else the heat of the hold [of the ship] will rott them, and looke whasoever you send me be it nev[e]r so much looke what I make of yt I will deale trulie with you I will send it ov[e]r, and beg the profit to redeeme me, and if I die before it Come I have intreated Goodman Jackson to send you the worth of it, who hath promised he will; If you send you must direct yo[u]r letters to Goodman Jackson, at James Towne a Gunsmith. (you must sett downe his frayt) because there bee more of his name there; good ffather doe not forget me, but have mercie and pittye my miserable Case. I know if you did but see me you would weepe to see me, for I have but one suite, but it is a strange one, it is very well guarded, wherefore for Gods sake pittie me, I pray you to remember my love my love to all my ffreinds, and kindred, I hope all my Brothers and Sisters are in good health, and as for my part I have set downe my resoluc[i]on that certainelie Wilbe, that is, that the Answeare of this letter wilbee life or death to me, therefore good ffather send as soone as you can, and if you send me anie thing let this be the marke. ROT

Richard Ffrethorne
Martyn's Hundred

April 2, 1623

[Here are t]he names of them that bee dead of the Companie came ov[e]r with us to serve under our L[ieutenants] . . . [a list of twenty names: seventeen men, two women, and a child]. All theis died out of my m[aster's] house since I came, and wee came in but at Christmas, and this is the 20th day of March and the Saylers say that ther is two thirds of the 150 dead already and thus I end prayeing to God to send me good successe that I may be redeemed out of Egypt. So vale in Christo.

Loveing ffather I pray you to use this man [who delivers this letter] verie exceeding kindly for he hath done much for me, both on my Journy and since, I intreate you not to forget me, but by anie meanes redeeme me, for this day we heare that there is 26 of English men slayne by the Indians, and they have taken a Pinnace [small boat] of Mr Pountis, and have gotten peeces [muskets], Armour, swords, all them from English, till it is too late, that they bee upon us, and then ther is no mercie, therefore if you love or respect me, as yo[u]r Child release me from this bondage, and save my life, now you may save me, or let me bee slayne, with Infidelle, aske this man [who delivers this letter], he knoweth that all is true and Just that I say here; if you do redeeme me the Companie must send for me to my Mr Harrod for so is this M[aster's] name.

Yo[u]r loving sonne
Richard Ffrethorne

April 3, 1623

Moreover, on the third day of Aprill wee heard that after theis Rogues had gotten the Pinnace, and had taken all the furnitures as peeces, swords, armour, Coats of male, Powder, shot and all the thinges that they had to trade withal, they killed the Captaine, and Cut of his head, and rowing with the taile of the boat foremost they set up a pole and put the Captaines head upon it, and so rowed home, then the Devill set them on againe, so that they furnished about 200 Canoes with above 1000 Indians, and came and thought to have taken the ship, but shee was too quicke for them wch thing was very much talked of, for they always feared a ship, but now the Rogues growe verie bold, and can use peeces, some of them, as well or better than an Englishman, ffor an Indian did shoote with Mr Charles my M[aster's] Kindsman at a marke of white paper, and hee hit it at the first, but Mr Charles Could not hit it, But see the Envie of theis slaves, for when they Could not take the ship then o[u]r men saw them threaten Accomack that is the next Plantac[i]on and now ether is no Way but starveing ffor the Governour told us and Sir George, that except the [ship] Seaflower come in or that wee can fall foule of theis Rogues and get some Corne from them, above halfe the land will surelie be starved, for they had no Crop last yeare by reason of theis Rogues, so that wee have no Corne but as ships do relieve us, nor wee shall hardlie have anie Crop this yeare, and Wee are as like to perish first as anie Plantac[i]on, for wee have but two Hogsheads of meale left to serve us this two Monethes, if the Seaflower doe stay so long before shee come in, and that meale is but 3 Weeks bread for us, at a loafe for 4 about the bignes of a pennie loafe in England, that is but a halfepenny loafe a day for a man: is it not straunge to me thinke you? But What will it bee when wee shall goe a moneth or two and never see a bit of bread. As my M[aster] doth say Wee must doe, and he said hee is not able to keepe us all, then wee shalbe turned up to the land and eate barks of trees, or moulds or the Ground therefore and with weeping teares I beg of you to helpe me. O that you did see [my] daylie and hourelie sighes, grones, and teares, and thumpes that I afford mine owne brest, and rue and Curse the time of my birth with holy Job. I thought no head had been able to hold so much water as hath and doth dailie flow from mine eyes.

But this is Certaine I never felt the want of ffather and mother till now, but now deare ffrends full well I knowe and rue it although it were too late before I knew it.

I pray you talke with this honest man [who delivers this letter] he will tell you more then now in my hast I can set downe.

Yo[u]r loving sonne
Richard Ffrethorne

14

Clement Downing, "The History of John Plantain, Called King of Ranter-Bay, &c." (1737)

Clement Downing served on a variety of ships in the Indian Ocean as an officer in the British Navy through-out the early 18th century. During his ship's efforts to counter piracy in the ocean basin, Downing visited a small island off the coast of Madagascar, St. Mary's, and a particularly fascinating pirate settlement on the mainland in a place called Ranter-Bay. Landing in Ranter-Bay, Downing and his men encountered for-mer pirates with most unusual stories and titles. In fact, their leader, one John Plantain of Chocolate-Hole, Jamaica, styled himself "King of Ranter-Bay" and ruled as de facto monarch of all Madagascar. From his "castle" on the bayside cliffs, Plantain and his hundreds of pirate followers drawn from the land and seas alike conquered and subjugated rival kings until the entire island paid tribute to the pirate overlords.

Plantain was born in Jamaica near the turn of the 17th century to parents of means enough to send him to school. Formal education did not agree with Plantain's constitution, and at age 13 he joined an English privateer, sailed against the Spanish for some time, and eventually (and eagerly) turned pirate under the pernicious influence of Rhode Islanders. Plantain and his fellow pirates sailing under Captain Edward England eventually worked their way to Madagascar, where they dissolved their crews, settled among the indigenous inhabitants, intermarried, and creolized life and politics in the southwestern Indian Ocean.

With a mix of personal ambition, lustful passion for rapine and conquest, and greed to accumulate money and power in whatever ways were available to him, Plantain invested his earnings from a career of piracy (he was estimated to be the wealthiest of his associates) in the purchase of slaves in Madagascar. He ordered his slaves to construct a "castle," to which he added guns with every further conquest of ships and territory. Plantain projected strong, well-armed, battle-tested pirate-soldiers throughout the region, forcing all rivals to bend to his will.

In my view, the bizarre and bloody story of John Plantain, King of Ranter-Bay, illustrates that an almost limitless desire for power can possess the hearts of men great and small alike. It challenges us to consider who among us would turn down the opportunity to play master to a small continent, let alone petty tyrant around the office or over one's family. Would we respect the lives and liberties of those weaker than ourselves, or would we too, given the right opportunities, proclaim ourselves kings of our very own private fiefdoms? In the end, Plantain's violence and exploitation provoked rebellion among his serfs. He escaped Madagascar with his life and legend intact, but was King of Ranter-Bay no more.[37]

A Compendious History of the Indian Wars; with an Account of the Rise, Progress, Strength, and Forces of Angria the Pyrate (London: T. Cooper, 1737)

News of the Indian Seas being incumbered with Pyrates of our Nation, so far alarmed the Court of Directors, as to petition the Crown to grant a Squadron of Men of War to be sent thither to suppress them, who for near two Years continued to infest those Parts. . . . They made the Island of Madagascar their Rendezvous, where they committed all manner of Enormities, and every one did as his own vicious Heart directed him. . . .

"The History of John Plantain, Called King of Ranter-Bay, &c."

John Plantain was born in *Chocolate-Hole*, on the Island of *Jamaica*, of *English* Parents, who took care to bestow on him the best Education, they themselves were possess'd of; which was to curse, swear, and blaspheme, from the time of his first learning to speak. This is generally the chief Education bestowed on the Children of the common People in those Parts. He was sent to School to learn to read, which he once could do tolerably well; but he quickly forgot the same, for want of practicing it. The Account he gave of his first falling into that wicked and irregular Course of Life, was, That after he was about thirteen Years of Age, he went as Master's Servant on board a small Sloop belonging to *Spanish-Town*, on the Island of *Jamaica*, and they went out a privateering and to cut Logwood in the Bay of *Campeacy*; where they generally used to maroon the *Spaniards*, and the *Spaniards* used to maroon them, as the one or t'other happened to be strongest. He followed this Course of Life till he was near 20 Years of Age, when he came to *Rhode-Island*; there he fell into company with several Men who belonged to a Pyrate Sloop. These try'd to persuade him, with several others, to go with them; shewing great Sums of Gold, and treating him and others in a profuse and expensive Manner. His own wicked Inclinations soon led him to accept the Offer, without much Hesitation. . . .

From *Rhode-Island* they shaped their Course for the Coast of *Guinea*, and in their way took three Ships. . . . They pretended to give Liberty to those Ships Crews either to go or stay with them. . . . Now they had got a Ship of near 300 Tuns, which mounted 30 Guns, well mann'd and well stored with Provisions. They usually are at no certain Allowance amongst themselves, till they are in a Likelihood of being short of Provision, but every

Man is allowed to eat what he pleases. Then they put all under the care of their Quarter-master, who discharges all things with an Equality to them all, every Man and Boy faring alike; and even their Captain, or any other Officer, is allowed no more than another Man; nay, the Captain cannot keep his own Cabbin to himself, for their Bulk heads are all down, and every Man stands to his Quarters, where they lie and mess, tho' they take the liberty of ranging all over the Ships. . . .

Plantain and his Companions were daily increasing their Store. . . .

They daily now increased their number, and were not for keeping so many Ships, imagining they should soon have a Squadron of Men of War after them, which they did not care to have any Correspondence with. Now Capt. *England* proposed a new Voyage to them, which might be the making of them all very rich; and as they had got such good Ships under their Command, they were resolved to make the best of their present Situation. . . . They had now six or seven Ships with them, of which account it was resolved, that *England* and [Capt.] *Roberts* should separate, for fear of a Civil War amongst themselves. *England* was to take the *Fancy*, the *Snow* and the Ship they called the *Victory*, and go away for the *East-Indies*; and *Roberts* and the rest were to continue and range about those Seas, as they thought fit. . . .

Capt. *England* took to the Eastern Seas, and came away for *St. Augustine*'s Bay, on the Island of *Madagascar*, and his People being very sickly, the Doctor had them sent on shore for the Recovery of their Healths; but several died. . . . [After several more trips throughout the region for provisions,] They then made the best of their way for *Madagascar*, and went to *St. Mary's* Island, where none of their Fraternity had been for many Years, and were very joyfully received by the King. This Island joins to the Continent of *Madagascar*, and is generally a Place of Residence for Pyrates. Here they made a sad Massacre of the poor Moors Men, they had taken in the Ship above-mentioned, and abused their Women in a very vile manner. Some say, that Capt. *England* kept one or two of the *Moors* Women for his own Use, there being some of Distinction amongst them, whose Fathers were in high Posts under the Great Mogul. . . .

Plantain, *James Adair*, and *Hans Burgen*, the *Dane*, had fortified themselves very strongly at *Ranter-Bay*; and taken possession of a large Tract of Country. *Plantain* having the most Money of them all, called himself King of *Ranter-Bay*, and the Natives commonly sing Songs in praise of *Plantain*. He brought great Numbers of the Inhabitants to be subject to him, and seem'd to govern them arbitrarily; tho' he paid his Soldiers very much to their Satisfaction. He would frequently send Parties of Men into other Dominions, and seize the Inhabitants Cattle. He took upon him to make War, and to extort Tribute from several of the petty Kings and his Neighbours, and to increase his own Dominions.

James Adair's Birth and Education was something superior to that of *Plantain*; for he was learnt to write as well as read; and had been brought up in the Town of *Leith*, by a sober and industrious Father and Mother. Not behaving to the Satisfaction of his Parents, he went for *London*, and from thence, for the *West-Indies*; but was taken by the Pyrates, and after that entered voluntarily with them. He was a young Man of a very hard Countenance, but something inclined to Good-Nature. When we bartered with the Pyrates at *Ranter-Bay* for Provisions, they frequently shewed the Wickedness of their Dispositions, by quarelling and fighting with each other upon the most trifling Occasions. It was their Custom never to go abroad, except armed with Pistols or a naked Sword in their Hand, to be in Readiness to defend themselves or to attack others.

Hans Burgen, the *Dane*, was born at *Copenhagen*, and had been brought up a Cooper; but coming to *London*, he entered himself with Capt. *Creed* for *Guinea*; the Ship being taken by the Pyrates, he agreed to go with them, and became a Comerade to King *Plantain*. This *Plantain*'s House was built in as commodious a manner as the Nature of the Place would admit; and for his further State and Recreation, he took a great many Wives and Servants, whom he kept in great Subjection; and after the English manner, called them *Moll*, *Kate*, Sue or *Pegg*. These Women were dressed in the richest Silks, and some of them had Diamond Necklaces. He frequently came over from his own Territories to *St. Mary*'s Island, and there began to repair several Parts of Capt. *Avery*'s Fortifications.

The King of *Massaleage* had with him a very beautiful Grand-daughter, said to be the Daughter of an *English* Man, who commanded a *Bristol* Ship, that came there on the Slaving Trade. This Lady was called *Eleonora Brown*, so named by her Father; she had been taught to speak a little *English*; but this is common on the Island of *Madagascar*. . . . Plantain being desirous of having a Lady of *English* Extraction, sent to the King of *Massaleage* (whom the Pyrates called *Long Dick*, or King *Dick*) to demand his Grand-daughter for a Wife. Capt. *England*, with 60 or 70 Men had dispersed themselves about the Island, and inhabited amongst the Negroes: but Capt. *England* being very poor, was obliged to be beholden to several of the white Men for his Subsistence. Several of these People had join'd King *Dick* at *Massaleage*; and persuaded him to refuse *Plantain*'s Demand, to put himself in a Posture of Defence, and to prohibit all Correspondence between any of his Subjects and those of *Plantain*. The chief Weapon used by the Natives is the Lance, which they are very dexterous in throwing. But *Plantain* had got some hundreds of Firelocks, which he distributed among his Subjects, and had learned them to exercise in a pretty regular manner. He also had great Store of Powder and Ball, and a good Magazine provided with all manner of Necessaries. He was a Man of undaunted Courage. . . .

He sent to tell him, that if he did not comply directly he would bring such an arm'd Force against him, that should drive him out of his Dominions; and if he happened to fall into his Hands, he would certainly send him to Prince *William* of *St. Augustine*'s Bay, who would sell him to the first English Ship which put in there. . . . He still refused his Demands, and boldly sent word, that he would not give him the Trouble to come quite to his Home, but that he would certainly meet him half way. This Answer so much inrag'd *Plantain*, that he called his chief Officers together to consult what he should do; tho', let their Advice be what it would, he always followed his own Inclination. . . .

[*Plantain* attacks and defeats King *Dick*.]

After this Success, he resolved to be revenged on King *Kelly*, who had deserted him, and had been join'd by Part of King *Dick*'s scattered Forces. To this end, he put himself on his March with his Forces, and came up with *Kelly*; on which ensued a smart Encounter which lasted a whole Day, each Party being supported by the *English*, some of whom were on one side, some on the other . . . but early in the Morning *Plantain*'s Men attack'd them with fresh Vigour, put them to the Rout, and took many of them Prisoners. . . . Capt. *England* was now in great Distress, and could well tell how to live; but coming to Prince *William* of *St. Augustine*'s Bay, he there met with seven or eight of his old Ship-mates, who supported him for some time, and Prince *William* resolving to come down to *Plantain*'s Assistance, they agreed to accompany him.

Plantain, to make the most he could of his Victory, pursued the Enemy over to the Town of *Masseleage*; but found a stronger Resistance there, than he imagin'd; for he could not force the Town, the Enemy firing from Houses, &c. which obliged him to retreat. This so enraged *Plantain*, that he resolved to cut the two Kings of *Masseleage* and *Mannagore* to pieces, or put them to the most cruel Deaths whenever he had them in his Power.

The *Europeans* who were dispersed about the Island, came soon to hear of these Disturbances; and some of them propos'd to attempt the taking of *Plantain*'s Castle; but the Place being guarded by Cannon, and a River very near the Place, the Design was laid aside. . . .

[At *St. Mary*'s Island, a man named *Thomas Lloyd*] said he was left with six more of their Men on the Island, and had suffered very much by a petty Prince called King *Caleb*; that had it not been for Prince *William*, they should have been murder'd. . . . That these Pyrates live in a most wicked profligate manner, and would often ramble from Place to Place, and sometimes have the Misfortune of meeting some of the Natives, who would put them to lingering Deaths, by tying their Arms to a Tree, and putting lighted Matches between their Fingers; that they served two of his Ship-Mates in the like manner, and would stand and laugh at them during the time of their Agonies. This I think was a just Retaliation to the Pyrates for the inhuman Barbarities they are guilty of. . . .

The Wars between *Plantain* and these petty Princes were carried on for near two Years; when *Plantain* having got the better of them, put several of his Enemies to Death in a most barbarous manner. . . .

King *Dick*, and all that belong'd to him, were taken by *Plantain*; however the Lady on whose account these Wars were begun, prov'd to be with Child by one of the *Englishmen* which *Plantain* had murder'd. This so much inrag'd him, that he ordered King *Dick* to be put to the same cruel Death as the *English* and *Dutchmen* had suffered. . . .

After *Plantain* had put King *Dick* to death, and those *Dutch* and *English* who had fought against him, he march'd to the King of *Massaleage*'s Dominions, and found a great deal of Treasure at King *Dick*'s House, and great Store of such Sort of Grain as the Island produc'd, which *Plantain* order'd to be pack'd up, and sent to *Ranter-Bay*. As to the Inhabitants, he sent great Numbers of them down to *Ranter-Bay*, made Slaves of them, and caused them to form several Plantations of Sugar-Canes, and after brought the same to great Perfection. So soon as he had cleared the Town, he caused his Men to set the same on fire, and then went to King *Kelly*'s chief Town, and did the same there. He found but little Subsistance in all these Dominions. . . . For he now tyranniz'd over the Natives all over the Island . . . bringing the Lady before mention'd with him, which he accounted the chief Trophy of his Victory; who tho' she was with Child, he accepted of, and was much enamoured with her. . . .

During the Season that *Plantain* was at his Castle, the time was spent in great Mirth and Entertainments amongst the *English* that were there under his Protection. Several new Songs were made in token of his Victories, and at the End of almost every Verse was pronounced, Plantain *King of* Ranter-Bay; which he seem'd mightily pleas'd with, as well as with Dances perform'd by great Bodies of the Natives. After he had destroy'd King *Dick*, and King *Kelly*, he established two Kings in their stead, leaving them to rebuild and make good what he had demolished. They were also tributary to him, and sent him in every Month, a certain number of Cattle of all sorts that the Places afforded; and they were to keep the Lands in good order, and to pay him Tribute for all sorts of Grain, Sugar-Canes, &c. . . .

But the Natives in *Plantain*'s Army were very much frighted at the sight of the Guns, and he was informed that some of them design'd to betray him, if possible. *Molatto Tom*, or young Capt. *Avery*, immediately seized some of those suspected, and by torturing two or three of them severely, entirely quash'd their Design. . . .

Plantain was resolved that he would now make himself King of *Madagascar*, and govern there with absolute Power and Authority. He kept now near 1000 Slaves, which he employed constantly on the Fortifications of his Castle; and had he acted as Capt. *Avery* did, would certainly have made a very strong Place of his chief Residence; for Capt. *Avery* only took to the Island of *St. Mary*, and seldom or ever troubled the Inhabitants of *Madagascar* for any thing except Supplies of Provision. . . .

Plantain now arrived near *Port Dolphin*, being resolved to make an end of the War that Summer: In his March he destroy'd several Towns . . . putting Men, Women and Children to the Sword. . . .

Having subdued *Port Dolphin*, he made Prince *William* Viceroy of that Dominion; and several other Districts he appointed to the petty Princes who had assisted him in his Wars, and who were to be tributary to him. He was now absolute Monarch of the whole Island, and the Inhabitants brought in all manner of Refreshments to him with great Submission. When we were there in the *Salisbury*, the Natives seem'd very subject to him; tho' I think we might at that time have surprised him, and brought him away, which would have prevented the Mischiefs he has since done. . . .

Plantain being now weary of his Kingship, resolved to quit his Territories (with the Advice and Consent of his Comrades) and to leave the Natives in quiet possession of their Properties; either urg'd to it by the Remorse of his own Conscience, or acting on the Principle of Self-Preservation (which is most likely) as he found his Associates decrease daily, and could not depend on the Fidelity of the Natives, whom he had used in so barbarous a manner. To this End he determined to build a Sloop big enough to carry them and their chief Effects to the Coast of *India*; and provided they found no Refuge in any other place, they would all go to *Angria*, and offer him their Service for some time at least, till Opportunity should suit for their getting to *Europe*. . . .

When they declared on what Account they were come, they were receiv'd very joyfully, and word was sent directly to *Angria*. . . . When *Angria* saw them, he was mightily pleas'd, judging them to be good Sailors, which he much wanted. Some time after, six of them run away to the *Portuguese*, pretending they were made cast away on *Angria*'s Coast, and had made their Escape; and by this means they got to *Bengal*, where I had a large Account of all their Proceedings.

When *Angria* came to understand what course of Life *Plantain* had lived, and what a valiant fighting Man he was, he entertained him in a magnificent manner. . . . They were entertained with such Grandeur, that *Plantain* was at a loss how to behave himself, having been so used to a brutish way of living at *Madagascar*: for tho' *Angria* is an Enemy to the *English* Nation, he is a Sovereign in his own Dominions, which are now pretty extensive.

15

Captain Charles Johnson, "Of Captain Misson and His Crew," or the Legend of Libertalia (1728)

One of the most important primary sources of any kind for the history of piracy in the Atlantic world is Captain Charles Johnson's *General History of the Pyrates* (1724) and its subsequent editions.[38] Although throughout most of the 20th century, historians believed "Charles Johnson" was pseudonymous for Daniel Defoe, most scholars now believe that Johnson must be considered an original and independent source of information on piracy. Although the vast majority of Johnson's work on pirates was based on trial transcripts and personal accounts, it is widely assumed that one chapter in the *History* is entirely fictional. Through his legendary tales of the ideas and exploits of Captain Misson and the founding of "Libertalia," Johnson explored his society's yearning for liberty in an historical age when power visibly expanded its reach wherever one might look.

Johnson describes Misson as a reasonably well-educated, respectable youth possessed by ambitions to travel the world, exploring new cultures and ideas. Misson joins a merchantman and sails the Mediterranean, learning invaluable skills while at sea. From Naples, Misson travels to Rome and meets a highly unusual and irreligious priest, one Signior Caraccioli. Caraccioli explains to Misson that religion, no less than politics, is simply a mechanism by which the powerful control and exploit the weak. Reason alone, Caraccioli argues, should guide men's actions, and reason demanded peace, harmony, and cooperation between individuals.

Misson was deeply affected by the priest's radical ideas, which the two busily spread among the ship's crew. When the captain and first officer are killed in an engagement with the English, Misson and his radical converts seized the opportunity to withdraw from their privateering mission. The crew peacefully reassembled itself, elected Misson its leader, and democratically determined their course. Although they were aware that the world would likely condemn them as pirates, they resolved to forever live as free men, in charge of their own lives and destinies, holding each other to strict standards of social morality through the bonds of ideology and fraternity. The "pirates" declared themselves permanently for liberty and at permanent war with all earthly power.

The men democratically determine their new course in a new life. Spontaneous, largely democratic order reigned aboard Misson's *Victoire*, and all shared in the common stocks of provisions and wealth. The *Victoire*'s crewmen freed all slaves they encountered while seizing European vessels in the Atlantic. Misson clearly prides himself on treating captives humanely and fairly, even granting captured captains new vessels to ensure their safe return home.

After some time at sea and the accumulation of great wealth, Misson's crew sails for Madagascar, where they are welcomed in friendship by the queen of Johanna. The crew intermarried with the Johannans, in the process joining the queen in her war against the neighboring state of Mohila. Misson is careful, however, not to become too involved in the domestic affairs of indigenous Madagascar governments. His focus remained the establishment of a permanent colony in which he and his like-minded fellows could live freely and without interference from abroad.

After a disastrous and nearly devastating encounter with the English, Misson determines to finally found his colony at the northernmost tip of Madagascar, near what is today called Diego-Suarez or Antsiranana. By virtue of his treaty with the queen of Johanna, Misson and several hundred of his followers and Johannans began constructing the settlement its residents named "Libertalia." Calling themselves the "Liberi," the settlers built their new world in direct opposition to the Old, flouting the all-pervasive nationalist-imperialist sociopolitical order. Although the "Legend of Libertalia" is almost certainly a work of fiction, it nonetheless reflects the hope of dispossessed, marginalized, and exploited people from virtually all societies and ages: that out there somewhere, in some forgotten corner of a planet crowded with courts, armies, and imperial agents, the individual may still carve space for the exercise of freedom.

Captain Charles Johnson, *A General History of the Pyrates, from Their first Rise and Settlement in the Island of Providence, to the present Time*, vol. 2 (London: T. Warner, 1728)

He was born in *Provence*, of an ancient Family; his Father, whose true Name he conceals, was Master of a plentiful Fortune; but having a great Number of Children, our Rover had but little Hopes of other Fortune than what he could carve out for himself with his Sword. His Parents took Care to give him an Education equal to his Birth. After he had passed his Humanity and Logick, and was a tolerable Mathematician, at the Age of Fifteen he was sent to *Angiers*, where he was a Year learning His Exercises. His Father, at his Return home, would have put him into the Musketeers; but as he was of a roving Temper, and much affected with the Accounts he had read in Books of Travels, he chose the Sea as a Life which abounds with more Variety, and would afford him an Opportunity to gratify his Curiosity, by the Change of Countries. Having made this Choice, his Father, with Letters of Recommendation, and every Thing fitting for him, sent him Voluntier on board the *Victoire*. . . . Nothing could be more agreeable to the Inclinations of our Voluntier than this Cruize, which made him acquainted with the most noted Ports of the *Mediterranean*, and gave him a great Insight into the practical Part of Navigation. He grew fond of this Life, and was resolved to be a compleat Sailor. . . . His Discourse was turn'd on no other Subject. . . . The Ship being at *Naples*, he obtained Leave of his Captain to go to *Rome*, which he had a great Desire to visit. Hence we may date his Misfortunes; for, remarking the licentious Lives of the Clergy . . . the Luxury of the Papal Court, and that nothing but Hulls of Religion was to be found in the Metropolis of the Christian Church, he began to figure to himself that all Religion was no more than a Curb upon the Minds of the Weaker, which the wiser Sort yielded to, in Appearance only. These Sentiments, so disadvantageous to Religion and himself, were strongly riveted by accidentally becoming acquainted with a lewd Priest, who was, at his Arrival (by meer Chance) his Confessor, and after that his Procurer and Companion, for he kept him Company to his Death. One Day, having an Opportunity, he told *Misson*, a Religious was a very good Life, where a Man had a subtle enterprising Genius, and some Friends; for such a one wou'd, in a short Time, rise to such Dignities in the Church. . . . That the ecclesiastical State was govern'd with the same Policy as were secular Principalities and Kingdoms; that what was beneficial, not what was meritorious and virtuous, would be alone regarded. . . . For its a Maxim, that Religion and Politicks can never set up in one House. As to our Statesmen, don't imagine that the Purple makes 'em less Courtiers than are those of other Nations; they know and pursue [self-interest] . . . with as much Cunning and as little Conscience as any Secular; and are as artful where Art is required, and as barefaced and impudent when their Power is great enough to support 'em, in the oppressing the People, and aggrandizing their Families. . . .

I shall only observe, that Signior *Caraccioli*, who was as ambitious as he was irreligious, had, by this Time, made a perfect Deist of *Misson*, and thereby convinc'd him, that all Religion was no other than human Policy, and shew'd him that the Law of *Moses* was no more than what were necessary, as well for the Preservation as the Governing of the People; for Instance, said he, the *African* Negroes never heard of the Institution of Circumcision, which is said to be the Sign of the Covenant made between God and this People, and yet they circumcise their Children; doubtless for the same Reason the *Jews* and other Nations do, who inhabit the Southern Climes, the Prepuce consolidating the perspired Matter, which is of a fatal Consequence. In short, he ran through all the Ceremonies of the *Jewish*, Christian and *Mahometan* Religion, and convinced him these were, as might be observed by the Absurdity of many, far from being Indications of Men inspired; and that *Moses*, in his Account of the Creation, was guilty of known Blunders; and the Miracles, both in the New and Old Testament, inconsistent with Reason. That God had given us this Blessing, to make Use of for our present and future Happiness, and whatever was contrary to it, notwithstanding their School Distinctions of contrary and above Reason, must be false. This Reason teaches us, that there is a first Cause of all Things . . . which we call God, and our Reason will also suggest, that he must be eternal, and, as the Author of every Thing perfect, he must be infinitely perfect.

If so, he can be subject to no Passions, and neither loves nor hates; he must be ever the same, and cannot rashly do to Day what he shall repent to Morrow. He must be perfectly happy, consequently nothing can add to an eternal State of Tranquillity, and though it becomes us to adore him, yet can our Adorations neither augment, nor our Sins take from this Happiness.

But his Arguments on this Head are too long, and too dangerous to translate; and as they are work'd up with great Subtlety, they may be pernicious to weak Men, who cannot discover their Fallacy; or, who finding 'em agreeable to their Inclinations, and would be glad to shake off the Yoke of the Christian Religion, which galls and curbs their Passions, would not give themselves the Trouble to examine them to the Bottom, but give into what pleases, glad of finding some Excuse to their Consciences. . . .

As he had privately held these Discourses among the Crew, he had gained a Number of Proselytes, who look'd upon him as a new Prophet risen up to reform the Abuses in Religion; and a great Number being *Rochellers*, and, as yet, tainted with *Calvinism*, his Doctrine was the more readily embrac'd. When he had experienced the Effects of his religious Arguments, he fell upon Government, and shew'd, that every Man was born free, and had as much Right to what would support him, as to the Air he respired.

A contrary Way of arguing would be accusing the Deity with Cruelty and Injustice, for he brought into the World no Man to pass a Life of Penury, and to miserably want a necessary Support; that the vast Difference between Man and Man, the one wallowing in Luxury, and the other in the most pinching Necessity, was owing only to Avarice and Ambition on the one Hand, and a pusillanimous Subjection on the other; that at first no other than a Natural was known, a paternal Government, every Father was the Head, the Prince and Monarch of his Family, and Obedience to such was both just and easy, for a Father had a compassionate Tenderness for his Children; but Ambition creeping in by Degrees, the stronger Family set upon and enslaved the Weaker; and this additional Strength over-run a third, by every Conquest gathering Force to make others, and this was the first Foundation of Monarchy. Pride encreasing with Power, Man usurped the Prerogative of God, over his Creatures, that of depriving them of Life, which was a Privilege no one had over his own; for as he did not come into the World by his own Election, he ought to stay the determined Time of his Creator: That indeed, Death given in War, was by the Law of Nature allowable, because it is for the Preservation of our own Lives; but no Crime ought to be thus punished, nor indeed any War undertaken, but in Defence of our natural Right, which is such a Share of Earth as is necessary for our Support. . . .

These Topicks he often declaimed on, and very often advised with *Misson* about the setting up for themselves; he was as ambitious as the other, and as resolute. . . . *Caraccioli* had sounded a great many of the Men on this Subject, and found them very inclineable to listen to him. An Accident happen'd which gave *Caraccioli* a fair Opportunity to put his Designs in Execution, and he laid Hold of it; they went off *Martinico* on a Cruize, and met with the *Winchelsea*, an *English* Man of War of 40 Guns, commanded by Captain *Jones*; they made for each other, and a very smart Engagement followed, the first Broadside killed the Captain, second Captain, and the three Lieutenants, on Board the *Victoire* and left only the Master, who would have struck, but *Misson* took up the Sword, order'd *Caraccioli* to act as Lieutenant . . . when by some Accident, the *Winchelsea* blew up. . . . After this Engagement, *Caraccioli* came to *Misson* and saluted him Captain, and desired to know if he would chuse a momentary or a lasting Command. . . . That he might with the Ship he had under Foot, and the brave Fellows under Command, bid Defiance to the Power of *Europe*, enjoy every Thing he wish'd, reign Sovereign of the Southern Seas, and lawfully make War on all the World, since it would deprive him of that Liberty to which he had a Right by the Laws of Nature: That he might in Time, become as great as *Alexander* was to the *Persians*; and by encreasing his Forces by his Captures, he would every Day strengthen the Justice of his Cause, for who has Power is always in the Right. . . .

In a Word he said so much that *Misson* resolved to follow his Advice, and calling up all Hands, he told them, "That a great Number of them had resolved with him upon a Life of Liberty, and had done him the Honour to create him Chief: That he designed to force no Man, and be guilty of that Injustice he blamed in others; therefore, if any were averse to the following his Fortune, which he promised should be the same to all, he desired they would declare themselves, and he would set them ashore, whence they might return with Conveniency;" having made an End, they one and all cryed . . . God bless Capt. *Misson* and his learned Lieutenant *Caraccioli*. *Misson* thanked them for the Honour they conferr'd upon him, and promised he would use the Power they gave for the publick Good only, and hoped, as they had the Bravery to assert their Liberty, they would be as unanimous in the preserving it, and stand by him in what should be found expedient for the Good of all; that he was their Friend and Companion, and should never exert his Power, or think himself other than their Comrade, but when the Necessity of Affairs should oblige him. . . .

The Boatswain then asked what Colours they should fight under, and advised Black as most terrifying; but *Caraccioli* objected, that they were no Pyrates, but Men who were resolved to assert that Liberty which God and Nature gave them, and own no Subjection to any, farther than was for the common Good of all: That indeed, Obedience to Governors was necessary, when they knew and acted up to the Duty of their Function; were vigilant Guardians of the Peoples Rights and Liberties; saw that Justice was equally distributed; were Barriers against the Rich and Powerful, when they attempted to oppress the Weaker; when they suffered none of the one Hand to grow immensely rich, either by his own or his Ancestors Encroachments; nor on the other, any to be wretchedly miserable, either by falling into the Hands of Villains, unmerciful Creditors, or other Misfortunes. While he had Eyes impartial, and allowed nothing but Merit to distinguish between Man and Man; and instead of being a Burthen to the People by his luxurious life, he was by his Care for, and Protection of them, a real Father, and in every Thing acted with the equal and impartial Justice of a Parent: But when a Governor, who is the Minister of the People, thinks himself rais'd to this Dignity, that he may spend his Days in Pomp and Luxury, looking upon his Subjects as so many Slaves, created for his Use and Pleasure, and therefore leaves them and their Affairs to the immeasurable Avarice and Tyranny of some one whom he has chosen for his Favourite, when nothing but Oppression, Poverty, and all the Miseries of Life flow from such an Administration; that he lavishes away the Lives and Fortunes of the People, either to gratify his Ambition, or to support the Cause of some neighbouring Prince, that he may in Return, strengthen his Hands should his People exert themselves in Defence of their native Rights; or should he run into unnecessary Wars, by the rash and thoughtless Councils of his Favourite, and not able to make Head against the Enemy he has rashly or wantonly brought upon his Hands, and buy a Peace (which is the present Case of *France*, as every one knows, by supporting King *James*, and afterwards proclaiming his Son) and drain the Subject; should the Peoples Trade be wilfully neglected, for private Interests, and while their Ships of War lie idle in their Harbours, suffer their Vessels to be taken; and the Enemy not only intercepts all Commerce, but insults their Coasts: It speaks a generous and great Soul to shake off the Yoak; and if we cannot redress our Wrongs, withdraw from sharing the Miseries which meaner Spirits submit to, and scorn to yield to the Tyranny. Such Men are we, and, if the World, as Experience may convince us it will, makes War upon us, the Law of Nature empowers us not only to be on the defensive, but also on the offensive Part. As we then do not proceed upon the same Ground with Pyrates, who are Men of dissolute Lives and no Principles, let us scorn to take their Colours: Ours is a brave, a just, an innocent, and a noble Cause; the Cause of Liberty. I therefore advise a white Ensign, with Liberty painted in the Fly, and if you like the Motto . . . for God and Liberty, as an Emblem of our Uprightness and Resolution.

The Cabbin Door was left open, and the Bulk Head which was of Canvas rowled up, the Steerage being full of Men, who lent an attentive Ear, they cried, *Liberty, Liberty; we are free Men: Vive the brave Captain* Misson *and the noble Lieutenant* Caraccioli. This short Council breaking up, every Thing belonging to the deceased Captain, and the other Officers, and Men lost in the Engagement, was brought upon Deck and over-hawled; the Money ordered to be put into a Chest, and the Carpenter to clap on a Padlock for, and give a Key to, every one of the Council: *Misson* telling them, all should be in common, and the particular Avarice of no one should defraud the Publick. . . .

Misson from the Baracade, spoke to the following Purpose, "That since they had unanimously resolved to seize upon and defend their Liberty, which ambitious Men had usurped . . . he was under an Obligation to recommend to them a brotherly Love to each other; the Banishment of all private Piques and Grudges, and a swift Agreement and Harmony among themselves: That in throwing off the Yoak of Tyranny of which the Action spoke an Abhorrence, he hoped none would follow the Example of Tyrants, and turn his Back upon Justice; for when Equity was trodden under Foot, Misery, Confusion, and mutual Distrust naturally followed."—He also advised them . . . That he was satisfied Men who were born and bred in Slavery, by which their Spirits were broke, and were incapable of so generous a Way of thinking, who, ignorant of their Birth-Right, and the Sweets of Liberty, dance to the Musick of their Chains, which was, indeed, the greater Part of the Inhabitants of the Globe, would brand this generous Crew with the insidious Name of Pyrates, and think it meritorious, to be instrumental in their Destruction.— Self-Preservation therefore, and not a cruel Disposition, obliged him to declare War against all such as should refuse him the Entry of their Ports, and against all, who should not immediately surrender and give up what their Necessities required; but in a more particular Manner against all European Ships and Vessels, as concluded implacable Enemies. *And I do now*, said he, d*eclare such War*. . . .

After Affairs were thus settled, they shaped their Course. . . .

[At one point in their travels, *Misson*] called all Hands up, and declar'd, that if any Man repented him of the Course of Life he had chosen, his just Dividend should be counted to him, and he would set him on Shoar, either near the *Havanna*, or some other convenient Place; but not one accepted the Offer, and the fourteen Prisoners unanimously resolved to join in with 'em; to which Resolution, no doubt, the Hopes of a good Booty from the *St. Joseph*, and this Offer of Liberty greatly contributed. . . .

An Account of the Provisions were taken, and finding they had Provisions for four Months, Captain *Misson* called all Hands upon Deck, and told them, as the Council differed in the Course they should steer, he thought it reasonable to have it put to the

Vote of the whole Company. . . . He then gave the Sentiments of those who were against him, and their Reasons, and begg'd that every one would give his Opinion and Vote according as he thought most conducive to the Good of all. That he should be far from taking it ill if they should reject what he had proposed, since he had no private Views to serve. The Majority of Votes fell on the Captain's Side, and they accordingly shaped their Course for the Coast of *Guiney*, in which Voyage nothing remarkable happened. . . .

[The pirates seize the *Nieuwstadt*, which] had some Gold-Dust on Board, to the Value of about 2000 l. Sterling, and a few Slaves to the Number of Seventeen, for she had but begun to Trade; the Slaves were a strengthening of their Hands, for the Captain order'd them to be cloathed out of *Dutch* Mariners Chests, and told his Men, "That the Trading for those of our own Species, cou'd never be agreeable to the Eyes of divine Justice: That no Man had Power or the Liberty of another; and while those who profess'd a more enlightened Knowledge of the Deity, sold Men like Beasts; they prov'd that their Religion was no more than Grimace, and that they differ'd from the Barbarians in Name only, since their Practice was in nothing more humane: For his Part, and he hop'd, he spoke the Sentiments of all his brave Companions, he had not exempted his Neck from the galling Yoak of Slavery, and asserted his own Liberty, to enslave others. That however, these Men were distinguish'd from the *Europeans* by their Colour, Customs, or religious Rites, they were the Work of the same omnipotent Being, and endued with equal Reason: Wherefore, he desired they might be treated like Freemen (for he wou'd banish even the Name of Slavery from among them)" and divided into Messes among them, to the End they might the sooner learn their Language, be sensible of the Obligation they had to them, and more capable and zealous to defend that Liberty they owed to their Justice and Humanity.

This Speech of *Misson*'s was received with general Applause, and the Ship rang with . . . Long live Capt. *Misson*.—The Negroes were divided among the *French*, one to a Mess, who, by their Gesticulations, shew'd they were gratefully sensible of their being delivered from their Chains. . . .

Upon the Coast of *Angola*, they met with a second *Dutch* Ship, the Cargo of which consisted of Silk and Woolen Stuffs, Cloath, Lace, Wine, Brandy, Oyl, Spice, and hard Ware; the Prize gave Chase and engaged her, but upon the coming up of the *Victoire* she struck. This Ship opportunely came in their Way, and gave full Employ to the Taylors, who were on Board, for the whole Crew began to be out at Elbows: They plundered her of what was of Use to their own Ship, and then sunk her.

The Captain having about ninety Prisoners on Board, proposed the giving them the Prize, with what was necessary for their Voyage, and sending them away; which being agreed to, they shifted her Ammunition on Board the *Victoire*, and giving them Provision to carry them to the Settlements the Dutch have on the Coast, *Misson* called them up, told them what was his Design, and ask'd if any of them was willing to share his Fortune: Eleven *Dutch* came into him, two of which were Sail-makers, one an Armourer, and one a Carpenter, necessary Hands; the rest he let go, not a little surprised at the Regularity, Tranquillity, and Humanity, which they found among these new fashioned Pyrates.

[The pirates encounter and capture an *English* ship.] They found on Board the Prize some Bales of *English* Broad-Cloath, and about 60000 l. in *English* Crown Pieces, and *Spanish* Pieces of Eight. The *English* Captain was killed in the Engagement, and 14 of his Men: The *French* lost 12, which was no small Mortification, but did not, however provoke them to use their Prisoners harshly. Captain *Misson* was sorry for the Death of the Commander, whom he buried on the Shoar, and one of his Men being a Stone-Cutter, he raised a Stone over his Grave with these Words . . . Here lies a gallant *English* Man; when he was buried he made a tripple Discharge of 50 small Arms, and fired Minute Guns.

The *English*, knowing whose Hands they were fallen into, charm'd with *Misson*'s Humanity, 30 of them, in 3 Days Space, desired to take on with him. He accepted 'em, but at the same Time gave 'em to understand, that in taking on with him they were not to expect they should be indulged in a dissolute and immoral Life. He now divided his Company between the two Ships, and made *Caraccioli* Captain of the Prize, giving him Officers chosen by the publick Suffrage. The 17 Negroes began to understand a little *French*, and to be useful Hands, and in less than a Month all the *English* Prisoners came over to him, except their Officers.

He had two Ships well mann'd with resolute Fellows; they now doubled the Cape, and made the South End of *Madagascar*, and one of the *English* Men telling Captain *Misson*, that the *European* Ships bound for Surat commonly touch'd at the Island of *Johanna*, he sent for Captain *Caraccioli* on Board, and it was agreed to cruise off that Island. They accordingly sailed on the West-Side of *Madagascar* and off the Bay *de Diego*. . . .

They arrived at *Johanna*, and were kindly received by the Queen-Regent and her Brother, on account of the *English* on the one Hand, and of their Strength on the other, which the Queen's Brother, who had the Administration of Affairs, was not able to make Head against, and hoped they might assist him against the King of *Mohila*, who threaten'd him with a Visit.

This is an Island which is contiguous, in a manner, to *Johanna*, and lies about N. W. and by N. from it. *Caraccioli* told *Misson* he might make his Advantage in widening the Breach between these two little Monarchies, and, by offering his Assistance to that of *Johanna*, in a manner rule both, For these would count him as their Protector, and those come to any Terms to buy his Friendship, by which Means he would hold the Ballance of Power between them. He followed this Advice, and offered his Friendship and Assistance to the Queen, who very readily embraced it.

I must advise the Reader, that many of this Island speak *English*, and that the *English* Men who were of *Misson*'s Crew, and his Interpreters, told them, their Captain, though not an *Englishman*, was their Friend and Ally, and a Friend and Brother to the *Johanna* Men, for they esteem the *English* beyond all other Nations.

They were supplied by the Queen with all Necessaries of Life, and *Misson* married her Sister, as *Caraccioli* did the Daughter of her Brother, whose Armory, which consisted before of no more than two rusty Fire-Locks, and three Pistols, he furnish'd with thirty Fuzils, as many Pair of Pistols, and gave him two Barrels of Powder, and four of Ball.

Several of his Men took Wives, and some requited their Share of the Prizes, which was justly given them, they designing to settle in this Island, but the Number of these did not exceed ten, which Loss was repaired by thirty of the Crew (they had saved from perishing) coming in to him.

While they past their Time in all manner of Diversions the Place would afford them, as hunting, feasting, and visiting the Island, the King of *Mohila* made a Descent, and alarm'd the whole Country. . . . The Party which went by Land, fell in with, and beat the *Mohilians* with great Ease, who were in the greatest Consternation, to find their Retreat cut off by *Misson's* Boats. . . . The Party of *Europeans* and *Johannians* then marched to their Metropolis, without Resistance, which they reduced to Ashes, and the *Johannians* cut down all the Cocoa Walks that they could for the Time, for towards Evening they returned to their Ships, and stood off to Sea.

At their Return to *Johanna* the Queen made a Festival, and magnified the Bravery and Service of her Guests, Friends, and Allies. This Feast lasted four Days, at the Expiration of which Time the Queen's Brother proposed to Captain *Misson* the making another Descent, in which he would go in Person, and did not doubt subjecting the *Mohilians*; but this was not the Design of *Misson*, who had Thoughts of fixing a Retreat on the North West Side of *Madagascar*, and look'd upon the Feuds between these two Islands advantageous to his Views, and therefore no way his Interest to suffer the one to overcome the other; for while the Variance was kept up, and their Forces pretty much upon a Level, it was evident their Interest would make both Sides caress him; he therefore answer'd, that they ought to deliberate on the Consequences, for they might be deceived in their Hopes, and find the Conquest less easy than they imagined. . . . The Queen gave intirely into *Misson*'s Sentiments. . . .

After the Council had concluded, they were again call'd upon, and the Queen told them, that by the Advice of her good Friends, the *Europeans*, and those of her Council, she agreed to make a Peace, which she wish'd might banish all Memory of former Injuries That they must own the War was begun by them, and that she was far from being the Agressor; she only defended her self in her own Kingdom, which they had often invaded, though, till within few Days, she had never molested their Coasts. If then they really desired to live amicably with her, they must resolve to send two of the King's Children, and ten of the first Nobility, as Hostages, that they might, when they pleased, return, for that was the only Terms on which she would desist prosecuting the Advantages she now had, with the utmost Vigour.

[The *Mohilians* orchestrate a ruse and assassinate several *European-Johannian* ambassadors.]

The Crew were resolved to revenge the Blood of their Officers and Comrades the next Day, and were accordingly on the Point of Landing . . . but *Misson* was for no such violent Measures, he was averse to every Thing that bore the Face of Cruelty and thought a bloody Revenge, if Necessity did not enforce it, spoke a groveling and timid Soul. . . .

After their Recovery, *Misson* proposes a Cruize, on the Coast of *Zangueber* [Zanzibar], which being agreed to, he and *Caraccioli* took Leave of the Queen and her Brother, and would have left their Wives on the Island, but they could by no Means be induced to the Separation. . . .

In a Word they were obliged to yield to them, but told them, if the Wives of their Men should insist as strongly on following their Example, their Tenderness, would be their Ruin, and make them a Prey to their Enemies; they answer'd the Queen should prevent that, by ordering no Woman should go on board, and if any were in the Ships, they should return on Shore: This Order was accordingly made, and they set Sail for the River of *Mozembique*. In about ten Days Cruize after they had left *Johanna*, and about 15 Leagues to the Eastward of this River, they fell in with a stout *Portuguese* Ship of 60 Guns, which engaged them from Break of Day till Two in the Afternoon, when the Captain being killed, and a great Number of Men lost, she struck: This proved a very rich Prize, for she had the Value of 250000 L. Sterling on Board, in Gold-Dust. The two Women never quitted the Decks all the Time of the Engagement, neither gave they the least Mark of Fear, except for their Husbands: This Engagement cost them thirty Men, and *Caraccioli* lost his right Leg; the Slaughter fell mostly on the *English*, for of the above Number, twenty were of that Nation: The *Portuguese* lost double the Number. *Caraccioli's* Wound made them resolve to make the best of their Way for *Johanna* where the greatest Care was taken of their wounded, not one of whom died, tho' their Number amounted to Twenty seven.

Caraccioli kept his Bed two Months, but *Misson* seeing him in a fair way of Recovery, took what Hands could be spar'd. . . . He stretched over to *Madagascar*, and coasted along this Island to the Northward, as far as the most northerly Point, when turning back, he enter'd a Bay to the northward of *Diego Suares*. He run ten Leagues up this Bay, and on the larboard Side found it afforded a large, and safe, Harbour, with plenty of fresh Water. He came here to an Anchor, went ashore and examined into the Nature of the Soil, which he found rich, the Air wholesome, and the Country level. He told his Men, that this was an excellent Place for an Asylum, and that he determined here to fortify and raise a small Town, and make Docks for Shipping, that they might have some Place to call their own; and a Receptacle, when Age or Wounds had render'd them incapable of Hardship, where they might enjoy the Fruits of their Labour, and go to their Graves in Peace. That he would not, however, set about this, till he had the Approbation of the whole Company; and were he sure they would all approve this Design, which he hoped, it being evidently for the general Good, he should not think it adviseable to begin any Works, lest the Natives should, in his Absence, destroy them; but however, as they had nothing upon their Hands, if they were of his Opinion, they might begin to fall and square Timber, ready for the raising a wooden Fort, when they return'd with their Companions.

The Captain's Motion was universally applauded, and in ten Days they fell'd and rough hew'd a hundred and fifty large Trees, without any Interruption from, or seeing any of, the Inhabitants. They fell'd their Timber at the Waters Edge, so that they had not the Trouble of hawling them any way, which would have employ'd a great deal more Time: They returned again, and acquainted their Companions with what they had seen and done, and with the Captain's Resolution, which they one and all came into.

Captain *Misson* then told the Queen, as he had been serviceable to her in her War with the Island of *Mohila*, and might continue to be of farther Use, he did not question her lending him Assistance in the settling himself on the Coast of *Madagascar*, and to that end, furnish him with 300 Men, to help in his Buildings. . . .

After a long Debate, in which every Inconvenience, and Advantage, was maturely considered, it was agreed to send with him the Number of Men he required, on Condition he should send them back in four Moons, make an Alliance with them, and War against *Mohila*; this being agreed to, they staid till *Caraccioli* was thoroughly recovered, then putting the *Johannians* on board the *Portuguese* Ship with 40 *French* and *English* and 15 *Portuguese* to work her, and setting Sail, they arrived at the Place where *Misson* designed his Settlement, which he called *Libertalia*, and gave the Name of *Liberi* to his People, desiring in that might be drown'd the distingush'd Names of *French*, *English*, *Dutch*, *Africans*, &c.

16

John L. O'Sullivan, "Retrospective View of the State of European Politics, Especially of Germany, since the Last Congress of Vienna," U.S. Magazine and Democratic Review, vol. 1, no. 1 (1837)

In the following excerpt from John L. O'Sullivan's *Democratic Review*, the author surveys the state of European aristocratic and democratic politics after the cataclysmic and transformative French Revolution and Napoleonic Wars (ca. 1789–1815).[39] Taking each major power in turn, O'Sullivan develops his concept of democratic-republican manifest destiny, arguing that if only the people of Europe would forsake their masters, democracy would proliferate across the continent. If common people forced their governments to obey the laws of nature, establish democratic-republican institutions, and never again interfere with the equal rights of individuals, democracy's historic triumph was unavoidable. Once the people were so resolved, neither kings nor even czars could stand in the way of democratic progress. Ultimately, O'Sullivan believed that ideas moved history and those ideas that conformed to the truths of nature were quite literally destined to prevail.

Perhaps most important for modern readers, the *Democratic Review* envisions virtually inevitable conflict between the autocratic despotism in Russia and the democratic forces of the West, led by Great Britain and inspired by American and French ideas. O'Sullivan argues that the incredibly complex diversity of ethnic, linguistic, and religious groups in the Russian Empire was held together as a single nation-state only by the czar's crushing power and authority. Far from offering a proto–Cold Warrior's scaremongering, however, O'Sullivan's *Democratic Review* declared even the czar a mere paper tiger in the face of a Russian population infected with democratic ideas. Autocratic despotism required, above all else, constant and strong military presences in any rebellious areas. Wherever the czar's soldiers mingled with democratic populations—notably in Poland—there spread the republican disease that would eventually, although ruthlessly and indiscriminately, exterminate aristocracies across the globe.

No sooner was the Corsican lion overpowered, and the great, but degenerate, representative of the French revolution trodden in the dust, than the same princes who, in Paris, had sued for the permission of wearing crowns, and plundering and selling the remnant of their subjects, assembled at the Congress of Vienna, to deliberate on the fate of Europe. England and the continent joined in exultation at the humiliation of the tyrant, whose eagle-bannered legions had been the terror of kings, and the woe and desolation of the people. But in the convulsive struggle of Europe against one man, whose great historic crime was the impious audacity with which he attempted to convert the principles of democracy, that had brought him into power, into a delusive phantom of military glory, for the re-establishment of a Byzantine empire, there were employed elements which could only act in concert on the spur of the moment, to avert a common danger, and must needs have assumed a mutually hostile attitude, from the moment they were gain left to their fate. England had nobly fought for conservative principles—for her lords and bishops; the nations on the continent had been thirsting for liberty, and were quenching their thirst with the blood of unfortunate France. . . .

As soon as the Congress of Vienna met, the people began to undeceive themselves. They became aware of their true position.

They found that they had chanced the gorgeous despotism of the great Emperor for the pusillanimous tyranny of their own sordid princes; the humiliating necessity of obeying, the mandate of a foreign dictator, for the abject condition of domestic slaves. The seed of liberty, which the Germans had sown on the battle-fields of Leipsic and Hanau, tilled with their sword; and moistened with their blood, had indeed sprung up and borne fruit; but their kings carried off the harvest. . . .

And what was the reward of the German people for the thousand sacrifices of lives and property during the long war of the revolution?— . . . *"an improved system of common schools"* was considered sufficient to heal the wounds of an hundred unfortunate battles. . . . Russia was the only European power which derived a signal advantage from the downfall of the French empire. . . . She opened to herself the road to Turkey and the wealth of India, and acquired a most powerful and pernicious influence on continental politics, especially on that of Germany. England, who had paid nearly two-thirds of all the expenses of the war, and who had involved herself in an immense national debt, lost nearly her whole influence on the continent, while the enormous sacrifices she had been obliged to make in order to exclude democratic principles from her dominions, only hastened their speedy introduction. . . .

France, in the midst of her humiliation, laid the foundation of a better government than that of which she had been deprived by the united efforts of her enemies. . . . As all conquering nations imbibe the manners and customs of the conquered, and, by this means, finally become themselves vanquished, so did the invasion of France do more for the spreading of liberal principles, and the overthrow of monarchy in Europe, than all the victories of the republic; and the doctrines of the revolution were never nearer inflaming the world than when their last representative was retiring from the field.

The armies of the allied powers left France with respect for the manners, custom; and laws of her inhabitants. They had seen more *equality* in France than they had ever before or after witnessed in their own countries; they had seen the dignity of man respected in the humblest of his species; and their hatred and prejudice against the French, which were constantly nursed by cunning politicians, had gradually yielded to feelings of forbearance and kindness. In short, France, though young and inexperienced in every liberal form of government, abounded, nevertheless, with all the *elements* of democracy, and had given proof of her deserving to be free, by the readiness with which her children were prepared to die for liberty. Her example was far from being lost even upon Russia; and many a rude warrior, like the crusaders of old, returned home to the confines of barbarism, there to plant the seed of new life and civilization. . . .

The ghost of the French revolution is staring them everywhere in the face, whether they look to Italy or Spain, to Portugal or Belgium, France or Poland, England or Germany. Nor is it confined there; it is haunting Turkey and Egypt, convulsing Asia and Africa, and, in its more remote consequences, is even felt in the United States. Herein consists the immortality of *principles* which, once born to light, cannot, by any earthly power, be deprived of their action, until they have produced all the ultimate consequences resulting from their single and combined application. No intolerance, no persecution, no martyrdom can prevent their promulgation; and they seem to acquire even an additional momentum from every obstacle they meet on their progress. . . .

England has, for the last ten years, made greater progress towards a pure democracy than any other country in Europe. Her nobility, the wealthiest and worthiest aristocracy in the world, is daily losing more of its moral influence in Parliament and on the minds of the people. Its riches and learning—its physical and moral power—will yet for years be felt in the councils of the nation; but it is no longer based upon, and entwined with, the affection and loyalty of the people. It has lost the magic of directing the multitudes and inspiring awe. . . .

Let us now turn our eyes to France, that land of political miracles and popular credulity, whose people has in scarcely fifty years accomplished the history of five centuries. . . . If we look upon a nation as representing the aggregate of intelligence and virtue of all the individuals composing it, we must at once admit that France has not only been regenerated by the revolution, but that her liberties—inconsiderable as they may appear to the English and Americans—are nevertheless resting on the firmest basis on which they can possibly be established in any country—on the determination of the people to be free, and their courage to assert that freedom, in opposition to every moral or physical obstacle. . . .

What statesman would now think it possible to lead the French people back to the state from which they emerged by the revolution? . . .

We consider the appearance of Louis Philippe as a mere interlude in the history of France, resembling some of Shakespeare's clowns, introduced to relieve the gravity of the drama;—a mere pause in the revolution. During this pause, the nations of Europe may fall asleep; but they will awake with fresh vigor at the first signal of battle, to conquer or die on the field. Louis Philippe has taught the people of all countries a memorable lesson, which, it is hoped, will not be lost upon them. . . .

Germany, of all countries, suffered most by the wars of the French revolution. . . . Twenty years in succession did the Germans combat the principle of liberty and supremacy in France; twenty long years were they beaten, insulted, and sacked by their victorious foes. . . . This time the people themselves took the field, and, in one great struggle for liberty, achieved their emancipation. That it was not the coalition, and especially, not the German princes, which produced the fall of Napoleon, was allowed by the Emperor himself when he declared that he had been defeated *by the power of liberal ideas in Germany*. . . .

The philosophy of the Germans is indeed an armor which renders them perfectly invulnerable. Oppress them with an iron rod, insult them, ridicule them, strike them, extort from them their last penny, starve them, bury them, only do not separate them from their book, and they will be satisfied. . . . There is not a single principle of liberty or justice which may not there be found ably and satisfactorily commented upon; there exists, in Germany, *on paper*, the most perfect democracy which ever governed any community; there may be found, *in books*, enough of radicalism to break down the thrones of kings and emperors, to destroy the last remnant of feudalism, to banish bishops and nobles, ribbons and stars, and to drive the last tithe-gatherer out of the country—if a man will only put himself to the trouble of collecting it from the millions of volumes in her public libraries.

With such a people, the policy of the Prussian government must be eminently successful. It opens to them the treasures of science and literature, reserving to itself nothing but their application; it equalizes, as far as practicable, nobles and commoners, claiming but the privilege of elevating the servants of the crown; it establishes a military democracy, in which the king, as a true soldier, demands but implicit obedience; it abolishes, by the union of the tariff the odious system of excise in the interior, but taxes commerce on the frontiers, and there establishes monopolies; in short, it is a policy which is no more akin to liberalism than hypocrisy to religion; and is just as much more pernicious to the progress of liberty in Germany, than the open despotism of Prince Metternich, as a treacherous friend is more dangerous than a declared enemy.

Much praise has been bestowed, in and out of Germany, on the Prussian system of common schools. Excellent as this may be in many respects, it is nevertheless a powerful organ of perpetuating slavery. What, after all, can be more opposed to freedom than a system of instruction . . . *in which the whole population is taught to think, feel, and act, according to the political and religious catechism of a single man?* Were it ten times the best system ever invented, we would not recommend it to any state or empire in which the people claim to be more than mere wire-puppets in the hands of their legislators. . . .

The particular position of the Austrian empire is this. It cannot depend for its safety, or the stability of its institutions, on the voluntary submission of the people, or the assistance which so many different nations would, of their own accord, render it in time of danger. . . . The spirit of democracy has found its way to one-third of the Austrian empire, (Hungary and Transylvania having, together, more than 11,000,000 inhabitants,) and is there making even more rapid progress than in Germany. . . .

These indices cannot be mistaken. Hungary and Transylvania have caught the spirit of the Polish revolution. But the Hungarians are a stronger and more energetic people than the Poles; they are not divided amongst themselves, and *began* their popular movement by an attempt to *emancipate the lower classes.* They are the most warlike and chivalrous people of the whole Austrian empire, and in possession of the richest soil— A revolution in Hungary would be more fatal to Austria than the Polish revolution could ever have become to Russia, and would at once sever the empire. . . .

With the exception of Austria and Prussia, there exists no absolute monarchy in Germany; all the minor States possessing, more or less, liberal *constitutions.* These constitutions, insignificant as they are, when compared to the free institutions of Britain, or even France, were, nevertheless, extorted by the force of public opinion, or, as was the case in Bavaria, by the financial embarrassments of the country. The necessity of conceding certain rights and privileges *to the people* was implicitly acknowledged; and, though the princes afterwards regretted having made these concessions, it was no longer in their power wholly to retract them. . . .

The Liberal [German newspaper] went even so far as to advocate the re-union of the different States into a Germanic empire, not under the auspices of Austria or Prussia, but under those of duke Leopold of Baaden. This prince, one of the few virtuous of his class united the suffrages of nearly the whole liberal party, and was actually set up as a candidate for the dignity of emperor. . . .

The diet of 1832 abolished the liberty of the press, threw the most distinguished editors into prison, excluded the champions of liberty from the legislative assemblies, abolished the most liberal papers . . . and put an end to all freedom of speech. All this was done so abruptly and unexpectedly, that the people who had ventured to rely on the promises of their princes, and had consequently omitted to concert measures for their common defence, could not for several months recover from their astonishment; and when they did recover, the Austrians were at Frankfort.

Thus ended the first fair dream of liberty in Germany; but the dreamers are now roused from their sleep, and made sensible of their true position. They have now tested, to the fullest extent, the veracity and good faith of their princes, and will not soon trust again to their sincerity. . . .

"Battles," said Voltaire, "are not lost by the number of killed and wounded, but by the effect which these produce on the survivers." The same holds now of the principle of freedom. Let liberty be once firmly established in Spain; let it be known that freedom found its way through darkness and superstition, through despotism and the inquisition; and it will inspire the liberals of all Europe with fresh enthusiasm for their cause. They will learn from it, that a people is free from the moment it is resolved to be so. . . .

Opposed to the liberal principles and common interests of mankind is the power of Russia, hovering like an eagle over its prey, and threatening, at every moment, to seize upon its victims—the civilized nations of Europe. The power of Russia is unquestionably alarming, and on the increase; but it is nevertheless overrated by friends and foes.

Russia consists of an assemblage of forty-eight different nations, united into an empire by nothing but a military despotism. These forty-eight different nations speak so many different languages; are widely separated from each other by customs and manners; and among them are many, who, like the Polish, entertain the most implacable hatred against the Czar. So many heterogeneous elements can only act in concert as long as they are barbarous. Accustomed blindly to obey the mandates of their military chieftains, civilization separates them by attaching them to the soil and to the interests of their respective countries. These, it would teach them, are not identified with the growing despotism of Russia; but, on the contrary, with the destruction of its baneful influence. The different people of Russia cease to be *Russians* when brought under the humanizing influence of the arts and sciences. They then become *Europeans*—subjects of that great moral empire, which extends from the extreme west of America to the confines of Asia,—and rebels in their own country. Civilization *weakens* the Russian empire instead of giving it strength, as is the case with every other country. It cannot give the Russians a national impulse, because it pleads the cause of her enemies, and is identified with their political progress. . . . It must, therefore, be the policy of Russia to check the progress of civilization and the arts;

to diminish the means of instruction, and to prevent, as far as possible, the formation of a public spirit. She is thus forced to destroy the chief elements of a nation's greatness, and reduced to no other means of attack or defence than the huge masses of her soldiery. In case of a war, the power of Russia would rest on mere numerical elements, while national enthusiasm, love of country and of home, devotion to liberty, and the strong principle of national honor, would unite to increase the moral energy of her antagonists. . . .

Civilization, moreover, is no longer confined to one or two particular states, but, by the press, is spreading over the world. Every ship which enters a Russian port discharges its cargo of intelligence, and reclaims her subjects from barbarism. Russia will be partially civilized before she will attempt the conquest of Europe; but then the elements of her power will no longer act in her favor. . . .

The Russian army stationed in Poland has already imbibed many principles which it has combatted with the sword. The conquest of Poland is perhaps one of the surest means of scattering them amongst the Russian population; and who can foretell whether the very division of Poland may not, in its fatal retribution, destroy the powers which sullied history by the commission of that crime. . . .

So far then from seeing, in the growing democracy of England, a cause of her future decline, we view in it the providential development of a principle which imparts new life and vigor to her people, and is destined to save not only her, but the rest of mankind, from oppression and bondage. We look upon the genius of England as the good genius of history, and trust that England will be true to it.

17

A Reporter, "Glances at Congress: No. 1," United States Magazine and Democratic Review, vol. 1, no. 1 (1837)

In the halls of the 25th U.S. Congress (1837–39), there lurked a curious sort of politician: the committed ideologue. They were widely considered chimerical monsters in the emerging world of Martin Van Buren's Second Party System, itself quickly solidifying a grasp on American political life. Yet these new men, these predominantly locofoco ideologues, rode from New York to Washington on the back of Van Buren's Democracy, having recently tamed the beast by successfully reviving Americans' instinctive spirit of Jeffersonian populism and anti-state radicalism. From 1835 to 1837, New Yorkers favoring some of the strictest libertarian policies ever offered by a political organization gained the balance of power in state Democratic Party politics and thereby gained critical influence in the new administration and Congress. The new Congress elected the fairly locofoco (or "Equal Rights") Democrat James K. Polk as Speaker of the House, and Van Burenites controlled both chambers. Although the union of radical and moderate Democratic forces ensured Van Buren's election and (briefly) the ascendancy of his party, the introduction of locofoco ideologues to the political process forever changed American political life.

The United States Magazine and Democratic Review, in its very first issue (1837), indicated with clarity and precision the source of this irrevocable change: the ideologues refused to keep their "gentlemanly" peace on the subject of slavery.[40] The *Democratic Review*'s sketches of the new Congress first identify "the voluntary principle" as the cornerstone of republican life in America. Such a principle was virtually embodied by Representatives Eli Moore and Churchill C. Cambreleng, both influential New York locofocos and "Equal Rights" Democrats, as well as former president John Quincy Adams. Although drawn from wildly different backgrounds and ideologies, locofocos like Moore and Churchill joined in anti-slavery coalition with Whiggish anti-partisans like Adams to defend Northern rights and liberties against the encroachments of Southern legislators and their partisan creatures in the North—creatures like Ogden Hoffman, the final sketch in the article. Hoffman was elected to Congress from New York as a locofoco, but his attachments to ideology crumbled during the Panic of 1837 and Whig attacks on the administration party. Then, as now, an "irate, tireless minority" often made the difference between good and bad policy, and its existence provided the means for a developing culture of dissent.

And what is it that brings together this remarkable body of men; the representatives of so many various sections, soils, characters, and interests—what is that bond of union that keeps together this wonderful *E pluribus Unum*? It is not the external forms of institutions and the organized machinery of government. It is a voluntary principle, existing in the bosom of every individual, a common sentiment of general mutuality of the most important interests, the knowledge that the spirit of democratic republicanism embodied in our system, protecting rights and punishing wrongs, and in all other respects leaving every man free to pursue his own happiness in his own way, contains the true secret which the nations have been so long and toilsomely in search of, from which alone the greatest and happiest results of social life are to proceed. This is the true principle of cohesion, the *anima* or informing soul, which cement our union, all the parts exciting a reciprocal influence of attraction upon each other. . . .

Distance and climate can have no influence upon this bond. It is wholly independent of them. There need be no fear of the effect of any possible extension of territory—though the representatives sent from the shores of the Atlantic and the Pacific oceans, from the Isthmus of Darien and the far wild regions of the north of our continent, on the very verge of that uninhabitable region, *domibus negata*, which the icy powers of the Pole claim as all their own—should one day meet in common friendly congress at some central point, the focus of the civilization of the western world, where not yet has even the solitary smoke of its first pioneer begun to curl up its thin, white, wavering column from out of the dark and deep heart of the ancient forest. The farther and wider our principles extend themselves, with peaceful and undisputed sway, accompanied with no poisonous elements of wrong or violence, the better! The greater the number of the oppressed of other countries who come to seek shelter under the shadow of the broad wings of our eagle, bringing with them strong hands and honest hearts, and a voluntary desire to enjoy the benefits of the free institutions denied to them in the land of their birth, the better!—provided, as the essential condition of safety, that the local action of the central government over domestic concerns and partial interests be restricted proportionately to its diffusion over a more extended surface of territory. . . .

Near to Mr. Wise sits a gentleman with an unhealthy complexion, and rather singular face—one of the most remarkable men of the body. His hair brushed back from his forehead, is long and curly; his eye is keen, stern, and intelligent; he generally dresses well, and his usual companion is a heavy ivory-headed cane.

He appears to be a nervous man; one of those men of deep but quiet enthusiasm who never fail to make themselves both marked and felt, whenever they put forth the lumbering powers within them. This gentleman is Eli Moore, of the city of New York. He may be said to be peculiarly the representative of the mechanics of that city, at whose head he stands, as a prominent member of the Typographical Society, and lately president of his favorite Trades Union. Mr. Moore is a quiet, silent, reserved man; but beneath that apparent cold calmness blow feelings of an intense enthusiasm for the principles of democracy, and of a bitter strength against whatever he regards as tinged with an aristocratic tone. In chartered banks he recognizes the privileged superiority of a fortunate or favored few over the great mass of the community, analogous in spirit and moral effects to the iron feudal aristocracy of the olden time, and considers them the moral upas of the age. He was formerly a journeyman printer of New York; but, possessing talents and ambition, and an enthusiasm in a cause which can never fail to draw forth the sympathies and support of the mass of our people, he soon raised himself over the shoulders of other aspirants, and won a seat in Congress.

Last winter Mr. Moore made his debut. Gen. Waddy Thompson, of South Carolina, believing that he saw in the Trades Unionists and the mechanics of the north the two great moving forces of the abolition cause, made some very bitter remarks in the course of one of his peculiarly sarcastic speeches against those interests. . . . The harshness of the charges rang discordantly on [Moore's] ear, and produced a high degree of mental and bodily excitement. In vain he daily left his sick room, and tottered into the hall, to retort upon General Thompson. The floor at that time was forever occupied. It seemed to be a springing-board for honorable members. Never before had there been so many to speak. The subject (abolition petitions) had aroused all the passionate, philanthropic, and partizan feelings of the House; the storm raged day after day, and angry glances and fierce words were exchanged on all sides; crimination and recrimination was the order of the day. The Speaker was compelled to bow his head to the howling hurricane, and permit it to rage in its full fury. Every man seemed to grow into vast pyramidal altitude in his own mind; and speak he must, or the country would be ruined.

At length Mr. Moore obtained the eye of the Speaker. There was quite a sensation in the gallery on the announcement. The large white-headed cane stood up with its master. The New York delegation was excited. Mr. Moore's reputation was high as a public speaker. I perceived at once that he was greatly enfeebled, but he seemed to nerve himself for his task. The House danced before his eyes: he saw but one object—the Speaker, in his black morocco chair, with his steady and earnest eyes fixed upon him. He commenced. His voice was remarkably strong. He laid down his premises with singular clearness, but wide of the subject-matter under consideration in the House. He took a review of the history of past ages; brought back to the mental vision the days of the feudal system—the fortress, the tournament, the plume, the helm, the lance, the gilded spur. His speech seemed to glitter with all the gallant splendor and bravery of the olden chivalry. But then his lip curled with indignation, and his voice sunk into a tone of deploring eloquence, when he brought up the other side of the picture—the serfs, with the iron collars around their necks. He pointed to the debased, enslaved multitude; and passing to a general application of the illustration to our own times, he proclaimed, in a voice tremulous with emotion, his creed to be founded in the equality of man. On this theme he enlarged, with a thrilling power of eloquence rarely equalled in that House. The impetuous force with which his reply bore upon the assailant, who had thus drawn him out, will not soon be forgotten. Mr. Moore's language was flowery and rhetorical: he possesses more genius than culture, and to one particular subject he seems to bend his thoughts entirely—that of the equality and rights of man. I understand that he has given himself up, of late, to deep application; and that when an occasion offers, he will splinter the lance of his cherished principles, against the system and mode of government as it is administered in detail.

I observed many among the auditors in the gallery who seemed to hang with rapture on his remarks. The whole House was excited at the novelty and boldness of his democratic doctrines, not less at the extraordinary manner in which he had turned aside from the current of debate, and struck fearlessly forward into a field to which few orators had before ventured to lead the attention of that body. I overheard some gentlemen from the south say, that they thought they heard the high priest of revolution singing his war song.

A bevy of members had gradually collected immediately behind the orator, whose voice still rang loud in the hall, in the midst of an impassioned passage. My eye was fixed upon him; I saw him grow paler than ever; till a deadly hue swept over his face; his hands were arrested in the air—he grasped at emptiness—a corpse seemed to stand with outstretched hands before the agitated crowd—his eyes were closed—he tottered, and, amid the rush and exclamations of the whole House, fell back insensible into the arms of one of his friends. Mr. Moore was borne from the hall. His wife had been watching him with emotions that may be imagined from the gallery. The scene had been worked up into a catastrophe, and never before had I seen the House so agitated as on this occasion.

Mr. Moore has never finished that speech; indeed he has not spoken since in the hall; his health is very bad, and I am under the impression that his friends will not allow him to address the House. He cannot control himself when he is up, and the consequence is that he soon becomes exhausted. . . .

Our attention is now attracted to a ray of light that glitters on the apex of a bald and noble head, "located" on the left of the House, in the neighbourhood of the Speaker's chair. It proceeds from that wonderful man who in his person combines the agitator, poet, philosopher, statesman, critic, and orator—John Quincy Adams. . . . What must be his thoughts as he ponders upon the past, in which he has played a part so conspicuous? We look at him and mark his cold and *tearful* eye, his stern and abstracted gaze, and conjure up phantoms of other scenes. We see him amid his festive and splendid halls ten years back, standing stiff and awkward, and shaking a tall military-looking man by the hand, in whose honor the gala was given, to commemorate the most splendid of America's victories. We see him again, years afterwards, the bitter foe of the same "military chieftain," and the competitor with him for the highest gift of a free people. We look upon a more than king, who has filled every department of honor in his native land, still at his post; he who was the President of millions, now the representative of forty odd thousand, quarrelling about trifles or advocating high principles. To-day growling and sneering at the House with an abolition petition in his trembling hand, and anon lording it over the passions, and lashing the members into the wildest state of enthusiasm by his indignant and emphatic eloquence. Alone, unspoken to, unconsulted, never consulting with others, he sits apart, wrapped in his reveries; and with his finger resting on his nose, he permits his mind to move like a gigantic pendulum, stirring up the hours of the past and disturbing those of the hidden future; or probably he is writing. . . . He looks enfeebled, but yet he is never tired; worn out, but ever ready for combat; melancholy, but let a witty thing fall from any member, and that old man's face is wreathed in smiles; he appears passive, but woe to the unfortunate member that hazards an arrow at him; the eagle is not swifter in his flight than Mr. Adams; with his agitated finger quivering in sarcastic gesticulation, he seizes upon his foe, and, amid the amusement of the House, rarely fails to take a signal vengeance. . . .

His manner of speaking is peculiar; he rises abruptly, his face reddens, and, in a moment throwing himself into the attitude of a veteran gladiator, he prepares for the attack then he becomes full of gesticulation, his body sways to and fro—self-command seems almost lost—his head is bent forward in his earnestness till it sometimes nearly touches the desk; his voice frequently breaks, but he pursues his subject through all its bearings;

nothing daunts him—the House may ring with the cries of order—order!—unmoved—contemptuous—he stands amid the tempest, and, like an oak that knows its gnarled and knotted strength, stretches his arm forth and defies the blast.

Opposite to Mr. Adams, on the right of the Hon. Speaker, sits a small man, who is engaged in the perusal of a huge mass of documents; occasionally he applies a double quizzing glass to his eye, raises his head and gazes earnestly around the hall. He is bald on the crown of the head, his forehead broad and high, and more striking than the lower part of his face. This gentleman is the Hon. C. C. Cambreleng, of New York, chairman of the committee of ways and means, and by his political opponents styled "the leader of the Administration Party in the House." . . .

He seldom converses with the other members, scarcely ever leaves his seat, but busies himself in the examination of papers; nor does he appear to pay the slightest attention to debate, and yet he never permits one word to escape; and should anything be said peculiarly unpleasant, from a political opponent, he is up, ready for a retort. Mr. Cambreleng's manner of elocution is sometimes a little inflated, but he is remarkably fluent, and his language is always chaste and appropriate. He is one of the ablest and most efficient members of the House; his consistency in an honest democratic creed of politics, his boldness and clear-sightedness, have placed him in a commanding position before the country. A statesman's real calibre for talent, importance, and future prospects, may, in general, be safely measured by the amount of abuse of which his opponents think him worthy.

Judged by this rule, the Hon. C. C. C. . . . is certainly stamped at once as one of the most formidable men of his party in the House, and before the country.

Dressed in a full suit of black, with a black silk bosom, light hair, and sunny face, the Hon. Ogden Hoffman, of New York city, has risen to address his maiden speech to the House. Mark with what graceful emphasis he delivers himself;—how musical his voice, though without much compass;—how apposite his gestures! A crowd has gathered around him; he evidently makes a sensation. He is bitterly opposed to the administration, and gives utterance to his sentiments with peculiar eloquence. . . . The last time I had heard Mr. Ogden Hoffman speak was in New York, on the occasion of the great democratic victory of the election of General Jackson and Mr. Van Buren, of whom he had been an ardent supporter, not quite one little lustre ago. I shall never forget the brilliancy and force of his eloquence at that period on that theme. However, the theme and the side are, it is to be presumed, immaterial to so ingenious a young lawyer. He was one of those "weaker vessels" who fell away from the truth during the panic period—that time that tried men's souls. In the city of New York, the tempest ran so high, and superior powers of clamor gave the bank cause such an apparent advantage, that many considered the democratic party there prostrated forever, and lost no time in being "off w' the old love" and "on wi' the new." Among these, Mr. Ogden Hoffman was perhaps the most conspicuous, as he doubtless considered himself one of the most sincere and patriotic. It is a pity, however, that such fine talents must hereafter be paralyzed by such a position. It can never be possible for him to exert any great moral force, whether in or out of Congress, in opposition to Mr. Van Buren's administration. The ghosts of his not yet forgotten sentiments and speeches (all murdered by that one ruthless blow, the removal of the deposites) must rise up too often in judgment before him, when on the eve of any intended exertion, with the depressing omen—

Let me sit heavy on thy soul to-morrow!

18

James Gemmel, "Two Years in Van Dieman's Land," Daily Plebeian, July 1, 1842

James Gemmel was your average mid-19th-century "Young American": he was an idealistic, romantic, *revolutionary* whose vision disastrously exceeded his real power and influence. During the heady, radical days of the Jackson–Van Buren administration, the most restless and hopeful of Democrats gathered together across the northern border to agitate republican revolution in Canada. The Canadians, for their part, did not rise to match the Americans' fury. Although there was indeed a flurry of relatively small battles between William Lyon Mackenzie's rebel forces and British-Canadian militiamen, the American filibusters constituted the largest corps of revolutionaries. Insisting on trying their own luck at whipping the British, a few particularly brave (or foolhardy) companies actually invaded Canadian territory to meet battle. Unsurprising to virtually all observers, British forces easily prevailed, meting out swift, unyielding military justice to the American prisoners.

James Gemmel, among many dozens of others, was convicted to transportation and prison labor in British Australia. In the following narrative, Gemmel describes to his audience the conditions of life aboard the convict ships and in the colony and the details of his fortuitous escape home to New York. Gemmel published his account of "Van Dieman's Land" (Tasmania) in Levi Slamm's *Daily Plebeian* and books circulated to eager locofoco, Democratic readers.[41] Those looking to Gemmel to reinforce Americans' gradually increasing feeling of imperial rivalry with Great Britain (see chapter 23) must have come away from his book sorely lacking, however.

James Gemmel, for all his youthful filibustering *gusto* for revolution, concluded his narrative with a plea for prudent *inaction*. "But let us avoid all frontier movements," he implored readers, "the best weapon . . . with which to revolutionize the world, is surely a strict adherence to that wise, just, and honest policy, which carries in its train prosperity and peace."

Mr. Editor:—The superintendent of the convict station on which I was employed last year, appointed me an overseer, a sort of spy upon my fellow prisoners, and insisted on my acceptance of that unpleasant office. To decline was to incense him, yet I flatly refused it, and was therefore immediately sent to the treadmill a month— very fatiguing for the legs it surely is, and the vile wretches whose company one is compelled to keep, double the punishment; I was next placed in the Bridgewater chain gang for two months, and kept standing in the water handling stones and building piers.

Linus W. Miller, the young law student from Chautauque County, made a bold defence at Niagara, when on trial for his life, though but 18 years of age. I presume that this boldness did him much injury with Sir John Franklin, for he was an object of special persecution on the island.

At length he joined [other prisoners] in a vain attempt to escape. They jumped into an open boat, and without rudder or compass, went out to sea, hoping that some vessel might be near that would aid their views. A storm overtook them—they were driven on the rocks on a desert island—their boat was smashed to pieces—and two weeks after that, they were found nearly famished, and carried back to Hobart Town.

When they were missed, the whole island was in an uproar. It was feared that they had got arms and joined the Bush Rangers . . . who, well armed and very resolute, keep the woods, and set the colonial authorities at defiance.

Miller and his comrades had no jury trial—two justices condemned them for two years to the coal mines at Port Arthur, a sentence the next in severity to the gallows—and there they were when I escaped.

It was to this place of torment, that Mr. Frost, late Mayor of Newport, with Williams and Jones, his comrades concerned in the Welsh outbreak, were sent, though some of the ablest lawyers and judges in England had declared their conviction and sentence to be at variance with law. They were at first treated better than the other wretched beings there, but bad is the best usage at Port Arthur, so they also put out to sea in a whale boat, were pursued, taken, and Williams was put in irons—in the day time he was made fast to a long and heavy chain fastened to an iron ring in the wall, and kept at hard labor stone-breaking, and Frost and Jones found their condition much changed for the worse. The editors were friendly to these Welshmen, but they could learn little and effect nothing. I am satisfied that in England they have no correct idea of Frost's sufferings; his letters dare not tell the truth. A convict or person in my situation would have been severely punished had we been seen talking to a free emigrant, or to any one not of our class and station. I have seen captive Americans flogged and sent to confinement on bread and water, for receiving a little tobacco or a slice of bread from a stranger, and for speaking to strangers. Our rules were printed, and, as enforced, no man could live up to them. . . .

After our arrival in England we were for some months on board the York Hulk, off Portsmouth. We were there taken into a square crib called a wash house, stripped naked, put into a big tub and well scrubbed by two convicts, our hair sheared quite close, and we attired in the convict garb. Grant and Miller came down with a gang of horrid looking wretches from Newgate, were sent to work, planned how to escape, but were informed on by Jacob Beemer, the Judas of the party, now a constable in Van Dieman's Land.

Elijah Woodman, of Maine, drew up a memorial, in the shape of a round-robin, addressed to Sir John Franklin, in July, 1840, setting forth that fellows guilty of the foulest and most revolting crimes, were our overseers—that many of us had to work long and hard barefooted, with wretched food and worn out garments, toiling whether it rained or whether we were in a burning sun, with no place to dry ourselves when wet and weary, till the bell called us to be locked up in our prisons at night. Sir John was incensed, mustered us, called us mutineers, ordered us to be dressed in magpie clothing—one leg and arm black, t'other yellow—with a military guard to shoot us down if disobedient. We were then sent to the worst station on the island, at Green Pond. There, however, we found a friend in the Hon. Capt. Erskine, son to Lord Chancellor Erskine, and brother to the Ambassador from England, who had married an American lady. This noble youth won the affections of us all by listening to our complaints when cruelly used, and doing justice on the felons who had maltreated us. His heart was full of kindness and humanity, but his conduct gave offence as being at variance with the policy Sir John Franklin had been directed to pursue, and the station was soon broken up.

On the 14th of last February, those of the captives not ordered to Port Arthur, were to have tickets by which they would be enabled to labor for their living, each man having a certain township far in the interior, beyond which if he dared to go, severe punishment would follow.

These townships extend perhaps ten miles by five, and contain, on the average, perhaps thirty landowners, who will unite to pay the poor captive just what they please, as he can go nowhere else; and if he demand a settlement, they may assert that he was saucy; and, any two of them being magistrates, can send him to the chaingang for a year, or otherwise coerce him. Redress is a thing not to be thought of. I have seen enough of this. If I were now a Van Dieman's-Land "relief captive," I would gladly exchange for slavery in Virginia, as far preferable.

Chandler and Waite are the exception to these remarks. They are much respected, and have been allowed to set up a blacksmith and wheelwright's shop; John Grant, of Toronto, being their hired assistant.

It is impossible for me fully to describe the state of society in Van Dieman's Land. Nine-tenths of the people are convicts. The men are bad enough. Some of their crimes are so revolting that I forbear to name them; and as for the London prostitutes, they are there in thousands, and infinitely worse than the worst of the men. —Virtue itself would soon be contaminated in such a polluted atmosphere. There are no distilleries but money is plentiful, and Van Dieman's Land is the most remarkable place for drunkenness I ever saw. The American and Canadian prisoners established temperance societies, at which sons of our ablest men lectured, and a very few of the English convicts joined us.

The law is administered in a very summary and severe manner. Sir George Arthur would sometimes sign eleven death warrants in a morning, and see them executed too. His severity was no doubt the reason why he was sent next to Canada, and is probably the cause of his promotion to the government of Bombay.

In April, 1841, Governor Franklin caused the American captives to be assembled, and made a speech to them. I think the pith of it was to this effect:—

He had received a letter from Secretary Lord John Russell, saying that our release rested entirely with the Governor General of Canada, who, if he could arrive at the conclusion that our return would not endanger the public safety, and prove the signal for renewed troubles on the frontier, might permit us to return home, but that so far as the condition of Canada was yet known to the government of England, our return was considered highly dangerous; that there was but little probability that we should ever be permitted to leave the island; and that his instructions were not to allow any of us a free pardon. He added, that as American vessels visited Launcestown and Hobart Town, he would keep us all in the interior, even after our first two years expired; that we might hope to be taken off by the sympathy of American seamen, but that if such a case should arise, the British and American governments being on the best possible terms, we would be demanded of the United States, authorities, given us, brought back, and receive a most exemplary punishment. As for Linus Wilson Miller, he would keep him in the coal mines, if he retained that government, to the last hour of his life, as a warning and example to others.

My object is to state plain facts, [I leave to] better informed men the task of applying them; but I may venture to remark, that it would surely be better for England to govern gently in Canada, and thereby gain the affections of the people, than to be careless there, and keep some hundreds of honest, well meaning men, who sought to get or give relief from a government acknowledged by the authorities of that nation to have been very wicked, 18,000 miles from their homes miserable, and among the most degraded of God's creation, under the pretext that their release would involved a million and a half of colonists in revolt.

So far as prudence will permit, I will not state the particulars of my escape.

Mr. Norries, a police magistrate, and formerly butler to Sir George Arthur, had received a large tract of land, which he was anxious to clear. I persuaded him that I could build a stump machine if I had the model from Mr. Woodman, of Maine, who lived beyond Hobart Town; and such was his anxiety, that he gave me a passport to that place, in which the ship that brought me, the places where I was born and tried, with my complexion and height, the color of my hair, eyes cheeks and eyebrows, the shape of my nose and chin, and size of my mouth, were faithfully inserted. . . .

This passport (which I yet have) was, in direct contempt of the public orders of the British government; accordingly, the moment I exhibited to Mr. Gunn, the superintendent, a letter from several of the prisoners, asking for their own clothes, that shrewd Caledonian suspected my design, arrested and gave me in charge to an armed constable, I being still attired in the conspicuous magpie garb in which I had reached the capital. I was ordered to be taken back into the interior immediately, was handcuffed, and being accompanied by several male and female criminals thither bound, set out on my weary journey. At noon the constable took off my handcuffs, that I might eat, when I seized his musket, declared I was off for the bush, and disappeared. In the night I left my hiding-place, crept into Hobart Town, told some whole-souled American tars my unfortunate history, and they required no coaxing to perform the part of honest men. The victim of oppression found deliverers, and entertains no fears whatever that John Tyler, President of the United States, will send him back again, but would rather hope that the friendly aid of this great nation, through its Executive, will soon effectually relieve those who yet groan in bondage, and restore them to their free and happy homes.

The American prisoners were not all put in cross-irons at first; but for one cause or other, the most of them were in the long run thus accommodated.

I joined the insurgents behind Toronto, of my own free will, and had long been anxious for such a movement. Sir George Arthur visited us occasionally while we were under sentence of death, and when he told me I had been deluded by Mackenzie, I replied that it was not so—that we were in the right—that if ever there was a just cause it was ours—and that I had weighed the matter and was sincerely sorry we had failed. Sir George's behavior to us was polite and affable. Of the justice of our cause, I have never since entertained nor expressed a different opinion; but this is not the time and place to discuss that question.

I was behind Toronto with the insurgents the first night, Monday—was in the Tuesday night's skirmish in the suburbs—took Sheriff Jarvis's fine blood mare, which Mackenzie rode until all was over on Thursday. I also brought in the Captain of Sir Francis's Artillery, of which we had none ourselves, nor even a bayonet—was of the small party on Wednesday who went and took the mails and carriages—and in the final fight at Montgomery's on Thursday. I parted with Mackenzie when he and Colonel Lount separated, (after the defeat), near Shepard's mills; and never saw him again till one of the refugees directed me to his home in this city, a week ago. I saw that he faithfully performed his duty behind Toronto, and if some who do not know have blamed him in the United States, I am sure that those who were his companions cannot have done so. . . .

In concluding, I would again entreat every friend of humanity to endeavor to get the United States government to interest itself in the matter of my unfortunate comrades. It is visionary to assert that the exertions of a few dozens of men, uninfluential, unconnected with politics, and worn down by pain and privation, could have the least effect in changing the destiny of Canada. And if not, why continue thus to torture them? But let us avoid all frontier movements—the best weapon in the hands of this great republic, with which to revolutionize the world, is surely a strict adherence to that wise, just, and honest policy, which carries in its train prosperity and peace. That is the true way to create admiration for institutions theoretically liberal and free. Had we succeeded in Canada in 1837, independence would have followed, but no war with America. War would only insure the oppression and captivity of tens of thousands who are happy in the bosoms of their families, would inflame the bad passions of two great nations, speaking one language, and capable, under such forms of government as they may respectively choose to uphold, of enlightening, benefitting and blessing mankind; but it would not soothe the griefs of the orphans and widows, the fathers and brothers, of those manly hearts which now beat on a far distant shore with fond and anxious confidence and hope that they will yet find opportune friends and deliverers in the land of Washington.

19

Levi Slamm and Frances Whipple, "From a Rhode Islander" and "An Unrepublican Anomaly," Daily Plebeian, August 3, 1842

In the summer of 1842, the Rhode Island "Dorr War" threatened to erupt into civil war throughout New England, from New Hampshire to Philadelphia. In question was the status of the state government. As of August 3, when Levi Slamm's *Daily Plebeian* published the following articles, Rhode Islanders possessed two governments: one claiming legitimacy through the royal charter of 1662, the other claiming its rights under the recently (although irregularly) approved "People's Constitution."[42]

Thomas W. Dorr (the "People's Governor") and his suffragist allies had long sought to liberalize the state government, especially by eliminating the landholding requirement for voting and reapportioning state representation. In search of a more democratic, republican government, the "Dorrites" spontaneously formed a "People's Convention"(1841), drafted the "People's Constitution," and successfully submitted the documents to voters for ratification. Voters overwhelmingly embraced the new government, whereas the old administration refused to give way.

In the ensuing standoff, suffragist forces embarrassingly lost several military contests and failed to organize a national political coalition in their favor. By August 1842, therefore, Rhode Island suffragists suffered at the hands of a reactionary regime, their movement floundering and their personal safety in jeopardy. In this context, Frances Whipple ("a Rhode Islander") wrote to New York newspaper editor Levi Slamm on the distressing affair and what many— including Whipple—saw blossoming into a wide-reaching revolutionary struggle. Although the suffrage cause failed for the moment, repressive reaction from the charter regime could only provoke deeper and wider responses from the ranks of average Americans.

In his own commentaries on the Rhode Island affair, Slamm echoed Whipple's sentiments, arguing that

Rhode Island represented a rare "anomaly" in the history of republican government. The thrust of American history, he believed, was undeniably in favor of expanding liberty. As the suffragist collapse in Rhode Island demonstrated, however, those who would protect and expand the scope of freedom must remain ever vigilant in pursuit of their goals. No encroachments of power on the liberties of the people can be tolerated, however anomalous and small they may appear.

"From a Rhode Islander"

Mr. Editor—I perceive the truth-loving Journal of Providence belabors you hard for espousing the cause of the suffrage party of Rhode Island, now crushed to the earth by mere brute force; and heaps upon you all manner of wicked intentions for the freedom and manliness with which you speak. That is not wonderful for the organ which proclaims "martial law," to prevent the liberty of speech, which arrests and imprisons men for expressing an opinion, or casting a vote; and which, in short, presents usurpations and despotism in its worst and most daring form. In no period of the French Revolution did Marat or Robespierre more directly violate the most sacred rights of man and the institutions of France, than have the Chartists in Rhode Island those of American Republicanism. They have arrested, imprisoned, slain innocent men; have broken open private dwellings, insulted and abused women and children, destroyed private property, broken down the "freedom of the press," forbidden the "freedom of speech," and prevented it by armed informers and eavesdroppers, and done just what was to be expected of desperate men, who know no law but their own creation, obey no power but their own ambition, and seek no object but party and selfish triumph.

You, Mr. Editor, having courage to speak in behalf of an injured, insulted, and down-trodden people, must expect to receive the curse of *such* beings. But condemnation from such a source is the highest praise. If they should praise you, you might forthwith hang yourself, to shun deeper disgrace.

I do not wonder that, with your democratic principles, you speak in favor of the right cause of the Suffrage party. I rather wonder you do not say more, for a vital principle is involved in that question, which lies at the foundation of our Government, and of Republicanism itself. I wonder that every *free press* does not speak out in thunder-tones against such an open violation of human rights by an armed aristocracy. Nay, I wonder even that every real friend of republican liberty does not arm himself and fly to the rescue of brother freemen suffering in our own land—the boasted land of the free. Fifty men from your city armed them-selves and came to Providence to put down the rights of freemen. Governor Davis lent 500 stand of arms to shoot down men who were willing to submit to a form of government guaranteed to them by the Federal Constitution. But that is all nothing. Oh, no; for the *rich*, the *aristocracy*, the Whigs, approve of that. But let the Plebeian say a word in favor of the poor and derided people, and it is "incendiary," and ought to be silenced! You would be, if you were in Rhode Island.

Some people lay the "flattering unction to their souls," that all is over, and that they can keep up the "martial law" until *such men* are chosen as will make a *good* Constitution. But they know better. They *feel* that they are sleeping on the top of a volcano. They hope to chain it down. They have just doubled their patrol, and are daily brushing their arms. Call that safely? They can have none by oppression. A spirit now slumbering, but just ready to be awakened, will take *sweet* vengeance on the enormities it has suffered. Clergymen may thank God "by law," and "Hard Ciderites" sing its requiem; but it "is not dead; but sleepeth." It will arise in giant strength, and hurl back its fetters, and wind aristocracy in the grave-clothes prepared for itself. Remember Haman's gallows. A thousand men driven from the State will not always keep away. It is now understood that Tyler will *not* intermeddle; so the very cause of their overthrow is taken away, and Suffrage men are beginning to feel the freedom they once felt, and to deem it worth some blood. Yes, sir, the Journal may yet have cause to thank you for the admonitions you have given them betimes. The Chartists may as well be picking up their duds, and preparing to make their peace with the great ruling power, the "*will of the People*." I can assure them it is coming. The Chronicle, a mere shade from the Journal office, may boast of the strong and ready force of the Royalists, but it is vain. They have taken, by force, the guns of the people, but they cannot take the armor of right. Those who fight in a right cause are not unaided. Some helping France, with a becoming fellow-feeling, will lend her aid to justice and human right. Let usurpers tremble.

Yours, in the love of freedom and right,
A Rhode Islander

"An Unrepublican Anomaly"

The condition of affairs in Rhode Island is anomalous in the history of republican government. A State, ostensibly one of our confederacy, in fact represented in both branches of our National Legislature under a Constitution which assumes to establish justice, provide for the common defence, and to secure the blessings of liberty, is at this moment a military despotism of the worst description, where neither persons nor property, youth nor age, is respected, and where the freedom of speech and of the press are trampled under foot with entire impunity. There is no possible excuse or apology for this state of things, which can satisfy the PEOPLE of the country. We are aware that a government, such as that under which the people of Rhode Island have tamely and ignobly live so long, must, at this time, when the light of political knowledge is reflected into every village and hamlet in the land, have recourse to violent means to maintain its ascendency. We are told as an excuse for the continuance of martial law, the encouragement of spies, informers and false witnesses; the persecution of the free suffrage people; the insults which are heaped upon them; the intrusions which are daily made into the houses of peaceable, honest and well meaning citizens; the imprisonment of husbands and brothers; and other outrages committed, not only upon residents, but upon citizens of other states, who may happen to sojourn there temporarily on business, that vile plots and conspiracies are on foot to overrun the state, burn down the dwellings, pillage the property, and ravish the women! These reports are base and willful fabrications. FEAR, the great principle of all despotisms, leads to the promulgation of these vile slanders. It is an old trick of despotism, which the masses are fully competent to comprehend. "Under Tiberius Caesar," so we are informed by Seneca, "the rage of accusing of informing was so common as to harass the peaceful citizens more than a civil war. The words of drunken men, and the unguarded joke of the thoughtless, were taken down and handed to the Emperor." And there have been periods in the history of England, when spies, informers, false-witnesses, and pretended plots and conspiracies were deemed lawful and useful expedients by the powers that were, to crush and trample upon the people. History will have recorded on its pages the same tyranny, the same despicable means, to crush the people of *republican* Rhode Island. It is not unfair to infer the existence of the same principles, the same motives, from a similarity of conduct. Anomalous, as it may seem, foul and disgraceful as it is, we make the inference.

Let not the powers that be in Rhode Island urge State necessity in defence of their odious and heart-rending despotism. Let them not say that those we have seen here, exiled from their native soil, intelligent, honest, industrious American citizens, must remain in exile as a matter of State necessity; that their appearance among their friends and relations would be hazardous to the peace of the State. We deny the existence of any such necessity. All will be peace and quiet, if justice, simple justice, republican justice, be done them. It is not a characteristic of the American people to be discontented, traitorous, or seditious. But they will complain, they have a right to complain, and they would be cravens and cowards would they not Act, when they see themselves despoiled of those

307

privileges which they of right should exercise by authority of God and the Constitution. With what reason can the dominant party in Rhode Island (we mean the armed and despotic minority) expect peace, when there is no peace, order when there is no order, law when there is no law? What! Do they hope that American citizens, when nothing is extended to them but villainous oppression, will yield to it a contemptible submission? Call they it law, and order, and tranquility, when the laws are iniquitously unequal, when persecution and insult must be submitted to without the privilege of complaint? The people of Rhode Island have already submitted too long, disgracefully submitted, to such law and order. We look upon it as the very bane and curse of humanity, and one entirely and emphatically anomalous to the character and institutions of the people of this country, antagonist to the spirit of the age in which we live, and disgraceful to those who hope to perpetuate it. We may speak warmly, but we fell [sic] what we speak when we say, in comparison to such law, and order, and tranquility as the people there now live under, we would gladly welcome all the feuds, animosities, and revolutions which the aristocracy falsely attribute to a state of political equality. These are the symptoms of life and robust health, while the inanimation, the repose, the quiet resulting from such a government as that now in existence in Rhode Island, is the deadness of a palsy. Who would not prefer life with all its activity and enterprise, to the silence of the grave and the stillness of desolation?

When is this unrepublican anomaly to be regulated? Can nothing be said or done, to advise or assist the down trodden and oppressed, as are the people of Rhode Island? We have extended our sympathies to the Greeks, the Poles, the Canadians, the persecuted of Old Ireland, and can we look on with calmness, and witness the operation of a military despotism within our own territory, almost at our very door? Cannot the enquiry be made to Congress, whether a military despotism be the Republican government which the United States are bound to guarantee to the citizens of each State of the Confederacy? Timid and nerveless as the majority of the Suffrage party are generally regarded, cannot they be warmed up to assemble peaceably, and demand with erect front, those rights which have been so long withheld from them? Twelve thousand voted for the People's Constitution—where are they? All quailing under the rod of the tyrant and the task master! It cannot be so. Let them unite, organize, concentrate, and in defiance of the martial law, demand its immediate abrogation. When this is done, let them send their own delegates to the coming convention, notwithstanding the inequality of representation and the injustice of the qualifications necessary to vote under the call. Twelve thousand men, armed with right, cannot be put down—twelve thousand men cannot be imprisoned, the Bastilles of Rhode Island are not sufficiently capacious to hold them. We must not be considered as intruding our advice in this matter. The principle the people there have attempted to establish, is an universal principle. We have the same interest in its establishment, that they have. Its failure there would tend to its subversion, and its success be the means of accelerating, its progress beyond the bounds of our territory to the present and the future benefit of mankind.

* * *

Since writing the above we have been informed that it is in contemplation to prepare an address to the people of the United States to emanate from a committee consisting of gentlemen of Philadelphia, this city and Boston. We are glad that this movement is suggested, and we trust that the address will contain a correct history of the wrongs which have been perpetrated upon the people of Rhode Island by the exclusive friends of "law and order." If all the facts are collected and arranged, the memories of the Kings and Whipples and Fenners, and such like, will be execrated by every human being to whom God has given a heart to feel, and a tongue to utter.

20

Marcus Morton, "Governor Morton's Letter to the Suffrage Clam Bake Committee," Daily Plebeian, September 6, 1842

Marcus Morton was born in East Freetown, Massachusetts, in 1784; studied at Brown and Taunton Universities; practiced law in Connecticut and Massachusetts for many years; and entered office as a judge during the opening days of the Jacksonian period. Always a radical Jeffersonian, Morton gradually found his intellectual allies in the so-called Loco-Foco Democracy represented at the national level by Martin Van Buren.

Morton represented Massachusetts in the Congress for two terms (1817–21) and served as William Eustis's lieutenant governor (1824–25), as acting governor upon Eustis's death (1825), and as a justice of the state Supreme Judicial Court (1825–40) before running perennially as the Democratic Party's gubernatorial candidate. Despite appearing on the ticket for the better part of a decade, Morton successfully (although by extremely narrow margins) won just two terms as governor. He presided over a sharply partisan, do-nothing government in 1839 and virtually endorsed civil war throughout New England while campaigning before his second term in 1842.

In the 1842 Massachusetts election, the issue at hand lay firmly in Rhode Island. Earlier that year, in Morton's troubled sister state, dueling governments vied for constitutional and military supremacy, battling at the state and national level for legitimacy and command of state authority in Rhode Island. For several years prior, a corps of "suffragists" in Rhode Island, led by Thomas Wilson Dorr, agitated for a new state constitution that would liberalize voting requirements and abolish the existing landholding provision.

Suffragists called for a constitutional convention in 1841, bypassing the state legislature, which remained committed to the state constitution—a document that did not provide for amendment and itself had not changed since King Charles II issued it in 1663.

Although the resultant "People's Constitution" received support from the vast majority of voters, the "charter" government refused to give way. Suffragists and Charterites amassed rival armies during the summer of 1842, and to many it seemed that New England was on the brink of civil war. Although the charter government successfully matched suffragist forces in the field, they diligently organized their own constitutional convention to subvert the suffragist cause.

During the subsequent fall of 1842 campaign season, Rhode Island ladies societies hosted a series of grand political fairs, "clam bakes," to which they invited sympathetic regional figures like Marcus Morton. In the following extract, Morton delivers a letter to the clam-baking "Dorrites" assembled at Medbury Grove, Massachusetts, clearly articulating the nature of "the Rhode Island question" and its importance for the history of republican government in the United States.[43]

Taunton, Aug. 27, 1842

Gentlemen—In declining to join *"The Friends of Equal Rights"* from Rhode Island in their gathering at Medury Grove, on Tuesday next, I beg leave to tender to them my hearty thanks for their obliging invitation.

No man has interfered less, in the recent affairs of Rhode Island, than myself. I have had no communication in relation to the great questions which have agitated and distracted your State, with any of its inhabitants, unless a very little conversation with some of the friends of the old Charter Party be an exception. I have, I trust, been an *impartial* observer of the passing events; but it would be worse than affectation to pretend that I have been an *indifferent* one. Every man alive to the welfare of our common country, must feel a deep interest in the occurrences which have there transpired, and the principles which they have developed. They have given rise to questions of portentous import to our democratic institutions, and brought to light doctrines which strike at the foundation of all free government.

But what magnifies their importance, and renders them of common concernment to the whole country, is the part which a great party, powerful by the wealth and talents of its leading members, now in possession of the government of the United States, has taken in relation to them.

The people of Rhode Island, acting in their original, sovereign capacity, without the aid of governmental regulation, but in a peaceable manner, and with all the formality which their circumstances would admit, called a convention, founded on an equal representation of their numbers, to form a constitution for their adoption or rejection. This convention performed the duty required of it, and submitted to the people a frame of Government, tending to secure equality of representation and universality of suffrage, which was adopted by the votes of a large majority of all the adult male population of the State. The validity of this constitution is denied by most of the inhabitants who exercised exclusive rights and privileges under the old Charter. Officers were elected and governments organized under both. It became an interesting question which was the valid instrument, and which the legitimate government. This has assumed a party character, and may be considered indicative of the political principles of the two great parties into which our country is divided.

The Whig party justifies the proceedings and defends the principles of the landholders' party of Rhode Island. The Whig President, doubtless with the advice of his Whig Cabinet; the acknowledged leader and supposed dictator of the Whig party; the Whig Governor of the greatest State in the Union; other Whig Governors and leaders; and all the Whig papers, with a very few exceptions, have taken the side of the old Charter and those who act under it; while all the Democratic papers, and, as far as I know, all the influential men of that party who have expressed an opinion, have advocated the validity of the new constitution. Indeed, no Democrat in principle, can deny to the people the right to form their own government, or justify that *rotten borough* system of unequal representation which gives to men in one town *ten* or *twenty* times the weight the same number of men in another possesses; or defend that restricted system of suffrage, which excludes one half the people from its exercise.

The questions, therefore, which are involved in this controversy, though local in their origin, have assumed a general interest, and are brought home to the breast of every citizen for his conscientious decision. Now, without intending to interfere with the transactions of the people of another State, or to give an opinion upon the proceedings of the two contending parties there, any farther than the examination of general principles renders necessary, I feel not only at liberty, but called upon, boldly and frankly, to discuss those principles.

It is neither my province nor my intention to judge of the constitution of another State. If a majority of the people of Rhode Island are satisfied with their new Constitution, no Democrat will deny their right to adopt it, or attempt to infringe the free exercise of that right. But in advocating its legal validity, I do not mean to be understood as approving of all its provisions.

But the enquiry presents itself, in the outset—what does this Constitution contain so extremely objectionable and pernicious, or what is there in the old Charter so very excellent and desirable, as to justify and require an appeal to arms to annul the one and sustain the other? If the Constitution be substantially wise and just, why should not the minority, who had not voted at all, have tacitly acquiesced, and suffered it to go into operation by general consent? If it contained defects it also contained provision for future amendments. The only reasons which can be found for resistance to it, must consist in objections to its adoption, or to the principles which it contains. It cannot be presumed that the men in office would expose their State to civil war for the sake of retaining the power.

But what are the great questions involved in this controversy? And what are the vital principles of government which the one party is supposed to maintain and the other deny? They are,

I. THE RIGHT OF THE PEOPLE TO GOVERN THEMSELVES, AND TO ESTABLISH THEIR OWN FORM OF GOVERNMENT.

II. FREE SUFFRAGE.

III. EQUALITY OF REPRESENTATION.

The friends of the new constitution *necessarily* maintain, and its enemies necessarily oppose these principles. I can see no escape from this conclusion. Let it not be denied that a majority of all the people voted for the constitution. The returns show about *three fifths*. They have been in the power of the opponents of the new constitution. Doubtless errors were committed, but they have been pointed out; and it would be unreasonable to suppose that they existed to the extent of the *thousands* which composed the majority. Besides, it is a common presumption, that those who omit to vote intend to acquiesce in the decision of those who choose to exercise that right, and this is believed to be the first instance in which a majority of all the qualified voters ever was required or obtained in favor of any constitution. If a majority of all the people were opposed to the adoption of the new constitution, why did they not turn out and reject it? This would have saved much of ill-will, confusion, expense and bloodshed. No. It cannot be so. The circumstances necessarily lead to the conclusion, not only that there was a large majority in favor of the constitution, but that its opponents well knew it to be so. Do they contend that the will of the *minority* should prevail over that of the *majority*? Do they maintain that there is a favored class who possess greater political rights and power than their fellow men, and that they cannot deprive of them without their own consent? *This is the rankest doctrine of* ARISTOCRACY.

Let it not be pretended that the new constitution was not adopted "*according to the form of law.*" Substance, rather than form, is now sought for. The *pettifogger's* plea in abatement, and the *special pleader's* special demurrer, are, in the light of the present day, discountenanced alike by legislative actions and judicial decisions. "FORMS OF LAW!" Constitutional questions are not to be embarrassed by legal quibbles and technical objections. They look through forms to the substance. But what are the forms prescribed to regulate the action of the people in the exercise of their highest sovereign power? Who can establish forms to govern their proceedings?

When the people have adopted constitutions, and in them provided the manner of making future alterations, some persons contend that they and their successors are bound by the regulations which they have made for themselves, and can make amendments in no other manner. Without admitting or stopping to discuss this position, I think that every believer in the doctrine of delegated power must admit, that, in the original formation of a government, the people must, as they proceed, determine their own forms of proceeding. The same rule applies where there is an existing form of government, which contains no provision for amendments. If this be not so, no new government could be formed, and no such old one could be amended.

If the community be so large that the people cannot meet and discuss the subject all together, some person must *assume* the power to introduce and bring it, in some way, before the people for their action. Such was the case in the old thirteen States, in the formation of their constitutions; for whether conventions, for the purpose, were proposed by the spontaneous action of the people, or by the recommendation of their Colonial Legislatures, they were alike unauthorized. The several charters never contemplated the establishment of independent governments, and never authorized the charter officers to take any steps towards the formation of democratic constitutions. But however a constitution is proposed to the people, it derives all its force from their action upon it. If they reject it, the proposal becomes a nullity. If they adopt it, it becomes the supreme law of the land. The mode of bringing the proposal before the people is not the most material part of the transaction. That which gives them the fullest opportunity for the fair expression of their opinions is doubtless the best. I am not aware that it has ever been objected against the new constitution, that every inhabitant of the State had not an opportunity to vote upon its adoption.

It will not be pretended that the Rhode Island Charter conferred upon the legislature the power to propose a constitution, or to call a convention for that purpose. It contains not a syllable to that effect. If they did either, they must *assume* the power. As no constitution could be formed without the exercise of this power, no very strong objection could exist to its assumption by the legislature; yet as they held unequal and unjust powers, which were the subject of complaint, there could be no peculiar propriety in their doing it rather than a meeting of the people themselves, or their delegates chosen for the purpose. But the assumption that the legislature alone can initiate proceedings for the formation of a constitution, and that none can be formed without their consent and preliminary action, seems to me to be founded in the most palpable usurpation. This, instead of keeping pace with the progress of the age, is retrograding some six hundred years into the dark ages—dark indeed for political liberty and the rights of the people—when British Kings undertook to *grant* to their subjects *charters* of their rights and liberties. One man *grant rights* to millions! *Liberties* depending on the *Charter* of a King! Do we derive our rights immediately from our Creator? Or do we depend on *rulers*, pretending to be ordained of God, to dole them out to us at their discretion, and according to their good pleasure? Will the American people, or the friends of free government any where, acknowledge the principle that the people can *only* make or amend their constitutions by the permission of their rulers?

But to recur to the great principles, opposition to which is implied in opposition to the people's constitution.

I. THE RIGHT OF THE PEOPLE TO GOVERN THEMSELVES, AND TO ESTABLISH THEIR OWN FORMS OF GOVERNMENT. This is declared to be a self-evident proposition, in the Declaration of Independence; is recognized as such in every constitution which has been formed under it; and has been acknowledged to be an unquestioned and fundamental principle of free government, by the most eminent statesmen, civilians and jurists of our country. This is now, for the first time, brought in question, by maintaining, that the people can make, alter, or amend their constitution *only* through the action of the legislature, and that too, whether the legislature has any constitutional power to act or not.

II. The doctrine of FREE SUFFRAGE is a *corollary* or rather branch of the last proposition. The right of self-government is inherent in *all men*, and not in a *part*; and should be secured to *every one*, unless he forfeit it by his own acts. Although this doctrine is not universally admitted, in its fullest extent, yet few heretofore have carried restrictions upon suffrage so far as to require *freehold* qualifications. This excludes more than *one-half* of the people from any participation in the government under which they live. And they, who are governed by laws in the making of which they have no voice, may be defined to be political slaves.

The revolutionary axiom that *"Representation and Taxation are inseparable,"* though sound and true in itself, has, I fear, had too much consideration given to it. By placing too great reliance upon it, we magnify the importance of property at the expense of moral and intellectual worth. No one holds the right of property more sacred than myself. But I am not willing to put them in the balance and make them preponderate against man, the noblest creation, and the express image of his Almighty Maker. The higher and more difficult duty of government is the protection of personal rights and the liberty of thinking, speaking and acting our own thoughts. Of what use is property if our persons are insecure? And why should not those who have personal rights to protect, have a voice in the government whose duty it is to protect them?

But the above axiom is as broad and extends as far as the warmest advocate of universal suffrage could desire. Who is there exempt from *taxation*? If such a person can be found, it must be one "who neither sweetens his tea nor salts his porridge."

What is there in the possession of land which confers superior intelligence and moral dignity?—What talismanic influence does it possess to inspire its owner with qualifications which depart the moment he parts with his land? May not the learned President of Brown University exercise the elective franchise as intelligibly as the most ignorant landholder in the State?

I well know that many who pretend to advocate free and representative governments are in favor of very restricted suffrage. In France only *one* person in *two hundred* is entitled to vote, and in parts of England the disproportion is quite as great. In our own country many desire to restrict rather than extend the elective franchise. But I can see no cause for doing it, and believe they mistake both the genius and the principles of democratic governments. The right of self-government belongs to *man* as *man*; and does not depend upon the accidents of birth, or of real or personal estate. And I have seen no reason to believe that power is more safe in the hands of the *rich* than the *poor*, or that the *former* are more honest than the *latter*. I should not, for the highest degree of perfection, look to either.

III. EQUALITY OF REPRESENTATION is a fundamental principle of our government, and without it we have no guaranty of its just, equal and beneficent operation. Unequal representation is but one grade better than no representation. Why should men residing in one town have greater weight than the same number of men in another? Let the advocates of the old charter and of the new convention, which give a disproportion of ten or twenty to one, answer the question.

I have now offered my views of the great principles which seem to be involved in the contest which has been carried on in Rhode Island, and which, theoretically at least, seem to have spread over the country, being maintained by those who advocate, and impugned by those who oppose the new constitution, wherever they may be. I have brought to the discussion no personal feeling, and I trust no bias or prejudice. My private friendships are altogether with the officers and members of the Charter party. I have endeavored, as far as practicable, to confine my remarks to the principles discussed. Their application to parties and individuals have been frankly made so far and no farther than was necessary for their explanation and elucidation. I have neither the means nor the inclination to judge of the various acts of the contending parties. Without, therefore, intending to impeach the motives of any one, or wishing to express any mere opinion, I cannot conceal, if I would, that the principles for which I have contended necessarily lead to the conclusion that the new constitution is the supreme law of the State, and of course that the success of the Charter government against it has been the triumph of *unauthorized power*, and of *military force*, over *political right and constitutional law*.

It is one of the beauties and excellencies of our admirable system of government that it provides for the redress of all grievances and the settlement of all controversies without a resort to physical force. And no one has less confidence in the justice of decisions by arms, or a greater abhorrence of an appeal to them, than myself. I yield to no one in respect for the civil authority, or (for reasons which will at once occur) in deference for judicial decisions. I cannot adequately express the depth of my regret and grief at the military movements which have occurred, and the demoralizing and distressing consequences of them. They certainly have added nothing to the happiness of the people or the reputation of the State. They seem to me to have been as needless and uncalled for as they were unwise and injurious.

The unhappy controversy might have easily been settled without bloodshed or a resort to arms. There were at least two ways obviously open for a civil decision; and assuming as I do that the great mass of both parties were honest, and actuated by good motives, it seems marvelous strange that the one or the other was not resorted to. Either would have produced a decision more satisfactory to honest minds than an appeal to the "God of Battles."

If either of the members of the United States Senate had resigned his seat, then the election of a successor by each of the Legislatures would have brought directly before the Senate the validity of the new constitution. Surely such a step would not have required a very high degree of patriotism in the resigning senator, when thereby he might avert civil war, especially if he, who doubtless would have been re-elected, had confidence in the unimpaired validity of the old charter.

But a better mode of settling the question would have been by an appeal to the highest judicial tribunal of our country. A mutual arrangement might have been made between the contending parties, by which a suit, putting directly in issue the validity of the new constitution, might have been commenced; carried in the most expeditious mode to the Supreme Court of the United States, and the earliest possible decision obtained. That the judgment would have been in favor of the new constitution I can entertain no doubt. But whatever it might have been, it would have commanded the acquiescence of the whole country, not excepting the people of Rhode Island.

I have learned from published statements, by both sides, that the friends of the new constitution were not only desirous of adopting this course, but willing to suspend all action under the new constitution until a decision could be had. This certainly was meeting their opponents more than half way and seeking an amicable adjustment at the extremest verge of honorable concession. If this proposition was made and rejected, whichever party may be in the right upon the constitutional question, the whole responsibility of the appeal to arms, of the loss of property, of blood and of life, and all the other physical and moral evils resulting from the military movements and government, rests upon the leaders of the *Charter party*. I hope their refusal to accede to this most conciliatory, just and reasonable proposal did not arise from an apprehension that the decision would be against them and a desire, by military operations, martial law and other arbitrary and oppressive measures, to overawe the people into the substitution of a less free and democratic constitution for the one heretofore adopted by them. . . .

I am Gentlemen, with respect, Your obedient serv't,
MARCUS MORTON

21

"The Canada Question," U.S. Magazine and Democratic Review, vol. 1, no. 2 (1838)

Locofoco energies surged during the Rhode Island affair, prompting waves of radicals to embrace hazy, emergent concepts of manifest destiny and heady visions of a continental republic. At the height of what may be called an "equal rights consensus," radicals exercised their greatest influence upon the Democratic Party, and in so doing, aided and abetted the Polk administration (1845–49). Although Martin Van Buren remained the darling of radicals everywhere, Southerners denied him the 1844 presidential nomination in return for his anti-Texas position. Proslavery expansionists found a great number of friends, however, in those locofocos who both harbored their own desires for a republican empire and were willing to overlook war and slavery to acquire it.

The radical vote in New York and Pennsylvania drove narrow margins for Polk, and a shift of merely a few thousand votes would have made Henry Clay president. Polk's illiberal policies and his patronage support for the locos' state-level enemies alienated most of the radicals, paving the way for the Martin Van Buren's Free Soil candidacy in 1848. The Free Soilers' belligerent agitation of the slavery issue did much to destroy the Whig Party and prepare the political and intellectual groundwork for what became the Republican Party over the next decade.

By 1860, a great number of important and influential locofocos joined ex-Whigs in support of Abraham Lincoln and the abolition of the worst monopoly in American life—Southern slavery. The hopeful, militant, revolutionary reformers who supported the Civil War, however, failed to defend the most important elements of classical liberal theory, and their failure buried their movement. Far too often, locofocos believed that state force wielded by a democratic republic could advance society's libertarian interests. They accepted the existence of powerful, imperial governments when they believed that the will of the people actually controlled the beast. During the Civil War, the beast became a virtually unstoppable juggernaut with unlimited funds, unlimited firepower, and an unlimited mandate to do the national will.

These generations of radicals bequeathed to their children a "second state" in American history—a bureaucratic, creepingly imperialistic corporate democracy. The second state grew fat on bloody shirts, protective tariffs, corporate charters, commercial imperialism using military resources, genocide against Native Americans, incessant corruption, machine politics, and any number of other modern horrors. As a result of their complicity in the growth of the second state, locofocos lost any coherent sense of their movement, and radical liberalism all but died in the United States around the turn of the century. As we will see in the conclusion, a "remnant" did indeed survive, providing the tools for later generations of radicals to fight their own battles for liberty against power.

* * *

Throughout the early 19th century, the rapidly developing movements that historians have called the "Market," "Industrial," and "Communications" Revolutions dramatically changed daily life and political institutions, often with violent and destructive, although decidedly generative, results. The Canadian rebellions of 1837–39 were just such an instance of radical, transformative upheaval. Following their locofoco, Jacksonian Democrat cousins in the United States, Canadian republicans protested the legally privileged land monopoly regime in Upper Canada, called the "Family Compact." Historian Jack Cahill describes the Family Compact as "a relatively small, tightly knit group of men that included the leading members of the administration—executive counselors, senior officials, and some members of the judiciary"—that dutifully relegated the choicest, largest lands in Canada to itself.

The Canadian Reformers adapted New York locofocoism to their own local context, aiming to sever the colonial relationship altogether, including existing ties to the history of the Old World. For their part, interested Americans wished to banish Britain from the continent once and for all, guaranteeing the future success of the American experiment in republicanism. Led primarily by reformer William Lyon MacKenzie, the Canadian rebel forces were disorganized and diminutive in 1837, likely dwarfed by the numbers of American filibusters prepared to pour across the border.

Pro-British forces quickly and easily quashed the uprising, dissolving any indigenous militant movements by early 1838. During the imperial counterrevolution, soldiers invaded and destroyed homes, burned property, and terrorized rebel sympathizers. Twenty-five thousand republicans, including Thomas Edison's parents, fled Canada and were welcomed by locofocos and Jacksonian Democrats in the United States. Although the Van Buren administration strictly adhered to a policy of international peace and goodwill, American "Patriot Hunters" invaded Canada only to face defeat at the Battle of the Windmill in November 1838.

Of those Americans captured, 157 were taken prisoner, 140 of the prisoners were court-martialed, 11 were then promptly executed, and 60 convicts were transported to Van Dieman's Land. Thirty prisoners aboard the *Marquis of Hastings* died in transit, their bodies cast overboard to be eaten by sharks and forgotten by time. The survivors were consigned to the brutal prison labor regime of British Australia. There they continued the intellectual and social cooperation that began in the loco networks of North America, their stories the stuff of legend among sympathizers.

Throughout the 1830s and 1840s, American locofocos and Canadian radicals exchanged ideas and fused their movements together in important ways too often overlooked in the history of classical liberalism. In the following article, John L. O'Sullivan's *Democratic Review* offers its interpretation of the Canadian rebellions and the historical stakes involved for all parties concerned.[44]

Civil war in the British North American Provinces! This event has come upon the people of the United States with something of apparent suddenness and surprise; and yet, to those who have attentively observed the progress of opinion in the two Canadas, the proceedings of the Assembly of Lower Canada, the discussions on the subject in the British Parliament, and the agitation of the Canadians themselves, the actual collision between the mother country and her colonies has been a matter neither strange nor unexpected. Indeed, if there be any thing remarkable in the fact, it has been, that, situated as the British Provinces are, in close contiguity with the United States, and exposed, as they thus have so long been, to the salutary contagion of democratic institutions and democratic principles, they have been content until this time to remain the subject colonies of Great Britain.

While, however, it has been apparent, of late especially, that change in the relations of Great Britain and her North American Provinces was at hand, it is right to observe that actual hostilities were precipitated by the violence of the royalist party in Lower Canada. The Canadians were pursuing *reform* in constitutional modes. Their House of Assembly had again and again presented the grievances of the colony to the notice of the mother country. They had refused, as they lawfully and constitutionally might, to make appropriations for the salaries of the officers of the Crown, unless the reforms, municipal and constitutional, which they deemed essential to the colony, were conceded by Great Britain. They were peacefully organizing themselves, as they had a right to do, for effective resistance,—forcible or not, as the case might require,—to any attempt of the Crown to coerce them into an abandonment of the objects of reform which the good of the colony demanded. They were discussing these objects in public meetings and in public journals, as they had full right to do. They were preparing to maintain their rights by force if assailed by force. But they did not strike the first blow. They did not explode the train of revolution. This was done by the persons and the party attached to the mother country, who assaulted individuals of an association called "Sons of Liberty," —mobbed the printing office, and destroyed the printing materials, of the principal journal of the Canadians, a paper conducted with great spirit and ability, the *Vindicator* arrested and imprisoned many of their number on charges of sedition or treason, and thus drove the Canadians to take up arms, and kindled the flame of civil war in the Province.

There can, we are inclined to think, be little doubt, that it was the *purpose* of the violent loyalists of Montreal, in those steps, to precipitate the outbreak, the near approach of which was self-evident,—in the belief that the rapidity of action, bravery, and discipline of the regular troops, would probably be able to crush at once the first insurrectionary gatherings, before the depth of the winter should open the communication across the St. Lawrence by means of the ice. Matters had, by this time, proceeded so far, the mutual feelings of the two parties had reached such a point of exasperation, and the organization of the Canadians, emanating from the central association of the "Sons of Liberty," in Montreal, was progressing so rapidly, that, in truth, the course adopted seemed the only one that afforded a chance of nipping the embryo revolution in the bud. By driving out into overt treason all the leaders,—whose designs were already scarce half concealed, while they pursued them so skilfully as to keep within the line of personal safety,—it was doubtless supposed that the result would either place their persons within the power of Government, as prisoners, or get rid of them as fugitive exiles.

The immediate crisis was brought on by measures of the British government, adopted in the aim to compel the Canadians to submit themselves to the will of the mother country, in respect of the questions of right raised by the House of Assembly of Lower Canada. To understand this point, however, and the merits of the controversy generally, it is necessary to go back to the former early history of the colony, and trace events down to the present day.

Canada, originally a French colony, it is known, came into the possession of Great Britain by conquest, being assured to her by treaty in 1763, just at the beginning of the controversy between her and the colonies now constituting the United States. The province contained at that time a small population, less than a hundred thousand souls. Being exclusively French, and having for many years been at war, more or less, with the old British Colonies in America, the Canadians did not, at the epoch of the Revolution, sympathize in feeling with the latter; and, unwilling, perhaps, to incur anew so soon the horrors of war, remained passively submissive to the authority of Great Britain,—governed, without institutions of their own, as a conquered colony.

But when the French revolution not long afterwards ensued,— an event, by which, from their French origin and language, the Canadians were likely to be more sensibly affected than by a revolution in the British colonies,—though on the same continent, the British government felt the necessity of anticipating any discontent in Canada by the voluntary concession of institutions, and by other measures which might conspire to secure their allegiance.

Accordingly, in 1791, an act of Parliament was introduced and passed by Mr. Pitt, which is commonly called the "Constitutional Act;" and by which the colony was divided into two governments, Upper and Lower Canada. The idea was, to organize each after the model of the constitution of Great Britain itself: answering to the King, a Governor,—for the Cabinet, an Executive Council,—for the House of Lords, a Legislative Council,—for the House of Commons, a Representative Assembly. The colony was divided, in order to have that part of it called Upper Canada peopled by emigrants from Great Britain, so as to balance the French colony of Lower Canada. . . .

It was objected that the theory of the "Constitutional Act" was radically defective, inasmuch as Canada had not, and no American colony could have, an hereditary aristocracy of sufficient number and weight to correspond to the peerage of Great Britain; and therefore the Legislative Council would either be nugatory, if it did not exercise its functions independently of the Assembly, or on the other hand, if it did, would become odious to the colony, as the mere instrument of the Crown, by whom its members were appointed.

Out of this inherent vice of the "Constitutional Act" a multitude of evils have flowed. As the Canadians grew in numbers and intelligence, they naturally desired to meliorate the condition of their country, in conformity with the spirit of the age. But the Legislative Council proved to be a perpetual drawback on all reform,—a standing conservator of every abuse.

Thus matters went on, until the war of 1812, between the United States and Great Britain, at which time, as before in 1774 and 1791, the government of Great Britain took pains, by politic conciliations, of one sort or another, to enlist the Canadas on their side, and against the natural ally of the Canadians.

Since that period, however, the discontents of the Canadians have been gradually growing to a head; until, in 1833, the supply bill, passed by the Assembly, was coupled with conditions of the reform of various gross abuses of the colonial administration; which the Government not consenting to reform, the supply bill was lost. This event was the beginning of the end; for the next year the House of Assembly set forth solemnly the grievances of the colony, in the celebrated "Ninety-two Resolutions." . . .

The Ministers were warned by the opposition that this was *the old question* between the thirteen colonies and the mother country; that things had been going on in the same train in Lower Canada now, as in Massachusetts Bay formerly; that Canada had precedents to refer to, and act by, in the history of the thirteen colonies, for any public contingency of her own case; that, *in general*, a populous and powerful colony could not be retained by Great Britain, without the consent of the colony itself; that especially the Canadas could not, being in the vicinity of the United States, imbued with democratic opinions by contact with a democratic people, and sure of being able to draw resources from, and find refuge in, the American republic; and that the Ministers had but one course to pursue,—to grant at once the reforms prayed for by the House of Assembly of Lower Canada. . . .

Our readers can now judge for themselves what are the merits of this great controversy between Great Britain and the Canadas. We say *the Canadas*, because, though Lower Canada has been foremost in the dispute, and though it was upon the resolutions of the Assembly of Lower Canada that parliament acted, and though the British party is much stronger in Upper than in

Lower Canada, yet the public question is the same in both, and the one must follow the fate of the other, so far as regards their ultimate relation to Great Britain. Our readers, we repeat, can judge for themselves, as to the merits of the question,—but there are two or three points in it, which we desire to present in relief from the others.

First, it must be admitted, that the Canadians have had ample cause of complaint; grievances enough to justify them in demanding redress, *and in persisting until they should obtain it.* The ministers of the Crown confessed this in the very resolutions they offered; Parliament confessed it; and it is a fact undeniable upon the record; proved by authentic state papers, of which we have given some idea in the preceding pages.

Secondly, those grievances were of a kind which seem to be of the very essence of a colonial government. The remoteness of an American colony from its European metropolis; the diverse and contrariant interest which of necessity grew up in such a case; the fact of being governed by officers, civil and military, sent from a foreign country—these, and a multitude of other considerations, which the colonial history of the United States renders familiar to all, tend to show that a colony on this continent, when it arrives at maturity, and acquires the feelings of self-respect belonging to maturity, *cannot* be satisfactorily governed, or well governed, by a Colonial Secretary in Europe. . . .

Thirdly, it is the right of every people, which possesses the inclination and physical power, to remodel and reform its institutions at will. This is the fundamental principle of the institutions of the United States, and cannot be denied or controverted, without impeachment of the wisdom and virtue of our fathers of the Revolution, nor without the renunciation of every thing which is peculiar or valuable in the constitutions, whether of the United States, or of the individual States. It is a right, which belongs *to every people;* and it belongs to a European colony in America, not less, but more, than to any other description of people. The Canadians have all these grounds of right to reform their government, and to institute a new one, in such form as may best promote their own happiness; and they have another, which is equally sacred, they are *a conquered people.* Great Britain acquired her dominion over them by *force;* they do not owe allegiance to her as an original colony of hers; and surely, if there be any case in which a people may of right throw off the authority of those who govern them, it is when these last are *foreign conquerors;* and which is the precise relation of Great Britain to the Canadas.

We do not propose to look at this question in any bearings which it may be presumed to have upon supposed interests of our own. Our aim has rather been to consider it as a question of political right. We look with solicitude, personally, to the issue of the event, because the triumph of the people will be a triumph of liberty—of democratic principle—of the right of self-government; but at all events, it must be the duty, and of course the determination and the endeavour, of the United States, to avoid any compromise of its neutrality, by taking sides either with the colonies against Great Britain, or of Great Britain against the colonies.

On a calm view of the whole subject, no one can, it appears to us, entertain the preposterous idea of the possibility of the continuance of the colonial relation between the Canadas and

Great Britain. It is utterly contrary to the spirit of the age. Thank God, the period of force, of armed violence, is passing away from the world, at least, from those countries enlightened and liberalized,—as England has been preeminently,—by the influence of the genius of Commerce. The idea of an armed struggle for dominion over a powerful colony, by England, at this day, is too absurd. A large proportion of the party now in the ascendency in that country, has long been utterly opposed to the whole system of foreign and colonial policy, maintained by England under the auspices of those anti-liberal principles which are now fast passing away in the mother country itself. A majority of the people of the Canadas desire to be free,—to govern themselves on the pure representative principles of which they have so glorious a model perpetually before their eyes; and they are so unreasonable as not to feel contented to go down to the sea shore to greet rulers sent to them from across an ocean three thousand miles wide! It is enough. They must become free whenever they will it.

The question is of no importance to us. There is nothing to be desired by us in the prospective annexation of the Canadas to our Union. That event may happen,—or those provinces may maintain a friendly independence. We have no material objection to the English neighbourhood. Any serious disturbance of friendly relations between the two commercial sister countries, Great Britain and our Union, is an event not less impossible, now, or hereafter, than it would be to roll back the lapse of time, and resuscitate the passed and buried centuries. Nor is there any thing to be either desired or deprecated in the proximity of a kindred republic on the banks of the St. Lawrence. It could not influence, in the slightest degree, either our safety or prosperity. Nor would there be any benefit to them in a participation in our federal union,—at least no greater benefit than would attend a sovereign independence, provided they should follow, which would doubtless be the case, our great principles of republican freedom at home, and peaceful commerce abroad.

And yet we are not haunted with that idea, which we hear so frequently expressed, of "the danger of extending our already overgrown territorial limits." This is one of those false ideas which has been bequeathed to us by the Past,—that Past which was terminated when the American experiment first dawned upon the world as the commencement of a new era. That idea is evidently correlative to the one of strong central governmental action. A strong central government cannot, indeed, maintain the cohesion of extended territories, of diversified peculiar interests, beyond certain limits. They follow the mathematical law of all radiating forces—the strength of their action diminishes in inverse proportion to the square of the distance; beyond a certain circular limit it must be inoperative, except by such convulsive effort as must derange and disorganize the whole system. Such a territorial dominion, is then "overgrown" and unmanageable. But those terms can have no proper applicability to a federal republican system, on the principle of diffusion of power on which ours is based. The peculiar characteristic of our system,—the distinctive evidence of its divine origin (that is to say, its foundation on those original principles of natural right and truth, implanted by the Creator, as the first moral elements of human nature),—is, that it may, if its theory is maintained pure in practice, be extended, with equal safety and efficiency, over any indefinite number of millions of population and territory. In such a federative system,—in which every individual portion is left free to its own self-government, and to the cultivation of its own peculiar interests, with the sole restriction, of respect for the equal rights of other portions, and under the protection of a federal union, of strictly defined powers, to give some degree of uniform national organization to the whole mass, in its relations with foreign powers,—every part has an equal interest in the maintainance of the system, and its great principles. The vitality is not forcibly propelled from the centre to the extremities, but is diffused equally throughout all the parts; and it is only necessary for the latter to contribute a sufficient degree of the vital energy *towards* the centre to keep alive the general unity of the national body. Such a system is, from its nature,—if its great principles are only preserved sound and pure,—as applicable on a large scale as on a small one; and we can see no reason why, at some future day, our "experiment" should not be in successful operation over the whole North American continent, from the isthmus to the pole. . . .

In discussing freely, therefore, the question of the relations between the Canadas and the mother country, we shall not be suspected of a hankering after an extension of our own territory. We look upon the subject only in the light of general principles,—and may, without impropriety, and without violating the spirit of perfect neutrality, express ourselves with entire freedom upon it. No American, sincerely and understandingly imbued with American principles, can refrain from feeling a deep sympathy in a cause so closely analogous with that of our own Revolution;—and feeling, there can exist no consideration to check the free expression of it. At the same time, we hold all actual participation in the contest, whether by individuals or bodies of men, to be highly improper, and equally a violation of our national neutrality (which the individual citizen is as much bound to hold sacred as the organized government) and inconsistent with a philosophical view of the principles involved. If the Canadian *people* will to be free from their dependence on a foreign country, they have but to arise in their strength of mass and say so;—they need no assistance of money or volunteers from us. If it is not the will of the *people*, or if that will is not sufficiently strong to carry them through the ordeal of revolution,—we ought not yet to desire it. . . . If freedom is the best of national blessings, if self-government is the first of national rights, and if the "fostering protection" of a "paternal government" is in reality the worst of national evils—in a word, if all our American ideas and feelings, so ardently cherished and proudly maintained, are not worse than a delusion and a mockery—then are we bound to sympathize with the cause of the Canadian rebellion, with the most earnest hope that success may, with as little effusion of blood as possible—Why should it flow!—crown it as a Revolution. . . . The end is at hand; and it would far better become the noble nation which would itself be the first to dare and sacrifice all in such a struggle, to resign at once, with magnanimity and mercy, an unnatural dominion which it will cost seas of human blood to attempt to retain. In fact, we look with not less deep interest to the news from England, than to the events of the contest in the Provinces. May she be true to her own best interests and highest glory!

22

Levi Slamm, "Oregon Territory" and "The Oregon Question," Daily Plebeian, June 1, 1843, and April 11, 1844

As the British Empire consolidated its grasp on territory across the globe, "Young American" republican nationalists like New York's Levi Slamm countered the Anglo establishment at every turn. Slamm supported the Irish nationalist movement, embraced Canadian independence (and eventual union with the United States), supported the American annexation of Texas, and advocated for American claims to the full Oregon territory in the Pacific Northwest.

To Slamm and the readers of his New York newspaper, the *Daily Plebeian*, the American republican project seemed qualitatively different from the British system of corporate aristocracy, and the future appeared uncertain at best. British territories, they observed, were won through rapine and conquest, death, destruction, and subjugation; whereas the Young Americans naively believed that the American republic expanded only through the voluntary application of territories or sister nations for statehood. They relegated the long, transatlantic history of genocide against Native Americans and massive forced migrations from Africa through the slave trade to the realm of natural history. These were events from the days before man rediscovered his ancient liberties and declared his independence from arbitrary rulers.

Slamm and his cohort believed that the United States thus represented a revolutionary break not simply with Great Britain, but with history itself. The Revolution of 1776 opened historical space for republicans in all countries to revolt against their aristocratic populations and arrayed people everywhere in a new system of ideological class identities. As democratic and republican ideas spread across the globe and republican nations entrenched themselves in the global political order, man's libertarian destiny would inevitably *manifest* itself.

Levi Slamm died in 1862, a year in which the United States appeared damaged perhaps beyond repair.

Locofoco expansionists from Slamm's era hoped that territorial acquisitions would bolster long-term global support for liberty against power. Most of them never seriously expected that annexations would, in the end, provoke disunion, civil war, and an unprecedented amount of centralization, militarization, and the con-solidation of a veritable American empire. In the follow-ing articles, Levi Slamm and his *Daily Plebeian* address the political and historical significance involved in "the Oregon question."[45]

"Oregon Territory," *Daily Plebeian*, June 9, 1843

Considerable excitement seems, at this time, to prevail throughout the whole western sections of our country, relative to a proposed immediate occupation of the Oregon Territory by emigrants from the United States. An expedition, consisting of five hundred per-sons, was to leave Jackson county, Mo., on the 20th of last month, for that remote region, to lay the foundation there of an American settlement. It has also been determined, by those who are deeply interested on the subject, to hold a Convention at Cincinnati, on the 3d, 4th and 5th days of July next, for the purpose of urging upon Congress the necessity of taking immediate possession of the territory. It will be proposed to base the action of the Conven-tion on Mr. Munroe's declaration of 1823—"That the American continents are not to be considered subject to colonization by any European powers; and that we should consider any attempt on their part to extend their systems to any portion of this hemi-sphere, as dangerous to our peace and safety."

The late outrageous robbery perpetrated by the British Government, in seizing upon the Sandwich Islands, should warn us against the encroachments which she meditates upon our own soil. Her lust of dominion is unbounded. Already it is truly said— "The morning drum-beat, rolling with the rising sun, and circling with the hours, girdles the earth with one continuous strain of the martial music of Old England." It was Daniel Webster who uttered this apostrophe to her power; and this same Daniel Webster has since given up to her rapacity a large portion of territory, of right belonging to the State of Maine—a territory which Lord Brougham has recently admitted that England had not the least shadow of just claim to. Her ministers are now intriguing for the purchase of California; and that country will, in all probability, be the next one seized upon by her hired cut-throats. She is intrenching herself in strong holds on our Northern and Southern borders to become complete mistress of the Pacific, so that, when she ultimately seizes upon the Oregon, her dominion there may at once be secure and her power permanently established. It is, perhaps, not much to be regretted that the late Treaty with Great Britain did not settle the line of boundary in that quarter. With such a statesman as Daniel Webster to conduct the negotiations, on the part of this country, our clear title to that territory would, most probably, have been surrendered, like that of Maine, to the arrogant and, unjust demands of England.

We hope that our Government will see the necessity of its speedy action on this question; and that, in order to secure our undoubted right of possession in the Oregon Territory, measures will be taken for its armed occupation before the great Brigand of the World pollutes our soil by planting upon it the freebooters standard of Great Britain.

"The Oregon Question," *Daily Plebeian*, April 11, 1844

The Oregon dispute promises to be one of the most vexed subjects that we have had to settle with Great Britain[,] perhaps not less tangled than was the North East boundary question. Much of this difficulty, we believe arises from the temporizing policy hitherto observed on our part, while Great Britain, by the possession she has so long quietly maintained there, now begins to look upon the whole country as her own. This is not as many suppose, a new question just started by some of the fiery spirits of the west. More than fifteen years ago, it attracted the attention of Congress, as likely to produce serious trouble for us, unless we then asserted our rights. Among those who entertained such views, was the Hon. I. R. Ingersoll, of this city, then a member of Congress from this State. On looking back to the congressional proceedings, we find that on the 7th of January, 1829, more than fifteen years ago, he moved in Congress to extend the laws of the United States over the territory, and followed up his proposition by a speech, from which we extract the following, as then published in the debates. Whatever difference of opinion there may be among our citizens as to the Oregon, the sentiments advanced then by Mr. Ingersoll, have the merit at least of coming from one who looked at the subject free from any sectional bias, and before it had in any way been mixed up in the politics of the day. His proposition did not obtain a majority of the House—the let alone policy prevailed, and has since continued, till now we find the difficulty one of the most embarrassing that we have in our foreign relations.

Mr. Ingersoll said, "the convention (with Great Britain) so often alluded to, stipulated that the country west of the Rocky Mountains, shall remain "free and open" to the citizens and subjects of the two contracting parties, during the continuance of the compact: and neither can recede, without giving twelve months notice to the other. The erection of a territorial government, therefore, and granting portions of the soil as a bounty to settlers, would be an exclusive occupancy on our part in the teeth of the treaty. But while he was restrained from going that length, satisfied as he was, that the title of the country was with us, he was not only willing, but anxious that some decisive act should be done on our part, which should indicate our determination not to surrender one particle of our claim—leaving the question of territorial government to be settled hereafter, when the existing convention would not be in our way. The British have erected and now maintain forts for the protection of their traders and hunters; they have gone further than this—they have covered the whole territory with their criminal and civil jurisdiction; and those who resort to it, are amenable to the courts of Canada and all violations of their laws. With this act of the British Parliament before me, (said Mr. I.) I cannot for one, refuse to send our laws along with our citizens, if they choose to go there, any more than I would to protect them by the erection of a fort. It was to meet the British legislation in all its bearings that he had offered the amendment; and he sincerely urged upon us hereafter, that we have at this day waived any of our rights, by silently acquiescing in the foreign jurisdiction now exercised there, or by refusing to spread our flag and our laws co-extensive with our rightful claims. . . .

Surely, if the "free and open" intercourse with that territory guarantied by the convention to the British, in common with ourselves, cannot be made secure to them, without carrying their laws along with their hunting expeditions, we have had abundant evidence in the repeated murders of our hunters beyond the mountains, that our citizens require at our hands a corresponding protection. Besides, Great Britain is estopped by her own acts from complaining of our going thus far; more than this he did not ask; but any thing less, would be injustice to ourselves.

Mr. I. said he was free to confess he had never formed a very flattering picture of the north-west coast of our continent—that is, of its attractions for an agricultural people. He preferred to see it remain a hunting ground, from which our fur traders can draw some of the treasures that are now monopolized by the Hudson Bay Co., rather than see it erected into a sovereign State. But whatever our preferences may be in this respect, it was our duty to protect our citizens whose enterprise may lead them there, and it was no less our interest to secure the harbor which the mouth of the Oregon offers to our hardy navigators who frequent the coast. He was not anxious to hasten the growth of a new State beyond the Rocky Mountains, for he was aware it would have but few tics, aside from its weakness, to bind it to this side of the continent. Its trade, if the country should ever become settled by a permanent agricultural population, as it must be, before it can grow into a State, would not probably cross the mountains to come to us, but would naturally seek the waters of the Pacific. For all commercial purposes, India, and the islands of the South Seas, would be to a thriving population there, what Europe and the Atlantic islands are to us. But although he entertained these opinions, still, when the question was put—and turn it as you may, it will come to this, whether we shall surrender this vast territory into the hands of the British, or maintain our own jurisdiction there, he was ready to give a positive and decisive answer. It should not, with his consent, go into the hands of a foreign power.

That country once annexed to Canada, with its formidable Indian tribes in the train of the agents of the Hudson's Bay Company, would be to our advancing frontiers, what Canada has been in all our Indian wars. Sir, we are not without experience on this subject. The history of our western settlements gives us ample evidence of Indian aggressions, stimulated by the influence of white men, within the bounds of Canada. We have felt this hidden influence in all our frontier contests, from the days of the Revolution, down to the declaration of the late war with England, or rather to the battle of Tippecanoe, which shortly preceded it. Nor have we since ceased to feel its effects; you felt it to the quick, on the frontiers throughout the war with England, and you feel it now. Yes, in the very territory about which we are told not to legislate, our citizens are shot down by Indians, armed with British rifles. And with these facts staring us in the face, are we to hold back, and hesitate, lest we give offence to the British government, in deciding to protect our own citizens by the establishment of a fort, or the extension of our laws into this territory? Let it not be said that the soil of the country is not sufficiently inviting to induce the British to occupy it.

To say nothing of the immense fur trade derived from it, the harbor at the mouth of the Oregon, commanding the upper country, convenient in its position in reference to India, the Sandwich Islands, and the new nations bounding on the west coast of our continent, presented sufficient attractions for the colonial grasp of Great Britain. . . . He verily believed, that not 12 months would elapse after we should abandon our claim to this position, before the mouth of that river would be controlled by the guns of a fortress, manned by our great commercial rival. Is it asked what reasons we have to suppose this? The answer will be found in the policy of that nation, which is to plant a colony from her super abundant population, wherever she can penetrate with a fleet. This policy is identified with the immense power which she wields; and which will be always pushed to its farthest limits. Small in territory at home, her extensive possessions abroad, are the towers of her strength in every part of the world. No spot however sterile, is lost sight of, if it can furnish new facilities to her commerce. She will fortify, at the expense of millions, a rock in the ocean, if it can be made a safe resting place for the merchantmen or a convenient rendezvous for her ships of war.

23

"Annexation of Texas" and Related Articles, Daily Plebeian *(1843–44)*

As of 1843, the "lone star" Republic of Texas counted itself among the family of independent nations. Although the Mexican government continued efforts to reintegrate the rebellious territory, it was clear to most observers that Mexico could not reconquer Texas without Herculean efforts. As such, Texas's relatively continuous attempt to enter the American union appeared more fruitful than ever before. Whereas the Democratic Party took a general turn toward expansionary hawkishness in the early 1840s, a sizable contingent of Jacksonians consistently opposed the territorial spread of slavery and Southern planter aristocracy.

In his New York newspaper, the *Daily Plebeian*, editor Levi Slamm allowed both sides of "the Texas Question" to voice their opinions.[46] Although he officially with-held judgment on the matter, Slamm plainly favored the annexation of Texas as strongly as he favored the "reoccupation" of the full Oregon Territory. Slamm devoted most of his Texas-related editorial space to the pro-annexation side, which raised numerous anti-slavery voices against him from his readership. Anti-expansionist Democrats too made their voices heard on Slamm's pages. Mere months before the 1844 nominating conventions, both Henry Clay and Martin Van Buren proclaimed themselves opposed to annexing Texas on the grounds that it would disturb international peace and domestic political relations between the sections. Slamm praised his chieftain's positioning, although the stance made it impossible for the former president to win the support of Southern delegates.

The convention chose James K. Polk as its nominee, and Slamm's New York provided the swing votes elevating Polk to the White House. Lame-duck President John Tyler saw Polk's election as a mandate for Texas and immediately sought a treaty, which soon passed. As Polk entered office, Texans prepared themselves to become the newest American citizens. With Texas came war on Mexico. The spoils of war rotted the Second Party System, polluted relations between the United States and its southern neighbors, and condemned Americans to sectional conflicts that were only resolved with an even more terrible war. Levi Slamm died in 1862, and we can only wonder whether he ever seriously repented for the damage caused by a generation that so mixed the ideas of democratic-republicanism and territorial expansionism.

"Annexation of Texas," November 21, 1843

We admit into our columns to-day two communications, from different sources, on the subject of the contemplated annexation of Texas to the Union. This question has of late become a frequent topic of discussion, and must be considered as one of the most serious importance. The project of the annexation is urged on the ground that there is a negotiation on foot for the transfer of that territory to Great Britain. We do not wish to be understood as endorsing the views of our correspondents in relation to the matter. It is our intention to take up this matter shortly and give our opinions at length as to the merits of the proposition. Much yet remains to be said on the subject.

"For the Plebeian—The Annexation of Texas"

[It] is now distinctly before the people, and as a question deeply affecting the future interest of the United States, it is receiving, though somewhat tardily, the attention of the press. There is, however, one peculiarity in the mode of handling it which deserves notice. In settling the terms on which the annexation would be allowed, Texas is always spoken of as if she would of course accept any conditions and be thankful. They who reason in this way, forget their own Saxon blood flows in its moat unconquerable energy in Texan veins. Those who fought the battle of San Jacinto, were the sons of those who woke the thunders of

Bunker Hill, and penned the Declaration of Independence. The Republic of Texas is the daughter of the Republic of the United States, and the child will no more submit to undue control than did the sire. With devout and filial love, Texas boasts that she owes her birth, her progress, the means of her independence, to the United States, and entreats that in policy and government, as in blood, principles and affection they may remain one. In all her legislative and diplomatic proceedings she has carefully avoided every act which might put obstacles to this cherished view.

At first to her prayers for admission, it was objected that she was still a colony of Mexico, and it would interfere with the amicable relations of the two governments, if the United States should become a party to and a gainer by the dismemberment of a friendly nation. This was indeed a just and reasonable argument, but it is now outlawed. Texas is independent, is recognized as such by the greatest powers of Europe and by the United States—and Mexico herself tacitly admits it would cost too much to reconquer her. Whether fairly or not Texas has taken the position to make her own bargains. The next objection was, that Texas was in debt and would be an incumbrance to the Union. It is now conceded that her ample domain is sufficient to pay her own debts, and instead of incumbrance would ultimately bring vast wealth into the general treasury. To refuse that rich territory for such a reason would be exactly like an individual refusing the gift of an estate worth an hundred thousand dollars, because there was a mortgage on it for one thousand.

The great—the specious objection to Texas, however, is the slavery question, and on this quicksand it is much to be feared the best interests of the Union will be wrecked. Narrow minded and cunning politicians have managed to present this subject in an unjust and false view. They talk as if a new race of slaves had been created, and were to be perpetuated in Texas, instead of their being in truth their own colored population, ruled by their own citizens according to the Constitution of the United States, upon a soil and in a region that by their own construction, should belong to the slave holding portion of the Union. Texas has no foreign slaves more than Louisiana, and to receive her into the Union just as she stands, is only to receive back a portion of our citizens who have been tempted by a fertile soil to move a little farther into the wilderness, and who took with them the slave property guaranteed them by the laws of the United States. To abolish slavery at once in Texas, would not be consented to, as it would place her in antagonism with the Southern States, and would break up with too rude a shock her existing social relations. It is nonsense to say that England would insist upon the abolition of slavery—England would do no such thing. England never lost an inch of dominion from scruples of conscience, and never will. Her morals are as wide and as capable of extension as her Indian empire. When Texas came to her for aid and recognition, she might possibly (and only possibly) have made the abolition of slavery the price of her favors, but she saw how useful Texas will be, and she took especial care not to alienate her by pressing distasteful conditions. After Texas was recognized, and would know how to answer to please herself, England began to incite the anti-slavery party in the United States to press their views in the most absolute manner. Nothing could be better managed. Although

England has avoided giving offence to Texas, yet she has made an interesting demonstration of her philanthrophy, and without any trouble or expense to herself, set the Northern States to fight her battles. By rejecting Texas we give to England a country on our Southern frontier equivalent to Canada on the Northern, from which she can at pleasure pour invasion and distress into the border States. It should be remembered that Texas, if admitted to the Union, brings as many advantages as she gains, and that it will be equally ungenerous and impolitic to insist upon what she will inevitably refuse[:] the instant abolition of slavery.

Antonia

"For the Plebeian—Annexation of Texas"

This subject is becoming of daily importance, and the impression is rapidly gaining ground that it will form a very important portion of the forthcoming message of President Tyler. It is a question calculated to create more or less excitement, as it will become a mere party or sectional subject or a great national one. That it ought to be looked upon and discussed in the latter point of view, no friend of his country will for a moment doubt. Party may seize hold of it and endeavor to distort and use it for their own base purposes, and seek to play upon the weaker judgments of the people by raising dire alarms about the extension of slavery.

There may be many who would [oppose] it, honestly perhaps, on these grounds alone, looking upon any movement or proposition calculated to extend or increase the slave population of the Union detrimental to our interests, and not in harmony with the philanthropic spirit of the age. But such should recollect that the slave population is not increased by the annexation of Texas. The institution already exists there, it forms a part and parcel of her government, and the mere transfer from an independent state to one of the sovereign states of this Union, is neither calculated to increase or diminish the number of slaves. If it is to have any effect at all, will it not rather tend to diminish the number of slave States than otherwise? Will it not prove an easy and natural outlet for the slave population of Maryland, North Carolina, Virginia, Kentucky, &c., &c.? Looks upon in this light, it become a question which even the sensitive philanthropists of the present age, including the Hon. John Quincy Adams, may view with a favorable eye.

But there are higher questions involved in this subject—questions of national policy, involving power and right, and possibly peace or war.

From late developments, it is almost certain that a transfer of all that vast and fertile country to the all grasping power of Great Britain is in contemplation—that negotiations are already on foot between British authorities and the Mexican government, who claim the territory, and Gen. Houston, President of Texas; and for certain considerations it is said the latter consents to the transfer. Allow Great Britain to get possession, in what condition are the United States? With her Canadian possessions stretching along our whole northern frontier, pressing down upon us through the Oregon on the West, Texas filled with British vagrants on the South, and her West India possession filled with armed soldiers while in their harbors float a large portion of the British navy, ready at a moment's warning to pounce upon us—thus hemmed in on every side, we shall virtually become subjects of Her Britannic Majesty Queen Victoria.

Texas of right belongs to us. Originally explored and taken possession of by French adventurers, under the protection of the French flag—held with other portions of the South Western Territory by the government of France, she undoubtedly had priority of right and had as undoubted a claim to that section of country as she had to the Territory of Louisiana, when she ceded the latter to the United States. Every consideration seems to favor the project of annexation. The institutions of Texas are already established, and in full operation under a Republican Constitution. Her population is essentially American—bone of our bone, flesh of our flesh—and without doubt a vast majority of her people look to this Union for protection from external foes as well as from traitors within. Shall the stars and stripes wave over this beautiful and fertile region, an emblem of power, proving a shield to her just rights and liberties, and bidding defiance to all foreign aggressors; or shall the British Lion quietly take possession and add this to other trophies of greatness and guilt? Texas relinquished to Great Britain, and war—war with all its horrors is inevitable. Bring it, with the Oregon Territory, into the Union, and we but take possession of our own, add to our means of wealth and happiness, and preserve the peace of the country.

T.

"For the Plebeian—Texas," November 28, 1843

The editor of the Plebeian is respectfully required, by an old Democrat, to take notice that we ask for no more territory. We have too much already. It was the besetting sin of Napoleon that he would go out of the ancient limits of France. What did he provoke? The world in arms. We do not want Texas. We ask not for the annexation of a State of Gamblers. Let them remain as they are, half-way between civilization and brutality. The moment you admit Texas, that moment you admit the most worthless population in Christendom to a participation of the privileges of freemen. Did you observe, sir, with what contumely the braggart Houston treated one of our own sons—I mean the Commodore Moore— did you see that; and are you possessed of stuff to commend, after that, any thing that is recommended by that Kentucky outcast? If he recommends the annexation of Texas, I for one object. He is too great a scoundrel to treat with upon honorable principles.

Besides all this, you seem to have a sort of latent leaning towards Texas; and, if I do not mistake the tone of your paper, you would be rejoiced to receive her with an open embrace. Beware, sir! The seeds of destruction to our excellent Republic are in that embrace.

It is hinted by one of your correspondents that Texas will pass into the hands of the petticoat monarch of Britain. Let it. Who cares a pin? Let her surround us if she chooses. There is more clear grit in the United States of America than would suffice to conquer twenty British empires. We can out-shoot, out-fight, out-lick and out-kick anything living. Your correspondent must not think to frighten us in this matter. Let England take all the world—all the States of this Union besides our own, "Empire State," and we ask no odds of her. We are equal to anything living: and, therefore, what matters it to us that we are surrounded by other powers? Let Texas go to Great Britain if she pleases. She has a right to be a slave in her own way.

Junius

Levi Slamm, "The Annexation of Texas—Its Effects upon Slavery," June 25, 1844

The existence of the institution of Slavery in our Confederacy of States is an acknowledged evil, or admitted to be so, not only by a large majority of the people of those States in which Slavery is abolished, but by a majority of the people of those States in which it still exists. But whatever may be its evil it is an institution over which the General Government has no control. The people of the non-slaveholding States are as much responsible for its existence as the people in which it is yet tolerated. Slavery is a State institution and not an institution of the General Government. A continuance of our Union is of all things the most desirable, and of course a dismemberment, of all things the most to be dreaded.

Previous to the year 1808 the increase of Slavery was from two sources—importation and the natural increase of those born among us. But by a wise and humane provision in the Constitution of the United States the importation of slaves was prohibited after the year 1808; and in 1820, Congress declared the Slave Trade to be piracy and punished with death.

Suppose we take it for granted that Texas is to be admitted into the Union, and that slavery is not prohibited, what will be its effect upon the increase of the slave population and the hope of the ultimate extinction of slavery in the Union? . . . Indeed, we consider the most effectual method of eventually getting rid of the institution of slavery would be the annexation of Texas. We believe that the admission of Texas without any limitations or restrictions respecting the institution of slavery would do more towards accomplishing the desirable object of the final extinction of African slavery in the United States than all the Colonization or Abolition Societies ever have or ever will accomplish. We believe with Senator Walker that slavery would, if Texas should be annexed, soon cease to exist in some of the more northern slaveholding States. The acquisition of Louisiana and Florida has been the means of diminishing the number of slaves in some of the more northern slave States. Mississippi and Alabama are States formed out of territory acquired by the purchase of Louisiana, and now have a large slave population, while the number of slaves in Delaware and Maryland, Kentucky, and Virginia, more than half a million of slaves. If Texas should be annexed, the extinction of slavery in these States is certain. . . .

The result is, that no man who will reflect for a moment will object to annexation of account of slavery. We firmly believe that if Texas should become a dependency of England, and slavery not tolerated there; or even if it should be annexed to the Union as a free state, slavery in the United States would be perpetuated, or cease only by revolution. The area of the states in which slavery now exists, is sufficient to maintain a population of at least 100,000. And surround this slave territory with free States— confine slavery in the heart of the Union, and what prospect is there for its extinction? Admit Texas as a slave territory, and the philanthropist may hope, with some prospect at least, that the curse of slavery may disappear, not only from the Union, but from the continent of North America. At all events, admit Texas as a slave territory, and you open a door, through which, in time, perhaps not far distant, the African race will make its exit, and become incorporated with the various colored races that inhabit Mexico, Central and North America.

If we had no other reason to offer for desiring the admission of Texas but the probable extinction of slavery, that would be sufficient. The admission of Texas we consider the first step that will finally and peaceably lead to the freedom of the African race in the United States. Slavery cannot be abolished, and the slaves remain among us and be happy. All experience, all history proves it. The very prejudices, if you please, of the North, are against it— prejudices that do not exist among the different races that inhabit Mexico and South America.

Lois Waisbrooker, "The Sex Question and the Money Power: How Shall This Power Be Made to Serve Instead of Ruling Us?"

Lois Waisbrooker was born during modern America's fledgling days (1826). She came of age in the Jacksonian and Civil War eras; her career and influence flourished during Reconstruction, the Gilded Age, and the Progressive era. As an independent individualist-feminist, Waisbrooker lectured and wrote fiction and nonfiction for decades. She published her first novel in 1871 and her final "scientific" book in 1907. Waisbrooker was the archetypical "thick" libertarian: she followed her political principles through to anarchism; her radical

365

individualism led her to feminism; and her deep anti-clericalism inspired her conversion to spiritualism and her attendant activities as a spirit medium.

In many ways, Americans throughout the 19th century experienced an endless series of personal existential crises. Adrift in a swiftly changing world, Americans struggled to find purpose and meaning for themselves. Those of a radical and libertarian temperament often followed their inclinations as far as they might go. To individuals like Lois Waisbrooker, spirit mediumship and feminism offered piercing and magnetic explanations for why the world was the way it was. What's more, they offered radical women opportunities to express themselves as unlimited individuals with existential purpose of their own making.

In her 1873 lecture, "The Sex Question and the Money Power," Waisbrooker proposes to explain the connections between the American economic system and feminism. She begins by noting the abject failure of individualists to capture the course of history from those who wield economic and political power. She argues that those people—especially poor men—who have felt themselves ground under the wheels of the powerful do not need to wield power themselves. In fact, oppressed men need feminism. Ideas move history, she believed, and the feminist idea could turn money "from master to servant." If men, especially, learned to temper their masculinity with a healthy, equal regard for femininity, humanity could combine in its natural strength to break history's fetters, "though it rock the nations from centre to circumference."[47]

In a world abounding with patriarchy and its grisly fruits, Waisbrooker argued that feminism offered a natural and necessary balance to social affairs. Most interestingly, she uses this portion of her lecture to combine Victorian science (including Darwinism, electromagnetism, and phrenology) with Christian eschatology, feminist theory, and even spirit mediumship. If only her audience could have channeled the same spirits—communed with "the wise ones of the ages"—they would also see the truth of her message.

She believed feminism was quite literally written in the laws of nature, and fighting for the unnatural maintenance of patriarchy was akin to denying evolution, forcing water to flow uphill, or making larger celestial bodies orbit smaller ones. Waisbrooker argues that the sexual recombination of individual traits from the male and the female is a simple fact of nature. Men need the influence of the feminine and vice versa. Although she and her fellow early Darwinists understood evolution through natural selection, they failed to grasp the mechanism through which offspring inherited parents' traits. Waisbrooker expresses the belief that "mental energies" formed through the electrical processes in the parents' brains and bodies combine during copulation. The same sorts of electrical forces that allowed women like Waisbrooker to channel spirits connected the principles of individualist-feminism and the act of sex, leveling the masculine and feminine both to the level of natural forces. The propagation of the species depended on pacific, equitable relationships between men and women, right down to the electrical forces that bind us all together with the material world. In her concluding remarks, Waisbrooker implored her audience to action: "Woman's freedom is the world's redemption." Too few listened, however, and although she remained active and influential in radical circles into the early 20th century, she died penniless and sick in a world still thoroughly controlled by patriarchal ideals.

Money or its equivalent rules . . . where it should, in justice, serve. In vain the benevolent man regrets this state of things; in vain the tears of the widow or the cries of the orphan. The plea of suffering is as vain under the shadow of the tall steeple as it is in the by-ways of degradation, for this power pervades every avenue of human life.

The head, the heart, the hands and the feet of the people are in its toils and forced to do its bidding.

We may assert our allegiance to humanity, to the divinity of love, to the guidance of wisdom; but hunger and cold are potent weapons and used as relentlessly as ever bigot drove the stake or piled the fagots.

We have failed, utterly failed, more than failed, in attempting to deal with the effects of this tyrannical control—have failed in our every effort to dethrone this selfish deity. But because we have thus failed shall we cease to struggle? Shall we give up in despair and say that there is no hope?

Shall we, with folded hands and benumbed brains, yield the conflict to the quiet of a grinding death? Shall we permit the heart's best blood to congeal a frozen river over which the triumphal car of this demon power shall pass without even a jar?

Shall we? Your response is: "No—a thousand times, no."

But what next? What new thing shall be tried; what new movement made? It must be something new, for there is no hope of the old. It has been tried and failed; "weighed in the balance and found wanting;" has been written against all its methods. Yes, we must have something new; but what shall it be?

Religion is powerless; Politics "a poison upas" (to use the language of one who was himself a politician, when arguing against woman's entering this field); Philanthrophy can only palliate the sorrows of the living and help to bury the dead; Morality is but a gilded name to attract wealth; and the fear or the love of God, whither have they fled?

The Alcoholic demon stalks through the land gathering in his harvest of victims and each or all of the above combined are powerless to stay its march.

Mother-love agonizes and father-hearts groan in smothered anguish, but still sons continue to stagger into drunkards' graves. Wives and children are made desolate by myriads, while this fiery demon sucks away the life blood of husbands and fathers. He fires the heart of the otherwise peaceful man with feelings of dire revenge, till red-handed Murder shrieks in the midnight air, and still there is none to rescue.

None can stay the havoc of his tread, for the power of Wealth sustains him; the money king has set his seal upon him, demon though he be, and, riding over your tall steeples, he intercepts your prayers to heaven or consumes them in the blue blaze of alcoholic fire.

Governments fail to enact just laws, or, having enacted, fail to execute, for the hand of the money king is upon the mouths of the witnesses; he bribes the jurors, sways the judge, fees the lawyers against the truth, and even buys the lawmakers themselves.

Invention fails, for the telegraph, the railroad and all the grand achievements of mechanical art, the result of brain-work, intended to lessen the labor of the poor while bringing them greater returns—these, all these, have been confiscated to this money king and are being used to fill the coffers of the rich. The poor gain nothing; their children and themselves are hopeless, grow more so each succeeding year, while the children of the rich ruin themselves and all with whom they come in contact, wherever Wealth can corrupt or Virtue be driven to the wall; and the 60 thousand of the so-called ministers of the eternal God bring us no relief.

At the command of this tyrant father forgets his home or remembers it only as a place to board and lodge. He buries himself in his business and leaves his children to go to moral ruin, that he may gain the wealth which will show to the world that he stands among the lords of this terrible king's court. The wife forgets her babes or murders them before birth, and all to the same end. Dress and show, parties and travel, stopping at first-class hotels, riding in first-class cars and paying first-class bills—all this that they may belong to this king's retinue; while the laborer, the honest toiler, is but the serf, the slave who bears the burdens of all above him.

How shall we dethrone this usurper who thus rides over hearts, grinding them into dust? How shall we escape the power of this bloated monster who feeds upon all beautiful, all holy, all divine things as his natural food? . . .

We need money; but shall it be as servant or master? . . .

Go, gather the hearts made desolate in a single year by his relentless power. Look at the mighty army of prostitutes—of homeless laborers made destitute and driven to desperation by financial crashes. Look at them as they plunge into crime and are then shut up in prison. See the poor needle-woman, as she stitches away her life to adorn the garments that are to cover the courtiers and mistresses of this king. Listen to the little ones as they cry for bread, while this king and his retinue waste the products of their fathers' toil. Gather them all together—all the victims. Let them stand out before you in all their misery. Look into their hollow eyes; mark their pale, sunken cheeks; note their ragged garments and the shiver which runs through their frames as the chill breath of Autumn tells of Winter. Great heavens! Look at them and then tell me if there is no way to save this motley host from an earthly hell—no way to remove the causes which have made them what they are.

It is for these that we toil. It is for these that our hearts agonize. It is for these, all these, and millions more who must follow in their track if we cannot bring about a different order of things, that we ask you to aid us in our work—to devote time, talent, means. . . .

The key that will unlock the door which leads to the guarded chamber of this monarch lies concealed in this vexed sex question. He draws his life-power from the sex fountain, and this fountain must be closed against him and open only to the demands of love, ere his reign will cease.

Yes, I know just what I am saying, and my position is as impregnable as are the axioms of mathematics. Solve the sex problem, free woman from her thraldom here, and Money, instead of being (as now) a tyrant king, will henceforth be the servant of Love. . . .

Swedenborg says that everyone "is as is the riding love." No matter how imperfect the results as to the carrying out the legitimate ends of that love, the love which rules decides the character. Is there any thinking man or woman who will deny that this is so?

Are not all our decisions as to the real character of an individual based upon the motive which prompts to action, rather than upon the result of the act itself? . . .

Another point: All the forces, all the powers of the being will be used (wisely or unwisely, as the intelligence of the individual shall determine); but all will necessarily be used, so far as they are used at all, to forward the objects of the ruling love. There can be no difference of opinion here; the statement has only to be understood to command assent.

Still another point: It has been demonstrated beyond the power of contradiction that without the union of the two forces known as masculine and feminine there is, there can be no form of life, of growth. And, still further, the nature of all forms of life is decided, first, by the ruling force or element of said compound; second, by the degree of the development of the elements entering in the compound.

I wish to state the above in still another form, for sexuality has been so degraded, so spit upon, so despised, that I sometimes wonder that we have not been permitted to fall into annihilation; and but for the continued action of this sex-law we should have done. I repeat: . . . Sex-union is the fountain from which springs all life—not merely human life but all forms and states of life.

When I speak of the sex fountain I do not mean an inactive, a stagnant fountain, neither one of which there is unnatural action; for the first is ice-bound death and the last putrid death. I mean a fountain in which there is the natural ebb and flow of reciprocal action between the positive and negative, the male and female forces, of which it is constituted.

LIFE IS POWER: consequently *the fountain of sex, if the source of all life, must be the source of all power.*

The degree, the range, of the life resulting from sex-union depends upon the channels through which it acts. If the two forces blend in the mineral kingdom we have iron, lead, silver, gold, the diamond, pearl, etc., and each pure, free from dross, just in accordance with the strength and purity of the different blendings; and so in the vegetable, the animal, the human, or the angel kingdoms. . . .

Or, in other words, the predominant feeling, the ruling love, takes control of, shapes and directs the life-power which flows both from sex-union and sex-blending. By "sex-blending" I mean that blending of sex atmosphere which takes place without sex contact.

We find, then, that *character*—both that of individuals and of communities—*is as is the ruling love.*

Now, what is the ruling love of society to-day?

Need we ask . . . when without it we are the slaves and with it we are masters of the situation?

Money has hitherto been spoken of as "king."

We will now take still stronger grounds and assert that, to all intents and purposes, "Money is god!"

Yes, Money is god—and all the people obey. Love, Tenderness, Charity, Religion, all—all! are bond servants to this money god—chained to his chariot-wheels—and crushed by his relentless tread if they dare to put themselves in his way!

But we must remember that all life, all activity, is generated by the union of the two forces known as masculine and feminine. . . .

We find that not only are certain forces necessary to the organization of individual life and of society life but that that upon which said life is continued must possess the same elements. The man whose ruling love is money is not at home with those whose ruling love is benevolence, for the atmosphere generated by the latter does not furnish the element needed to enable the money-love to hold its supremacy, and, being the ruling love, it takes the man to an atmosphere generated by the money power, for there only can it breathe freely . . . .

The man whose ruling love is money cannot breathe freely, cannot have an atmosphere suited to the supremacy of said love unless he mingles with women whose ruling love is also money; and he must not only mingle with them fraternally but sexually—that is, either directly or indirectly. . . .

So long as the money power is in the ascendancy woman must of necessity be mercenary in her love; and, if not naturally so, must be made and held so by the force of circumstances; and in no way could this have been done so effectually as it has by making her subject to man in the matter of sex—dependent on him for support, protection.

Woman's whole being is subject to man, in the present order of society, just so far as that which constitutes her woman affects her life or happiness. She must wait till man asks her to be his wife. She must not herself make a movement looking in that direction or she is considered unwomanly. So she must wait her natural life alone or accept something short of that which is recognized as marriage; and, if the latter, then she is ostracized, shut up to the merchandize of herself for support.

Man has control of the avenues of wealth and will hold woman's wages to the lowest point possible—that is, the wages of labor—while he uses the money that has been wrung from the virtuous woman's toil to pay for sex gratification. He does this at the command of the ruling love, which is that of money, and, true to the universal law (which demands two forces in union in order to obtain active, successful life), he tempts woman to a mercenary use of her sexual nature—tempts her from one direction and drives her from another—forces necessities upon her through the control of the wealth of the world and then tempts these necessities with money rewards.

Man's natural sphere is that of the accumulative, and it is right that he should gather, but not to abuse. Yet just so long as he controls as well as accumulates just so long will Acquisitiveness hold the reins of power—just so long will Wealth rule—Money be the god before which the people will bow. In a true state of society

Acquisitiveness will gather for Love to use. Acquisitiveness cannot use, distribute wisely, justly, any more than man can be mother or woman father. This latter is the work of Love, guided by the wisdom of Justice.

Man loves to acquire. It is his sphere—his delight. But the ruling love which uses wisely for the good of all—this love is woman's—it is the ruling power of her soul: love, devotion, maternal, filial or conjugal—love in some or all of these forms combined. And this is particularly true of her sex-nature; she yields it where she loves, and only there when left free from outside pressure. This sex-life of woman—controlled by and giving life to (first) the special and (secondly) the universal maternal—would, in freedom, control all the other organs of the brain, or the powers of the spirit through them, in the service of humanity, acquisitiveness not excepted.

With this, the ruling love of woman, to wit, the maternal, in the ascendancy—as it would be if she had the entire control of her sex-nature, making man subject to her in this direction—the sex magnetism, in vitalizing life's activities, would not then, could not be from the money but from the love plane. With this, the ruling love of woman, in the ascendancy, monopolies of wealth to the injury of the masses would be impossible, for the vitalizing life for such a condition would be wanting, and, of course, the condition itself could not exist.

The mockeries of wealth, in contrast with the wretchedness of hunger and rags, would no more be known; for the woman hand, guided by the woman heart unperverted by forced obedience to the money god—now god no longer—that hand, guided by the true, maternal heart of woman, would wipe the tears from off all faces.

Glorious consummation! One long prayed for; but when a few of us see the way to its realization and go to work in live earnest then comes the tug of war—then the hounds of Slander and Malice are let loose.

The prayer of words does not alarm in the least, but when the prayer of deeds commences then this money god begins to look after the slaves who have sustained his throne by holding their sex subject to his will, or, rather, submitting their sex to his use because they saw no way of escape. . . .

We have laid hands upon the *recognized standard* of marriage; we have claimed that woman shall be free, declared our belief in her innate soul purity and her right to the use of her maternal functions in spite of law or priest; and from the outcry made we know that we have found the vital point of the disease; and, further, we shall lay bare and probe, though it rock the nations from centre to circumference. . . .

They tell us that we must have nothing to do with this social question.

Nothing to do with the fountain of life, of power!

No wonder that apathy has reigned and still reigns where once there was life and vigor.

We must have something to do with this thing, with this question, or perish. We cannot escape it if we would; and, as the agitation increases—when the subject of freedom for woman is talked of—as misrepresentations multiply—as honest confession is met with repudiation, while sneaking hypocrisy comes to the front (or tries to) and talks long and loud of purity—we are led to ask, "Why is it? Why all this disturbance? Why is it, when prostitution runs riot on our streets, that leading reformers do not seem particularly distressed? When advertisements for the cure of disease brought on by abuse of the sex functions are posted upon almost every street corner no particular anxiety is manifested about the matter by those who are so afraid of being disgraced if this question is discussed?["]

Women prostitute their bodies nightly to legal brutes called "husband," and, *thinking* themselves virtuous, shrink from the very touch of the garments of the more-womanly woman who is prostituted illegally—forced thereto by the accursed edict of Respectability because she once loved in purity of soul and *trusted illegally*.

We know all this to be true; and know, also, that broken health and diseased, discordant children are the legitimate fruits of these legal prostitutions—evils fully as terrible as those that arise from illegal prostitution; and, further, we are all ready to admit that woman is less sensually inclined, loves more from the spiritual than does man. We admit this *in theory*. Why then is it that when a portion of us try to put this theory into practice by giving woman the control of her own person and demanding that the wealth of the world shall be so used that she'll not be pressed, either directly or indirectly, into giving herself from the money place; or, in other words, for a support—why is it when we demand this that the spasms of Respectability are so terrible? . . .

We are shaking the throne of power upon which this money god sits, and . . . he is riveting the chains of his captives . . . and talking of doing the will of the Father who is in Heaven. Alas, they cannot serve two masters if they try. And so humanity—a bleeding, dying humanity, stretches its hands to them in vain.

Brothels may exist all over the land; marital infidelity run rampant; sexual diseases poison the very fountains of life; Foeticide lift its red hands dripping with the blood of the innocents—this, all this, and a thousand times more, and yet those who claim to wish for better things are so carried by the tide, so held in the grasp of the dominant power that they seem very little troubled about the matter.

But when it is proposed to set woman entirely free from man's domination sexually, then the anxiety manifested for the preservation of purity is wonderful to behold. For the preservation of purity? We must first have before we can preserve it; and true purity we never can have so long as we are under the rule of the present order of things.

But purity we must and will have. The hour has come when woman is demanding to be freed from unwilling sex relations; neither will she much longer be held to sex isolation because not owned, because she has not been sealed, delivered over to the keeping of some man, as man-made statutes direct. Man-made, for woman has had no voice therein.

Woman must be free to use her sex functions only at the promptings of her love, and then the material of which the throne of the money god is built and sustained will no longer be manufactured. Sex life will nevermore flow forth at the beck of Wealth, of the money which tempts Poverty.

Thus Acquisitiveness will no longer rule, but take its place as the servant of Love—and Love worketh no ill to its neighbor.

But we can see the combined power that will be brought to bear against us in this the grandest work of the ages. Ah, yes, we see it.

We behold the thunderbolts of the money god's wrath, as he hurls them at our uncovered heads. We see the martyrdom which awaits us and may yet be ours. We see the gathering forces that are rallying for the final conflict, ere the millenial can be ushered in.

Though we see and feel all this bearing down upon us, we pale not. We are rebels in the fullest sense of that word. We are determined to overthrow the ruling power, to dethrone it and to place the Christ of love—existing in woman's soul—upon the throne. That Christ who has worn the crown of thorns and had the wormwood and the gall pressed to the lips, through the ages of the past, has been crucified between the two thieves of Marriage and Prostitution, till the very heavens are black with agony, and the veil of the temple of Hypocrisy is being rent in twain from the top to the bottom. Soon the passion of suffering will be finished and the resurrection morn be ushered in. Already the angels have descended to roll back the stone from the door of the sepulcher.

Yes, we are determined to accomplish this mighty work. The hosts of those who oppose us are many; they have wealth; they have the power of the present order of things upon their side; they may use the prison or the gallows; they will do what they can, for their case is desperate. But those who are with us are more than those who are against us.

Could you see the hosts of the unseen world as they urge us on; could you hear what I have heard, as with my soul's ears; I have caught the voices of the wise ones of the ages, whose benevolence has agonized till they have learned that they must have the aid of those who have passed through earth's hells, ere such hells can be removed; could you hear them as they called from the highlands of the other life to these in the valleys of degradation, saying: "come up and help us to solve the problem of redemption;" and could you hear the myriads of those who went down to death with the arms of despair encircling their souls—the drunkard, the outcast, and all of earth's untimely ones who have been torn from this life and its benefits; yea, the myriad millions, who came and sat upon the seat of council, with their darkened spirits quivering into new life 'neath the influence of an awakened hope—sat upon the seat of council and told their experiences, opened up the causes which crushed them—and could you have seen the faces of these listening ones, as they have glowed before me in my hours of exaltation— seen them as they gathered up item after item of evidence, till at last they saw the cause of it all—that cause, the slavery of woman.

Could you see the determination written upon their faces and upon the faces of those who, for the first time, realize that they too are needed in this work, you would know that we could not fail—you would know that woman must and will be free—that these myriad hosts have sworn it, and for this they are working. Kings, priests, principalities or powers of earth—be they what they may—cannot prevent, but must wheel into line or go down in the wreck of the old.

For this we live, and for this we will die if needs be. For this we ask your aid, for we know that woman's freedom is the world's redemption, and the renovation of the spirit spheres as well; and when it is accomplished there will be such a shout of "peace and good will" as the world has never heard.

A grand culmination! But mankind has been ruled so much through the emotional, have walked so little in the light of underlying and undying principles that I would fain return again to the law controlling this matter and by further illustrations impress it more fully upon your minds.

We have already seen that there are two forces acting in unison to bring into being all forms of life. We call these forces, these unfathomable, ever-acting life powers, "Father God" and "Mother Nature" or "Father and Mother God." We find these two forces embodied in the human as male and female, and we know that the union of these two gives another form of life. It is easy to recognize this truth when the form resulting is a physical one—another human being. When we look upon a child we know that there has been between some two persons a union of those two forces in the production of that child. We know this—we do not stop to question, to prove it.

But when we come to the intellectual, to the spiritual, it is hard to realize that all the beauty, all the life we have here, comes also from the fountain of sex. The aroma of the flower is as much a part of it as is the seed ripening in its bosom, and the same elements which blended in the grosser form are necessary in the finer blendings to produce the other; and so of the human.

Every one's sphere, their magnetic and electric emanations, *are as is the sex life*, and the sex life is determined as to the direction of its vitalizing power outside the special sex act, by the organ of the brain most active in the individual. The sex life gives strength, power, to said organ, and said organ gives direction to said power. . . .

The forms of all life are determined by the nature of the sex life which gives them form. The sex life, in its concentrated elements, must be like unto the form of life from which it is concentrated, otherwise it could not give the same or a similar form to the life which springs from it, when it is blended with its opposite. . . .

That the diffused elements flowing out from an object, whether animal or vegetable, will also be of the same nature, is also undeniable. We know that this is true of each individual object, and that, flowing out in so rarified a condition, these emanations blend and form a general atmosphere, such as surrounds the earth. This atmosphere we breathe into our lungs, and the health of our bodies depends much upon the elements of which it is composed. If it is loaded down with noxious vapors rising from pools of filth, from decaying vegetation, where there has been much moisture and little sun light; from swamps, where the waters are pent up and become putrid from inaction, then chills follow, fevers prevail and general distress takes the place of health and peace. It is of no use to cover up or turn your backs upon these conditions—the subtle element finds its way into every crack and crevice. Favorable situations and disinfectants may palliate but cannot wholly save from the effects which such putrid conditions generate.

But there is an atmosphere which sustains the same relation to the mental and spiritual as does this of which we have been speaking to the physical. Whence comes this mental, this spiritual atmosphere? From whence does it obtain its life or death-dealing power! From the sex life, acting through the brain organs. Those organs of the brain brought into action when the sex act is thought of, or consummated, give character to this atmosphere, make it moral or immoral, degrading or elevating in its vitalizing power.

If we think of this act as something low, enter into it under conditions that our self-respect disapproves, then we give off a degrading sex atmosphere, for the low thought, acting through the brain, poisons it. The lungs of the soul, or spirit body, breathe in this atmosphere, giving a healthy or diseased action, even as the lungs of the body take in the physical atmosphere, giving health or disease physically.

Would that I could so impress this truth, not only upon your minds but upon the minds of the entire human family, that it could never more pass from their active consciousness. Never since the dawning of creation's morn has a truth of more importance been announced to a waiting world; never one which showed so fully the destructive tendency of the sex act under any and all conditions but that of mutual sex love. . . .

Again I ask: What are the organs of the brain called into action in most cases under the present order of things? In legal marriage, where there is not mutual sex love it is submission or combative indignation combined with fear and disgust. Woman is, must be, repelled, disgusted, whenever she submits to an unwelcome embrace. This always, but it may be combined with fear and submission, in which the elements of cowardice are furnished; or it may be combined with fear of results, and bitter, resentful, combative elements accompanying. Is it any wonder that the world has become disgusted with this most beautiful, most holy of all relations, if entered into aright? Is it any wonder that the very air is replete with the elements of war, of red-handed murder, wholesale and retail?

But the brain organs called into action under such circumstances, on the part of the male, what are they? The combative resistance to the partner's dislike which overcomes—the persuasiveness which wakes into undue reciprocal action, thus destroying love, as hot-house plants die beneath the biting frost; or the enforcement of legal rights—in other words, legal rape.

Is it any wonder that with such a combination of vital elements permeating the mental, the spiritual atmosphere, that society is made up of the oppressor and the oppressed, of tyrants and slaves.

But both in and out of marriage this act is full often—yea, three times out of five the result of acquisitiveness. When a woman is so situated in life that money, support for herself and children, necessarily comes in as one of the chief considerations, even love in such a case is neutralized, or nearly so; but when there is no love then all the sex force called into action during the entire life goes to vitalize the money power—becomes a part of the very breath of the life of this god.

Love outside of legal marriage cannot be consummated only by calling into action the organs of the brain which, in their undue action, furnish the elements of hypocrisy, or of reckless, shameless defiance, except in these few—very few—cases where the law has been ignored from principle, and the parties stand to their acts in a noble self-approval. Such are the heroes that the world will one day crown with unfading immortelles.

But I will leave this subject with you, feeling that you must see, as I do, that woman's freedom is the world's redemption, and, seeing this, that you will aid in bringing it about, either by coming to the front yourselves or by sustaining those who do.

Part Three:

Closing

25

The Artist as Exemplar: Thomas Cole's Voyage of Life *(1842)*

Throughout this volume, we have explored the classical liberal theory of history in theory and practice, often in tandem and oftener at odds. The most hopeful, visionary, and romantic liberal activists embraced the American position in history and their own individual and collective abilities to shape time. The more pessimistic (perhaps *realistic*), cautious liberals inclined toward theory and doubted the tools activists chose to sculpt free society. While his optimistic, locofoco peers in the Young America movement championed national power and global republicanism, Thomas Cole lamented his country's feverish departures from pure theory. Cole and his democratic contemporaries largely shared the same liberal theory of history, explaining change over time throughout all social units with reference to the cyclical conflict between individuals' interests in liberty and power. Despite their shared theory, Cole and the democratic Young Americans were sharply divided in applying historical knowledge to present-day action.

In his paintings, Thomas Cole attempted to convey the wisdom of the ages to those precious few in the audience that may actually listen. *The Course of Empire* followed the life cycle of a full civilization, warning that a society that maintains insufficient virtue and reverence for liberty cannot check the growth of concentrated power. When a society's exercise of power so outstrips its love of liberty, that society invites its own destruction, whether from rebellion within or conquest from without.

From world history to civilizations, nation-states, communities, and every unit in between, right down to the individual life cycle, Cole believed this cyclical dynamic was *the narrative key to explaining change over time*. While exhibiting *The Course of Empire* in 1836, Cole was inspired to produce a similar series chronicling the same historical dynamics in the life cycle of an individual. From 1838 to 1843, Cole developed the idea for *The Voyage of Life* in verse and translated poetry and history into a masterful visual representation of theory and narrative.

In the poem that inspired the later series of paintings, Cole explored history through the microcosm of a single individual during the phases of the life cycle. Man begins life as an infant full of wonder upon encountering the natural world for the first time. In the days of *Childhood*, existence is lush and full of life and of nurturing abundance. The future appears magnificently bright on the horizon, and the river gently drifts the babe forward. The guiding angel steers life's vessel from the cavern's opening. The darkness of the cliffs and cave is firmly behind the newborn,

Part One: *Childhood*. (Credit: Munson-Williams-Proctor Arts Institute, Utica, New York.)

whereas nothing seems to await the infant but soft pastels and the stillness of undisturbed nature.

The poem uses the voice of an unnamed narrator to tell the story of the life cycle. While adventuring through a mountain cave, the narrator encounters the river, boat, child, and guardian angel with a mixture of wonder and concern. "What meaneth this," the narrator demands of the scene in general. The narrator's soul replies:

> By thee now standing midway on the height
> Of contemplation not alone are seen
> Pictures of the departing past; but sight
> Of future scenes is opened through a screen
> Of darkling clouds and mists fantastic lies
> Across the tearful vision of thy longing eyes.

Accepting the scene as a sort of prophetic vision, the narrator's soul continues:

> By mortal man that River of dark source
> Is named the "Stream of Life"; with constant flow
> With many a winding on its downward course,
> At times it lags along with motion slow,
> At times impetuous o'er the rocky steep
> It journeyeth onward toward The Eternal Deep.

The unwary traveler of this river—although undoubtedly pleased with the initial surroundings and situation—will all too soon plunge into

> that vast Profound—that darkest Dread
> That Silence—that immeasurable Gloom,
> The Breathless—Shoreless—the Un-islanded
> Of the great World—of mighty Time and Tomb.

The narrator's soul certainly strikes a chord with the pessimists among us, those of us who believe it better to learn hard lessons about life sooner rather than later. Far from promoting despair, however, our narrator reminds that

> human thought, thanks be to God, can soar
> Triumphant on the wings of light divine
> And take its flight above the Shadow hoar;
> Where Angels in a land of beauty shine
> In living light which is the Light of Light,
> The everlasting day, that suffereth not the night.

The narrator continues to muse about the relations between one life cycle and another, the comparison between the developing vision and his own life in the real world. The narrator's soul continues:

> Thou wert such infant Voyager, all men
> Have been—the thousands yet unborn will be.

The innocence of childhood shielded the ship-bourne subject:

> For withering sin, as yet, can claim no part
> Nor pale remorse bedim the beaming eye.
> Children are buds of Heaven 'tis earthly air
> That breeds the cankers, guilt and deadening despair.

Guarded by heaven's angels, individuals may rely upon God's protection throughout their lifetimes,

> And nought by Giant Sin can drag us thence
> Who grows and conquers by our disobedience.

When our narrator demands that the vision explain why innocent childhood does not last forever, the narrator's soul replies:

> A higher destiny is thine . . . through trial, sorrow, darkness, pain
> The road to far sublime joys does lead
> And lasting bliss by suffering we gain
> And by the gloomy value through which we tread
> We reach the bliss that makes all earthly joy seem dead.

During *Youth*, man gains greater knowledge and self-confidence, literally taking the helm of life's ship from the

Part Two: *Youth*. (Credit: Munson-Williams-Proctor Arts Institute, Utica, New York.)

personal angel. While the angel maintains a watchful, caring eye over the youth, our subject's gaze is fixed on the distant celestial temple. In a rush to reach the greatness and grandeur that lie ahead, our youth bids farewell to the stillness, beauty, and plenty in the current frame. Youth steers life's vessel away from shore, downriver to the twists and turns of fortune and fate. Self-assured, overconfident, and yet lacking in necessary experience and virtue, the youth exercises powers over nature in an effort to exercise mastery over the world, turning it to serve the youth's own ends. "So changed my thought from light to shade," comments Cole's poet-narrator,

> At times exulting in the glow of hope, at times
> In darkness cast by what my soul had said;

'Till sunk in reverie her words seemed chimes
From some far tower.

Even our narrator—blessed with the gift of historical foresight, fully aware of the dangers lurking beyond the bend—has fallen to the lustful, romantic passions of youth.

The youth's world is immediately exciting and pleasing. It bustles with fauna, bursts with flora, and continually beckons both subject and narrator alike. Entranced, they proceed ever onward,

Toward the ethereal mountains which did close
Fold beyond fold until they vanished
In the horizon's silver, whence uprose
A structure strangely beautiful and vast
Which every earthly fane Egyptian, Gothic, Greek
surpassed.

The youth's focus, irrevocably drawn forward with a passionate yearning for greater liberties to explore the world and greater powers with which to do so, is absorbed by the cloud temple. In fact, when one concentrated enough, intent on discovering all one might accomplish, a youth may catch sight of an endless array of gilded pinnacles and domed heights:

Above the columned pile sublimely rose
A Dome stupendous; like the moon it shone
When first upon the orient sky she glows
And moves along the Ocean's verge alone;

And yet beyond, above, another sphere
And yet another, vaster, dimly did appear.

Such was the dizzying, dazzling ambition of youth, it was
As though the blue supernal space were filled
With towers and temples, which the eye intent
Piercing the filmy atmosphere that veiled,
From glorious dome to dome rejoicing went,
And the deep folds of ether were unfurled
To show the splendors of a higher world.

Finally peeling the eye's gaze from the celestial temple, the narrator takes keener notice of the youthful voyager, remarking that

Now stood a Youth on manhood's verge, his eye
Flashing with confidence and hot expectancy.

The youth maintained singular focus on the cloudy castle and

His bosom heaved as if with the secret powers
Possessed to tread the deep—to outstrip the flying Hours.

The angel bids the youth farewell from the shore, and the narrator's soul returns to the scene to enlighten the narrator:

The scene before thee beautiful and bright
Is but a phantasm of Youth's heated brain
And doomed to fade as day before the night,
Fleeting its glory, transitory, vain;

Save that it teaches the meek humble soul
Earth's grandeur ne'er should be the spirit's Goal.

A truly virtuous life and real heavenly rewards required diligent toiling in one's own garden. "But mark the Youth," the soul continues,

how filled his eager eye
With the bright exaltation—See! He aims
To reach the portal of the palace high . . .
The tempting semblance of a conqueror's crown
And wreath to bind the brows of him who wins renown.

The narrator's soul stands in righteous judgment of the youth, whose actions betray a nature both reckless and acquisitive. "Weak and deluded one!" the soul-voice castigates *Youth*,

Dost thou not know
They Bark is hasting down the Stream of Life
And tarries not for any golden show . . .
Does not thine eye perceive that when yon towers
Are well nigh gained with sudden sweep the stream,
And growing swiftness, shoots away and pours
Impetuous, towards a shadowy raven deep
Cleft in the mountain's vast and misty side.

At the notion of *Youth*'s impending doom, the narrator again demands the vision account for the angel's absence given

That hand divine could steer
The willing Boat to where yon glittering domes uprear.

A loving god, it would seem, would provide that

> E'en youth might live a long long life of joy
> And shun perchance the torrent where it pours
> Adown yon dread descent.

The narrator's soul responds that there is no accounting for the ways of divinity, but the voyager is most obviously to blame. After all,

> Through feeble Infancy is steered the Bark of Life
> By Angel hands; but growing man demands
> The helm in confidence and dares the strife
> Of the far-sweeping waves. The lurking sands,
> The rapids foaming through the channel dim,
> The roaring cataract are all unknown to him.

Thus do heavenly forces create wisdom out of man's arrogant, youthful folly, as

> from man's conflicts with the world arise
> A sense of weakness and of chilling fear
> And driven from earth his hopes ascend the skies.
> Thus is he launched upon the stream alone
> To chasten pride and give young desire a holier tone.

Upon entering *Manhood*, our subject cannot help but realize the follies of youthful arrogance and inexperience. Clearly unaware that the once-calm river led directly and inevitably to a thicket of craggy rapids, the youth lusted after the power to reach the heavens. So badly did he yearn for selfish liberty and selfish power,

Part Three: *Manhood*. (Credit: Munson-Williams-Proctor Arts Institute, Utica, New York.)

that he endangered his own well-being in the pursuit. With age, man gains wisdom and repents his sins. The subject prostrates himself before the now-unknown forces mastering his world, begging them for clemency and protection. He is lost and virtually without hope. It is only when he has reached the point of no return and ultimate danger that man finds it in himself to admit his own failings. The ever-watchful angel, meanwhile, patiently waits for the subject to weather the struggles ahead; the angel waits to rebuild a battered, broken, and humbled man.

In the poem, it seems to our narrator that

the Earthquake there had oped his jaws
And fierce Convulsion rent the ribs of Earth;
Darkness and light forgot their ancient laws.

So dark were the depths of man's depravity and lust for power, the stretch of craggy rapids

> was a den where demons had their birth
> Where voices strange and many a dusky form
> Smote the strained ear and did the sky deform. . . .
> Where fear and death forever hover round.

The river coursed quickly onward, "with a tyrannic force," tossing jagged bits of rock as casually as it tossed sprays of foam, and

> Like famished wolves when the scared prey is nigh,
> The pale demoniac roared louder as for joy.

At the very moment of certain death, the voyager casts himself before nature's god, pleading with the unknown forces of his world. "This is the crisis," the narrator's soul explains,

> this the decisive hour
> In life's swift fever—balance Life and Death.
> Adversity's cold storm and Sorrow's power
> Temptation desperate with changeful breath
> Break with unmitigated fury on the Man,
> And Pleasure once so fair is sicklied o'er and wan.

The voyager's youthful lust for power has failed and mastery over the material powers of the earth remains well beyond his actual grasp. In the process, he has abandoned friends, acquired enemies, and lost his childhood innocence. The angel stands by to observe as man reaps the just and natural rewards for his inexperience and systematic lack of virtue.

Part Four: *Old Age*. (Credit: Munson-Williams-Proctor Arts Institute, Utica, New York.)

In *Old Age*, man once again returns to the serenity and stillness of childhood. He has sufficiently humbled himself before the god of nature and his angelic representatives. Man has given himself to the course of nature without exercising the selfish, reckless pursuit of either liberty or power. He has seen visions of grandeur and fallen prey to them. He has seen death pressing in from every corner, a sharp, angular world full of nothing but stabbing, rushing madness. He has, ultimately, realized that the world is no kingdom, and he is no king. He is, in fact, a lone individual trapped in nature's river of history. Man can choose to forsake the serenity and peace that attend individual humility, or man can exercise his extraordinary powers to warp nature into more pleasing forms.

Cole's lesson in *The Voyage of Life*, as in *The Course of Empire*, is that when we indulge ourselves with the belief that we can master nature and change the course of history, we are in fact simply pushing forward the cyclical course of the natural world. We can never master nature, and despite our pretensions to power and our abuses of natural liberty, we remain the subjects of nature and nature's god.

"There sat the voyager," the poem's narrator states with a note of pity,

> an ancient Man,
> Withered and blighted by the frosts of time:
> Furrowed his cheek, his forehead bare and wan
> As though the tempests of each earthly clime
> Had broken o'er him in their fiercest mood
> And he with patient soul their fury had withstood.

The guardian angel finally returns to her charge, the flames surrounding her lighting the way for the old man's ascension to heaven. With the man's death, our narrator is cast out of the vision and awakens thrown to the ground.

> There long I lay mingling my sighs and tears,
> Recalling all the Vision to my mind,
> Its varied scenes, its many hopes and fears
> Its seasons four mysteriously combined,
> How through bright Childhood's vale the river flowed
> Youth, Manhood, Age, to reach the mighty flood.

The narrator's soul once again responds by inciting him to action:

> Rise
> Dwell not inactive on the Vision true
> Remember that Life's River swiftly hies
> Toward the great Deep and thou hast much to do:
> The Vision teaches when divined aright
> That he must trust in God and strike,who conquers in
> the fight.[48]

Thomas Cole's inspirational, masterful, and thoroughly influential career as a visual artist propelled him to stardom in both elitist Knickerbocker and locofoco Young American cultural circles in New York City. He was accepted and loved by Americans of all sorts as an undoubtedly brilliant, original, and *wise* artist, a credit to his nation and its unique place in world history. Yet Cole himself was not nearly so optimistic, and as we saw in *The Course of Empire*, he feared impending national doom. In the Jacksonian period, pessimists like Cole may have inspired optimists like John L. O'Sullivan, the Loco-Focos, and others explored in this volume, but he feared their virtue failed to match their vigor. He was correct.

Young Americans surged to the polls behind James K. Polk in 1844 and rushed headlong into war with Mexico, their minds clouded with dreams of a great continental republic. Thomas Cole, the young Walt Whitman, and a sizable portion of the American population opposed the war as a barbaric attempt at annexation and a sop to the Southern Slave Power. They feared, too, that the impending firestorm over slavery in the territories would consume and destroy the country.

The Jacksonian era, then, was to Cole's mind the point of *Consummation*; the days of Polk ushered in *Destruction*, leaving the youth a *Desolation* fresh and new, ready to begin the cycle once again. Perhaps—if individuals such as himself could impute the right message in the right ways—future generations would have a better chance to improve history's course.

All such hopes, Cole suggests to his audience, rest on individual moral agents and their virtue. *The Voyage of Life* and its attendant series of paintings suggest a dual moral mandate: individuals have obligations to both "trust in God," *and* "strike." We have the opportunity to use history like the narrator's vision. Our knowledge of the past allows us to understand the world better and transcend the moral failings of our ancestors. When we fail to do so, we fail to heed God's commandments and cast away our angelic guardians.

Should we remain firmly rooted in our life's vessel, allowing ourselves to be guided entirely by our knowledge of the natural order, we would greatly ease our individual voyages through history. Doing so, we will *not* avoid life's calamities and catastrophes, but we *will* be sufficiently prepared to meet them and overcome a long series of celestial tests. Thomas Cole believed his own world of Jacksonian *Manhood* still unrepentant of its evils, but in that pessimistic view laid an entrancingly optimistic declaration: each and every one of us changes history when we resolve to change ourselves and to be better than our forebears.

Conclusion: Generations of Remnants—Libertarianism and the Mechanics of Historical Change

By the turn of the 20th century, the radical liberal tradition in the United States entered a sort of dismal twilight. Despite their decades of hopeful, optimistic attempts at reform, the Loco-Foco movement (ca. 1820s–70s) dissolved itself in a sea of political compromises, accommodations, and intellectual fracture. Those who still identified with Thomas Paine and William Leggett's brand of vociferous, firebrand radicalism found themselves cut adrift from any coherent movement, supplanted by what one historian has called the "second state," in American history—the bureaucratic, creepingly imperialistic nation-state birthed during the sectional and Civil War eras.

When locofocoism died throughout the late 19th century, no radical liberal movement surged to replace its vigor and vitality. As a consequence, isolated intellectuals and writers like Benjamin Tucker, Moses Harman, and Albert Jay Nock preserved and developed the creed with a distinct sense of having been abandoned by the swing of history. As Progressivism morphed into world wars and the New Deal, Americans built a permanently mobilized government capable of representing the people in their collective struggle against scarcity and insecurity. The voices of criticism during the statist historical upswing, however, remained precious few for many decades.

So few, in fact, that Nock saw himself as a sort of lone libertarian, bobbing along in a sea of statism. But Nock was *not* alone, and he knew as much. Despite their myriad and unceasing problems, human societies persisted and even flourished through global war and depression. The existence of progress meant that somehow, somewhere, behind the death, destruction, and retrograde motion that so often characterize events, there *must* have been a constant substratum of individuals essentially *responsible* for ongoing productivity. Although the masses of mankind unthinkingly, cold-heartedly, or even viciously organized themselves into warring factions, there was always a "remnant" of right-thinking, right-doing individuals who kept the world from going completely to hell. In what undoubtedly remains his most famous and important essay, Nock relates to readers the story of a personal conversation with a friend over the course of an autumn evening. When his European interlocutor confessed to Nock: "I have a mission to the masses. I feel that I am called to get the ear of the people. I shall devote the rest of my life to spreading my doctrine far and wide among the population," Nock replies that this was a fool's errand and a supreme mistake.[49]

As prime evidence against courting the masses toward radical liberalism, Nock marshals the biblical story of Isaiah. Isaiah was a prophet charged by God with preparing the "remnant" that would save civilization once it had gone to the dogs. The Lord exhorts Isaiah: "Tell them what a worthless lot they are. . . . Tell them what is wrong, and why and what is going to happen unless they have a change of heart and straighten up." "Don't mince matters," Jehovah continues, "Make it clear that they are positively down to their last chance. Give it to them good and strong and keep on giving it to them."[50]

Of course, under such conditions the vast majority of people will not listen. Not only that, they will probably run Isaiah out of town for fear of his life. But the Lord assures Isaiah that his preaching will not be in vain: "There is a Remnant there that you know nothing about. They are obscure, unorganized, inarticulate, each one rubbing along as best he can. They need to be encouraged and braced up because when everything has gone completely to the dogs, they are the ones who will come back and build up a new society. . . . Your job is to take care of the Remnant, so be off now and set about it."[51]

Nock takes it almost for granted that the great masses of people live for essentially small reasons. They want basic material comforts and a chance at success and happiness in life. So long as demagogues and tyrants ameliorate one's problems in life, then the tyranny was one the "common man" could apparently live with comfortably enough. Nock chides his guest for thinking only of "mass-acceptance and mass-approval. His great care is to put his doctrine in such shape as will capture the masses' attention and interest." In so doing, the message is always diluted, "Its effect on the masses is merely to harden them in their sins," and—even worse—there is on balance one less prophet preaching the unadulterated truth. Lacking truth, the prophet lacks his fundamental connection to the remnant, and God's community of civilization builders dissipates into nothingness or stumbles along blindly and without leadership.[52]

As we have seen, throughout the mid-19th century, the Loco-Foco movement captivated and moved radical liberals all over the United States for decades, but the Civil War and its attendant leviathan state effectively buried political liberalism for decades. The liberal movement languished in a crisis of leadership and momentum, especially with the deaths of old radicals like Lysander Spooner late in the century. When Spooner died, Benjamin Tucker lamented, "Our Nestor [has been] taken from us,"[53] and between then and the publication of Nock's essay "Isaiah's Job" in 1936, no significant radical liberal movement remained in the United States.

Disgruntled with the state of the world and probably profoundly intellectually lonely, figures like H. L. Mencken and Nock managed to maintain a distinctly hopeful sense of fatalism. Nock faithfully believed that as long as prophets preached and the remnant existed, the two *would find each other*. Their real work could begin, however, only when competing paradigms of social thought exhausted themselves in failure. The historical cycle must reach its trough before once again ascending to a new crest.

True, "working for the Remnant means working in impenetrable darkness," never truly knowing whether your protestations are affecting the world.[54] Because the remnant exists permanently out of power, their influence cannot be discerned by investigating the world from the top down. Rather, the "substratum of right-thinking and well-doing which [the historian] knows must have been here" is composed largely of liberty-interested individuals diligently pursuing their own private affairs with little desire to exercise power over their fellow creatures.[55] This, after all, is the secret to their civilization-building: voluntary interactions between liberty-loving individuals maximize prosperity. Because the remnant lived this idea as an article of personal honor and integrity, their daily lives were spent constructing a complex, civil society from the bottom up, "like coral insects."[56]

Whether he was a turn-of-the-century Isaiah or a particularly productive coral insect, Nock contributed profoundly to an emerging sense in 20th-century America that statism was perhaps the greatest danger facing the human species. With this fear came a sharpened sense of individual, *personal* historical duty.

The modern libertarian or classical liberal revival owes much of its historical mooring to midcentury thinkers from the radical and inspiring Rose Wilder Lane to the diligently studious, although equally inspiring Carroll Quigley. As one of the "founding mothers" of modern libertarianism, Lane published her immensely significant book *The Discovery of Freedom* in 1943 during the depths of the Second World War. Like Croce, Lane thought of history as the story of liberty, and despite the temporary triumphs of concentrated power, history's arc inevitably leads back to liberty. As the economist Hans Sennholz wrote about Lane's thinking, "The history of mankind could be understood only as the theater of two diverse forces, the authoritarians and the revolutionists, locked in an unending struggle for supremacy."[57] Roger Lea MacBride, the long-time libertarian activist in many ways raised as Lane's grandson, compared her book with *Common Sense*, not simply for its sparkling and simple prose, but for the fundamental arguments about human nature and change over time. To Lane, the Revolutionary generation revived ancient ideas about liberty and individuality, combining their Saxon background with modern Protestant and rationalist understandings of nature. In the post-1776 world, "the individual would be master of his own fate. Kings were just ordinary mortals. Government would be the servant and not the master of men." This was the "discovery of liberty," the fact that individuals are indeed free and solely responsible for their own actions.[58]

Practically all libertarian thinkers since Lane have felt her influence in one way or another, but Roy A. Childs Jr. was among the most perceptive proponents of her historical ideas. Childs saw the previous century as one of unrepentant, unrelenting statism in which the individual became ever more thoroughly separated from real power over his or her own life. For Childs, history was the story of "the age-old conflict between individual liberty in all of its forms and the political power of the state over the affairs of men." In a 1975 essay, he lamented the state of an absolutely government-sodden world:

> The twentieth century is the century of power, a century where state coercion and violence have become common-place. Every conceivable form of statism has been tried in this century: fascism, communism, social democracy, the corporate state and military dictatorships.

> The fruits of power, too, have become apparent. We have seen more human misery caused by the wielding of politi-cal power, more cruelty and destruction of human lives, than ever before in our history. It is as though all of the terrifying horrors of which human beings are capable were rounded up and paraded before our eyes. . . .

> The hopes awakened by the revolutions against power, on behalf of liberty, in the seventeenth, eighteenth and nineteenth centuries, have been nearly universally aban-doned today, and an all-pervading sense of despair seems to have conquered our spirits. On all counts, the political, social and economic problems we face today seem infi-nitely more complex than those of the last century. . . .

> Throughout the West, the system of "corporate statism," the alliance of elite business, intellectual and labor inter-ests with the government, is collapsing, unable to solve any of the most fundamental problems. Decades of "fine tuning" the economic system through political means, through regulations, controls, taxes, spending, privileges

and the like, have caused massive dislocations in the structure of our economic system. . . .

Communist nations still cannot feed their own people. "Central planning" hasn't worked and the hapless subjects of communist regimes find the course and direction of their lives totally shaped by the state apparatus. Civil liberties and economic freedom are non-existent. Exile or death awaits those heroic souls who protest such tyranny.[59]

Childs's reading of history, however dismal its tone, inspired a somewhat hopeful libertarian vision for the future. Following Lane and Murray Rothbard, Childs dated modern libertarianism to 17th-century Europeans' battles against feudal institutions. Liberals across the Western world waged a centuries-long revolution "against power by the forces of liberty." Although successfully dismantling much—and in some countries, most—of the feudal state, the liberal project collapsed during the First World War, "which destroyed so much of what was valuable in the West." Liberalism survived the First and Second World Wars, but only as a small remnant of what it once was. Childs wrote, "It was, alas, a tradition which never fully triumphed anywhere, a revolution which remained an incomplete revolution, touching only America and Western European society."[60]

As a member of that very remnant, Rose Wilder Lane felt a distinct duty to produce *The Discovery of Freedom*. During the interwar period, Lane "joined with the group of intellectuals who launched the modern libertarian movement: Leonard Read,

R. C. Hoiles, Henry Hazlitt, Isabel Paterson, Albert Jay Nock, Frank Chodorov and all the rest."[61] The secret to *Discovery*'s power, of course, is Lane's sense of the libertarian's role in historical change. As Childs noted: "We travel through the centuries, learning the story of the Middle East's tumultuous history, the Jews and their struggle for liberty, and the attempts in Europe and America to limit the power of government and institutionalize individual liberty. . . . There is a celebration of the meaning of America that remains unsurpassed." Childs loved *The Discovery of Freedom* so much that he happily declared: "More than any other book, it is this one that made me a libertarian. . . . It is a joy and an inspiration, and will live as long as human beings live who long for freedom—all across the world."[62]

In 1991, historians and consultants William Strauss and Neil Howe presented the world with their own model of historical change. Although by no means a particularly *liberal* theory of history, the "Strauss-Howe generational theory" offers libertarian historians and activists a powerful model for how they can affect the world. Like Carroll Quigley's model of civilizational rise and fall (or rejuvenation, in the case of the West), Strauss and Howe's generational approach recognizes that the personalities and actions of *individuals* ultimately build the historical experience. Individuals' inability to improve upon the world of the past condemns future generations to fighting the same timeworn battles of liberty against power.

In their book *Generations*, Strauss and Howe build a grand vision of Anglo-American history stretching in time from 1584 into the 2060s.[63] *Generations* argues that Americans periodically experienced spiritual-intellectual awakenings and institutional crises. As these major events shape the minds and actions of the youth, the young grow old and shape the world in turn. Their own children and grandchildren then rebel against the calcified world of inherited institutions that has surrounded them since birth. The *new* youth arise to adulthood as the heroic champions of a new order and a new world. The heroes—quite satisfied with themselves by midlife—bequeath to their children the same generational struggles for liberty and power, dressed to fit a new context.

Like Thomas Cole's voyager, each of us is born into a world not of our making. History pushes us inexorably through time; and in our struggles to exercise power over the natural world and to enjoy liberty of action, we stumble our way into maturity. Bearing catastrophic burdens and reflective spiritual reformations alike, individuals are battered, bruised, and *shaped* by the flow of time across their lives. When Cole then situates a society of voyagers living together in nascent civilization, the individual life cycle is irrevocably linked to the rise and fall of entire nations.[64]

Strauss and Howe later expanded on *Generations* with their 1997 book *The Fourth Turning*. Here, their theory reaches its peak of persuasiveness, backed by rich and varied historical research. Strauss and Howe revive an old and multicultural philosophy of time that argues that events proceed according to a "natural century," or long human lifespan. This roughly 80-year period is called a *saeculum*, and four generations of individuals occupy each cycle. Each generation is stamped by historical events and in turn stamps history with its own mark.

Our authors divide the *saeculum* into four "turnings," each associated with a particular generation and a particular zeitgeist. First turnings are "High" eras in which new institutions replace calcified old interests, and a strong civic spirit replaces narrow individualism. Second turnings are "Awakenings"—eras of spiritual, intellectual, and cultural turmoil that undermine the integrity of existing institutions. Third turnings are "Unravelings," in which the world seems lost beyond repair. Fourth turnings—like our current position in the model—are periods of "Crisis," characterized by institutional restructuring or collapse. Although not exactly representative of the classical liberal theory of history as such, the Strauss–Howe generational theory provides a valuable interpretive framework through which libertarians may interpret the past and apply their own ideas about human nature and human action as need be.[65]

The full model places each identifiable *saeculum* in succession dating from the "Arthurian" generation of 1433–60 to the millennials of today. The first major crisis included in their survey is the War of the Roses, which prepared England for both the Protestant Reformation (1517) and the nation-building process. Some 70 years later, the Armada crisis (1588) established England as a major naval power and a nation of Protestant warrior-adventurers.

The new prevailing ideas of Puritanism, missionary Protestantism, colonialism, nationalism, and eventually even republicanism led to the Glorious Revolution (1688) crisis and solidified parliamentary supremacy. In this period of deep and widespread Enlightenment, the American colonies learned to govern themselves and experimented in Lane's "discovery of freedom." The

Awakening generation (born 1701–23) carried from its youths a world of spiritual fervor reignited and ablaze after a century of Puritan misrule in New England. Awakened youths gave birth to liberty children like Washington and helped raise Republican visionary grandchildren like Jefferson. The Washingtons and Jeffersons in the colonies led Americans through the Revolutionary War crisis, leaving it to the Compromise generation (born 1767–91) of Andrew Jackson to make sure that the United States lasted.[66]

As it happened, the United States did *not* last as originally constituted. The constitutional settlement established in the decade after the Revolution proved incapable of restraining deep moral, economic, and social conflicts over slavery, nor could it effectively account for the caprice, ineptitude, and general viciousness of party politics. The old order of 1787 died during the Civil War crisis, replaced by a militarized, imperial, democratic-corporatist nation-state. One lifetime later, the "second state" bureaucracy born during the Civil War itself gave birth to the largest, richest, most powerful, and potentially destructive institutions that have ever existed in human history.

The Great Depression and the Second World War entrenched the very sort of unrepentant statism that so depressed Roy Childs. For nearly a full *saeculum*, silents (born 1925–42), baby boomers (born 1943–60), gen-Xers (born 1961–81), and millennials (born 1982–ca. 2000) have lived with the welfare-warfare state built by Progressives, New Dealers, and Cold Warriors. Strauss and Howe identify the late 20th-century "culture wars" as the latest third turning or Unraveling period, and if the model is to be believed, we currently occupy the fourth turning crisis. Millennials, as it happens, are the "hero" analogs to Thomas Jefferson's Republicans. The Second World War ended the "Great Power Saeculum," and the postwar boom years began what our authors call the "Millennial Saeculum." Modern libertarianism began in this era, inspired by generations that had come before.

Roy Childs was born in 1949, and although he grew to maturity in the optimistic postwar boom years, Childs essentially knew too much history to be terribly pleased with the world. Childs's reading of history helped inform modern libertarianism as it took root in small booksellers' offices, student newsletters, and basement press operations around the country. The heady years of Consciousness Revolution (1964–84) witnessed libertarianism's flowering into a full school of thought, a national political movement, and a genuine way of life. Defining themselves *against* the New Dealers and the Cold Warriors, many libertarians were primed and ready to join *both sides* of the 1990s culture wars. Millennial children, meanwhile, have waited long, learned much, and seem poised and ready to take the helm from elder guides. How this generation of "heroes" intends to resolve an endless array of potential calamities remains to be seen, but time flows on regardless.[67]

Every generation experiences a period of existential crisis in its lifetime, and the way we respond to our individual crises of identity accumulates into transformational changes in our culture and society, moments of revolution for nations, civilizations, and even the whole species. It is in our power as individuals, without regard to historical categories, to break with the patterns of the past and resolve to end the historical cycle. The fact that practically all people everywhere have failed to do so throughout all of history suggests that we are far from ending it now. Earth certainly does not seem like heaven, but studying history makes one sympathize with the idea that we are living in a sort of hell—doomed by our own wickedness to forever purge our sins in tortures of our own making, the butcheries and horrors we call "history."

The better we comport ourselves with the laws of nature, the more we lessen our earthly sufferings; and perhaps the classical liberal tradition's ultimate lesson of history, then, is that if we ever want to truly escape it, we must first individually rise ourselves above it and be better than those who came before us. Crises cannot be wished into oblivion, nor acquiesced in; they must be dealt with, for better or worse. Those who favor liberty in the historical battle against power would do well to recognize themselves as history's *agents*, rather than its *remnants*, meeting their futures with energy, humility, virtue, and *cautious* optimism.

Notes

Introduction

1. For a fuller discussion of ideological thickness and thinness, see Charles Johnson, "Libertarianism Through Thick and Thin," *Freeman* 58, no. 6 (2008): 35–39.

2. Harry J. Hogan, "Foreword," in *The Evolution of Civilizations: An Introduction to Historical Analysis* by Carroll Quigley (Indianapolis: Liberty Fund, 1979; originally published by Macmillan, 1961), pp. 13–22.

3. Ibid., p. 16.

4. Ibid., p. 17.

5. Ibid., pp. 17–18.

6. Ibid., p. 19.

7. Ibid., pp. 19–20.

8. Ibid. In a sadly ironic twist of narrative, Quigley's most influential and important student has, undoubtedly, been President Bill Clinton.

9. Thomas Paine, Common Sense (Mineola, NY: Dover Publications, 1997; originally published in 1776), p. 14.

10. Ibid., p. 33.

11. Stephen Davies, *Empiricism and History* (New York: Palgrave, 2003), p. 20.

12. Ibid., p. 28.

13. Ibid., p. 35.

14. Lilian Handlin, *George Bancroft: The Intellectual as Democrat* (New York: Harper & Row, 1984); Francois Guizot, *The History of Civilization in Europe* (Indianapolis: Liberty Fund, 2013; originally published in 1846).

15. Davies, *Empiricism and History*, p. 21.

16. For its richness of detail and wealth of information about 18th- and 19th-century intellectual life, Murray Rothbard, *An Austrian Perspective on the History of Economic Thought*. 2 vols. (Auburn, AL: Ludwig von Mises Institute, 1995) is unsurpassed. For general information on 19th-century Americans' thoughts about social order, politics, and history, see Harry L. Watson, *Liberty and Power: The Politics of Jacksonian America* (New York: Hill & Wang, 1990).

17. For a broad overview of the history of modernity, see C. A. Bayly, *The Birth of the Modern World, 1780–1914: Global Connections and Comparisons* (Oxford, UK: Blackwell Publishing, 2004).

18. Benedetto Croce, *History as the Story of Liberty* (Indianapolis, IN: Liberty Fund, 2000; originally published in 1941), pp. xi–xii.

19. Ibid.

Chapter 1

20. As historians have done a thorough job of neglecting the Loco-Focos, our terms require some clear defining. One should be careful to distinguish between those individuals actually and directly involved in third-party political efforts from those loosely associated with the wider movement. This book uses "Loco-Foco" to indicate membership in the Equal Rights (or Loco-Foco) Party, whereas "locofoco" simply refers to those in the broader movement's intellectual orbit.

21. For Young American cultural and political history and its relationship to Thomas Cole, see Peter Bellis, *Writing Revolution: Aesthetics and Politics in Hawthorne, Whitman, and Thoreau* (Athens: University of Georgia Press, 2003); James T. Callow, *Kindred Spirits: Knickerbocker Writers and American Artists, 1807–1855* (Chapel Hill: University of North Carolina Press, 1967), pp. 3–37, 68, 221–28; Linda Ferber, ed., *Kindred Spirits: Asher B. Durand and the American Landscape* (New York: Brooklyn Museum, 2007), pp. 15, 30, 84, 123; Andrew Lawson, "'Song of Myself' and the Class Struggle in Language," *Textual Practice* 18 (2004): 377–94; Perry Miller, *The Raven and the Whale: The War of Words and Wits in the Era of Poe and Melville* (New York: Harcourt, Brace, 1956), pp. 9–68, 69–117, 122; David S. Reynolds, *Walt Whitman's America: A Cultural Biography* (New York: Knopf, 1996), pp. 20, 30, 33–34, 62–63, 66, 83, 98–110, 115–22; John Stafford, *The Literary Criticism of "Young America": A Study in the Relationship of Politics and Literature, 1837–1850* (Berkeley: University of California Press, 1952); William H. Truettner and Alan Wallach, eds., *Thomas Cole: Landscape into History* (New Haven, CT: Yale University Press, 1994), pp. x, 3–21, 23–31, 33–49, 51–77, 79–101; Marshall Tymn, ed., *Thomas Cole's Poetry: The Collected Poems of America's Foremost Painter of the Hudson River School Reflecting His Feelings for Nature and*

the Romantic Spirit of the Nineteenth Century (York, PA: Liberty Cap Books, 1972), pp. 41, 123–25, 145–60, 185, 191; Sean Wilentz, *Chants Democratic: New York City and the Rise of the American Working Class, 1768–1850* (New York: Oxford University Press, 1984); Sean Wilentz, *The Rise of American Democracy: Jefferson to Lincoln* (New York: W. W. Norton, 2005); and Edward Widmer, *Young America: The Flowering of Democracy in New York City* (New York: Oxford University Press, 1999), pp. 3–26, 94–96, 127, 142–43, 148–50, 155–84.

22. John Bigelow, *William Cullen Bryant* (New York: Chelsea House, 1980, original published in 1890), pp. xiii–xiv, 69, 76–78, 79–83, 103–7; Charles H. Brown, *William Cullen Bryant* (New York: Scribner, 1971), pp. 18–31, 145, 212.

23. Widmer, *Young America*, p. 149.

Chapter 2

24. John Ponet, *A Short Treatise on Political Power* (Menston, England: Scolar Press, 1970), Originally Published: 1556.

25. John Adams, *The Works of John Adams, Second President of the United States: With A Life of the Author, Notes and Illustrations Vol. VI.*, Charles Francis Adams (ed.) (Boston: Charles C. Little and James Brown), 1851, pp. 3–4.

Chapter 3

26. See the Library of Congress collection of Thomas Jefferson papers. This version has been modified from the original.

Chapter 4

27. Levi Slamm, "Introductory," *Daily Plebeian*, July 2, 1842; Slamm, "The Plebeian," *Daily Plebeian*, July 2, 1842.

Chapter 5

28. John L. O'Sullivan, "European Views of American Democracy: M. de Tocqueville," *United States Magazine and Democratic Review* 1, no. 1 (1837): 91–107.

Chapter 6

29. John L. O'Sullivan, "Political Tolerance," *United States Magazine and Democratic Review* 3, no. 9 (1838): 58–65.

Chapter 7

30. François Pierre Guillaume Guizot, *History of Civilization in Europe*, trans. William Hazlitt (New York: Colonial Press, 1846).

Chapter 8

31. Levi Slamm and Michael Walsh, "Great Meeting of the Mechanics and Working Men at Tammany Hall!" *Daily Plebeian*, October 19, 1842.

Chapter 9

32. Henderson, Ernest F. (ed.) *Select Historical Documents of the Middle Ages* (London: George Bell and Sons, 1910), pp. 176–189.

Chapter 10

33. The Visigothic Code: (*Forum judicum*), ed. S. P. Scott, Library of Iberian Resources Online, http://www.documentacatholicaomnia.eu/03d/0506-0506,_AA_VV,_Leges_Romanae_Visigotorum_[Scott_JP_Curatore],_EN.pdf. (Accessed: 12 January, 2017).

Chapter 11

34. The Canons of Adamnan, or the Law of Innocents (ca 697), Edited and Translated by Kuno Meyer (Oxford: Clarendon Press, 1905).

Chapter 12

35. "Privileges and Prerogatives Granted by Their Catholic Majesties to Christopher Columbus" (1492); the "Charter to Sir Walter Raleigh" (1584), in Francis Newton Thorpe (ed.) *The Federal and State Constitutions Colonial Charters, and Other Organic Laws of the States, Territories, and Colonies Now or Heretofore Forming the United States of America Compiled and Edited Under the Act of Congress of June 30, 1906* (Washington, DC: Government Printing Office, 1909), available from the Yale Univerity Lillian Goldman Law Library at http://avalon.law.yale.edu/16th_century/raleigh.asp (Accessed: 1 January, 2017).

Chapter 13

36. *The Records of the Virginia Company of London*, ed. Susan Myra Kingbury, with an introduction and bibliography (Washington: Government Printing Office, 1905). See also Michael P. Johnson, ed., *Reading the American Past: Selected Historical Documents*, vol. 1 (Boston: Bedford/St. Martin's, 2012), pp. 37–41; and Alan Taylor, *American Colonies: The Settling of North America* (New York: Penguin, 2001), pp. 117–57.

Chapter 14

37. Clement Downing, "The History of John Plantain, Called King of Ranter-Bay, &c.," in *A Compendious History of the Indian Wars; with an Account of the Rise, Progress, Strength, and Forces of Angria the Pyrate* (London: T. Cooper, 1737), pp. 105–39.

Chapter 15

38. Captain Charles Johnson, "Of Captain Misson and His Crew," in *A General History of the Pyrates, from Their first Rise and Settlement in the Island of Providence, to the present Time*, vol. 2 (London: T. Warner, 1728), pp. 1–48.

Chapter 16

39. John L. O'Sullivan, "Retrospective View of the State of European Politics, Especially of Germany, since the Last Congress of Vienna," *U.S. Magazine and Democratic Review* 1, no. 1 (1837): 123–42.

Chapter 17

40. A Reporter, "Glances at Congress: No. 1," *United States Magazine and Democratic Review* 1, no. 1 (1837): 68–81.

Chapter 18

41. James Gemmel, "Two Years in Van Dieman's Land," *Daily Plebeian*, July 1, 1842.

Chapter 19

42. Frances Whipple, "From a Rhode Islander," *Daily Plebeian*, August 3, 1842; Levi Slamm, "An Unrepublican Anomaly," *Daily Plebeian*, August 3, 1842.

Chapter 20

43. Marcus Morton, "Governor Morton's Letter to the Suffrage Clam Bake Committee," *Daily Plebeian*, September 6, 1842.

Chapter 21

44. John L. O'Sullivan, "The Canada Question," *U.S. Magazine and Democratic Review* 1, no. 2 (1838): 205–20.

Chapter 22

45. Levi Slamm, "Oregon Territory," *Daily Plebeian*, June 1, 1843; Slamm, "The Oregon Question," *Daily Plebeian*, April 11, 1844.

Chapter 23

46. "Annexation of Texas," *Daily Plebeian*, November 21, 1843; "For the Plebeian— Texas," *Daily Plebeian*, November 28, 1843; Levi Slamm, "The Annexation of Texas— Its Effects upon Slavery," *Daily Plebeian*, June 25, 1844.

Chapter 24

47. Lois Waisbrooker, "The Sex Question and the Money Power," originally delivered as a lecture at Jackson, Michigan, December 14, 1873. See *Three Pamphlets on the Occult Forces of Sex* (New York: Murray Hill Publishing Co., 1891).

Chapter 25

48. Tymn, *Thomas Cole's Poetry*, pp. 144–72.

Conclusion

49. Albert Jay Nock, "Isaiah's Job," *Atlantic Monthly* (1936): 641–49.

50. Ibid.

51. Ibid.

52. Ibid.

53. Benjamin Tucker, "Our Nestor Taken From Us: Obituary for Lysander Spooner," *Liberty Magazine*, May 28, 1887.

54. Albert Jay Nock, "Isaiah's Job," *Atlantic Monthly* (1936): 641–49.

55. Ibid.

56. Ibid.

57. Hans F. Sennholz, "Foreword" in Rose Wilder Lane, *The Discovery of Freedom: Man's Struggle against Authority* (San Francisco: Fox & Wilkes, 1997; originally published in 1943), pp. vii-viii.

58. Roger Lea MacBride, "Foreword to the Fiftieth Anniversary of the First Publication of *The Discovery of Freedom*," and "Introduction to the 1984 Edition," in Lane, *The Discovery of Freedom*, pp. v-vi, ix-xii.

59. Joan Kennedy Taylor, ed., *Liberty against Power: Essays by Roy A. Childs, Jr.* (San Francisco: Fox & Wilkes, 1994), pp. 2–3.

60. Ibid., pp. 261-63.

61. Ibid., p. 262.

62. Ibid., p. 263.

63. William Strauss and Neil Howe, *Generations: The History of America's Future, 1854 to 2069* (New York: Morrow, 1991).

64. Strauss and Howe, *Generations*; Tymn, *Thomas Cole's Poetry*, pp. 144–72.

65. William Strauss and Neil Howe, *The Fourth Turning: An American Prophecy* (New York: Broadway Books, 1997), pp. 1–3.

66. Ibid., pp. 122–38.

67. Ibid.

Index

Note: Page numbers with letter f indicate figures; letter n indicates notes.

Libertarianism.org

Liberty. It's a simple idea and the linchpin of a complex system of values and practices: justice, prosperity, responsibility, toleration, cooperation, and peace. Many people believe that liberty is the core political value of modern civilization itself, the one that gives substance and form to all the other values of social life. They're called libertarians.

Libertarianism.org is the Cato Institute's treasury of resources about the theory and history of liberty. The book you're holding is a small part of what Libertarianism.org has to offer. In addition to hosting classic texts by historical libertarian figures and original articles from modern-day thinkers, Libertarianism.org publishes podcasts, videos, online introductory courses, and books on a variety of topics within the libertarian tradition.

Cato Institute

Founded in 1977, the Cato Institute is a public policy research foundation dedicated to broadening the parameters of policy debate to allow consideration of more options that are consistent with the principles of limited government, individual liberty, and peace. To that end, the Institute strives to achieve greater involvement of the intelligent, concerned lay public in questions of policy and the proper role of government.

The Institute is named for *Cato's Letters*, libertarian pamphlets that were widely read in the American Colonies in the early 18th century and played a major role in laying the philosophical foundation for the American Revolution.

Despite the achievement of the nation's Founders, today virtually no aspect of life is free from government encroachment. A pervasive intolerance for individual rights is shown by government's arbitrary intrusions into private economic transactions and its disregard for civil liberties. And while freedom around the globe has notably increased in the past several decades, many countries have moved in the opposite direction, and most governments still do not respect or safeguard the wide range of civil and economic liberties.

To address those issues, the Cato Institute undertakes an extensive publications program on the complete spectrum of policy issues. Books, monographs, and shorter studies are commissioned to examine the federal budget, Social Security, regulation, military spending, international trade, and myriad other issues. Major policy conferences are held throughout the year, from which papers are published thrice yearly in the *Cato Journal*. The Institute also publishes the quarterly magazine *Regulation*.

In order to maintain its independence, the Cato Institute accepts no government funding. Contributions are received from foundations, corporations, and individuals, and other revenue is generated from the sale of publications. The Institute is a nonprofit, tax-exempt, educational foundation under Section 501(c)3 of the Internal Revenue Code.

CATO INSTITUTE
1000 Massachusetts Ave., N.W.
Washington, D.C. 20001
www.cato.org